Clans and Families of Ireland and Scotland

An Ethnography of the Gael
A.D. 500-1750

C. Thomas Cairney, Ph.D.

HERITAGE BOOKS
2006

HERITAGE BOOKS

AN IMPRINT OF HERITAGE BOOKS, INC.

Books, CDs, and more—Worldwide

For our listing of thousands of titles see our website
at
www.HeritageBooks.com

Published 2006 by
HERITAGE BOOKS, INC.
Publishing Division
65 East Main Street
Westminster, Maryland 21157-5026

International Standard Book Number: 978-1-58549-070-9

To John Riley Sutthoff:
"The O'Reillys used to be kings, you know."

Acknowledgments

I am indebted to a number of people who have had a formative influence on this book, among them Tom Johnson, Valene Smith and Lowell Stratton at the California State University, Chico; Dan Crowley at the University of California, Davis, and Gilbert Youmans at the University of Missouri, Columbia. Thanks also go to John Foley, Ed Tyler and Sarah Feeny at the University of Missouri, Columbia, for introducing me to oral-formulaic theory, and for recommending books and articles on the subject. A special thanks is due to Connie Reece, also of the University of Missouri, who read the book in proof, and converted many awkward Cairney-isms into readable prose while struggling through the difficult Gaelic spellings in Part II. Finally, thanks is due to Art Lehmann, California State University, Chico, who introduced me to anthropology and inspired me with its possibilities as a tool for understanding cultural continuities past and present. This book is a direct result of that inspiration.

Table of Contents

Introduction

There be more than 60 countries, called regions, in Ireland, --- some regions as big as a shire, some more, some lesse; where reygneith more than 60 Chyef Capytaynes, whereof some callyth themselves Kings, some Kings Peers, in their language, some Princes, some Dukes, some Archedukes --- and every of the said Capytaynes makeyth war and peace for himself, and holdeith by sword, and hath imperial jurisdiction within his rome, and obeyeth to no other person.
A Tudor official in 1515

This book is dedicated to the heroic spirit of those "Chyef Capytaynes" of old, who reigned in wild but magnificent style in the numerous tribal kingdoms which once graced the Emerald Isle and the North of Britain. Part One of *Clans and Families* provides the reader with an historical overview of the lost tribal culture of Ireland and Scotland. In Part Two, the reader is provided with information on the origins of specific Irish and Scottish families/surnames as they developed from clan and tribal names/groups.

The idea for a book on the tribes and clans of Ireland and Scotland has been with me for a long time. There has certainly been a need for an authoritative, comprehensive yet relatively concise treatment of the subject, one faithful to the Gaelic reality as it was lived by the tribesmen of the sixteenth and seventeenth centuries. As a student of anthropology, I have long been interested in the tribal character and racio-ethnic origins of the Gaelic-speaking peoples of historical times. My personal interest in the rich lore and cultural heritage of the Irish and Highland Scottish people, including the history of the great kin groups and families, led me to the task of providing for general readership a guide to the subject less affected by Anglicized characterization and romance.

This book combines genealogical, historical and anthropological information on Irish and Scottish clan-families in one volume. Excellent work has been done on the origins and character of the early tribal populations by British and Irish scholars. *Clans and Families* bridges the gap between these early tribes and the great clan-families of the sixteenth and seventeenth centuries, showing their relationships and connection to each other through branches, subtribes, and clans. Herein I have brought together much diverse and specialized

xi

material from various fields in order to apply the best modern information in a unified way. Such information has been heretofore unavailable to the general public.

The purpose of this book is to provide in one volume an authoritative and comprehensive account of the Gaelic tribes and clans. Any serious treatment of Gaelic history, politics, sociology, anthropology or related fields should take this Gaelic tribalism into central account when dealing with the period preceding 1607 in Ireland and 1746 in Scotland. The reason for this is that throughout the historical period and even into the eighteenth century, Gaelic polity was built upon a framework of tribal groups with their intra- and inter-tribal political relationships.

Similarly, studies of traditional Gaelic literature which aim to examine its social context should strive to view it in light of its tribal background. Much folklore in the Gaelic oral tradition, inasmuch as it is an expression of cultural realities past and present, is also profitably viewed in this way.

It is not my purpose here to glorify a particular place or race by calling attention to some mystical quality. The men of the tribes were just men, and the places where they dwelt were just places. If anything must be glorified, let it be the human spirit; the spirit of men and women who would build a hearth and defend a family against ever-present dangers in a wild land. Think of the Gaelic tribes as an aspect of our Western heritage, for they have left us above all with a legacy of pride in the face of adversity, of family unity in the face of potential annihilation. This is the legacy of the tribes and clans, that men could unite with bonds of blood and friendship, to uphold their freedom, their chief and their way of life; that men could stand together with honor, and face their fears with dignity. Though often enough the Gael fell short of his best, yet more often he did not, and at the very least the scions of an heroic aristocracy could gather around a fire at night, and listen to their ancient tales, reaffirming the morals and values of their people.

In many ways Gaelic society stood in bold contrast to the rest of Europe. To correctly interpret a society so strikingly different from its neighbors in the rest of Europe requires knowledge of the nature of its separate identity. This book should greatly aid that task.

C. Thomas Cairney
October 1988

Part One

I. The Identity of the Gaels

This book is about the origins of the Irish and Scottish surnames of millions of Americans and Canadians. Much of the genealogical and cultural legacy of our Irish and Scottish ancestors has not been made available to the common English-speaking culture of North America. This state of affairs reflects the fact that much good scholarly work bearing on the subject has been "locked way" in academic works, often very old, by either Irish or British authors dealing primarily with their own respective geographical or subject areas. Specialized information from diverse academic sources (long overlooked by North American writers) is presented here in a unified text for the benefit of Irish and Scottish Canadians and Americans.

Though prior to the seventeenth century Ireland and Scotland were in many ways a single cultural unit, scholars since have skirted this issue, along with the issue of past Irish and Scottish Gaelic tribalism, and this is probably a result of their not spending the time to break into the enigma of Gaelic language and culture. As a result, they have tried to categorize Ireland and Scotland separately, and generally as a backwater of English history. This book provides a fresh, historically accurate treatment of the subject by considering both Gaelic areas, Ireland and Scotland, at once, and in the light of the best modern information from such fields as anthropology, history, folklore, genealogy, heraldry, literature and linguistics.

A close affinity has always existed between Ireland and Scotland, especially northern Scotland. The native peoples of these places, the Irish on the one hand, and the Scottish Highlanders on the other, are known collectively as "the Gaels," and share as well the common heritage of the Gaelic culture and tongue. Because of its continuity with its Indo-European past, this culture could during its sixteenth-century heyday be described as the most ancient, the most unaffected, and the most unchanged and unchanging in all of Europe. The earliest literature and history of the Gaels are particularly interesting for they provide a unique window on the Iron Age. But the history of Gaeldom involves an apparent cultural paradox, for Gaelic society enjoyed many of the benefits of "civilization" without being itself "civilized" in the sense of being organized around concentrated population centers, or cities.

The basic organization of Gaelic society before the seventeenth century remained tribal; changes brought on by outside influences were secondary in nature and were generally adapted to the existing social order. Thus the society expressed the vitality of an unbroken connection with its most ancient origins until the power of the Gaelic tribes in Ireland and Scotland was broken by the English. The English facilitated their conquest of Gaeldom with great cruelty, conquering with bravery, political treachery and great military and logistical strength. The Gaelic people were completely disenfranchised and denied education as well. This struck at the very heart of Gaelic society, one of the truly great learned societies since ancient times. However, education did not entirely die. Traditions continued to be passed down, and some semiformal education continued in furtive "hedge row" schools, often run by priests on pain of death.

The Christian church in Gaelic Ireland and Scotland (the Celtic church) had a unique character, and maintained its independence and power from about the time of St. Patrick (ca. 400) to the coming of the Normans (ca. 1200). It was not fully submerged until after the end of the Gaelic period in the seventeenth and eighteenth centuries. The Celtic church was from the beginning very important both in missionary activity and in the advancement of learning in Europe. Indeed, many of the oldest European religious houses were founded by Gaelic saints, or had Gaelic pilgrims associated with their beginnings. Throughout history, Gaelic scholar-clerics continued to find a welcome at the courts and monasteries of the Continent. Gaelic missionary and monastic activity (sixth to twelfth centuries) also show a Gaelic wanderlust which is mirrored in the military sphere by Gaelic mercenaries of the thirteenth to sixteenth centuries, who fought for hire under foreign lords, as antecedents to the so-called "Wild Geese" of the seventeenth and eighteenth centuries.

During the nineteenth century, Gaels in great numbers were cleared from their once-healthy homeland to make way for British agriculture and livestock; the removal was a dirty business which the English rationalized by quaint economic theories proclaiming the Gaelic situation as "hopeless in any case." There was, however, a population explosion in Ireland at this time, and with the coming of the Great Potato Famine of the late 1840s in Ireland, millions of Gaels starved for want of potatoes, while the real agricultural fruit of the land passed on unhindered into England, as per British policy. No less tragic was the clearing of the loyal Highlanders of northern Scotland from the homes of their ancestors of a thousand years, to make way for sheep. On the brighter side of irony is the fact that there are, as a result of immigration (especially in North America), many millions more Gaels in the world community than could ever have been nurtured on the "old sod" of Ireland and Scotland alone.

II. Gaelic Society

Before their political eclipse in the seventeenth and eighteenth centuries, the Gaelic people of Ireland and northern Scotland had lived since prehistoric times in a society which was tribal and pastoral in nature, and whose essential elements had come together toward the beginning of the medieval period. Gaelic society in the early eighth century A.D. thus represented a fusion between the old pagan, Heroic traditions and culture and the new Christian society with its scholarship and monasticism.

This fusion, in its inception, was the bed upon which Gaelic society would flower. It was a cultural synthesis born of a long history of ethno-tribal relationships on Irish soil, and it would, through invasions by Vikings (mainly Norwegians) and Normans, attain new equilibriums with each contact, and continue on in its essentially Gaelic fashion. The resultant culture would maintain its vitality well into the modern period, retaining both its ancient flavor and the universality of its appeal. Far from being on the retreat, it would absorb the Viking and Norman invaders, while by its own expansion it would convert the Picts of Albany (North Scotland) and the Britons of Strathclyde (South Scotland) as well, covering most of medieval Scotland in the process.

The absorption, however, of the Vikings and Normans who settled in Gaeldom worked both ways. The Vikings brought towns, merchant and seafaring expansion, and new blood. Their Norman cousins brought castles and mounted knights in armor, both of which came to play a central role in all later political struggles in the Gaelic areas. The Normans changed the face of Gaeldom forever with efficient land use, encouraging the development of the previously emergent "tribal-dynastic feudalism" of the native kings with a healthy infusion of their own purely Norman feudalism. Thus, while the Normans were Gaelicized, the Gaels were themselves Normanized as well.

Gaeldom in its sixteenth century heyday consisted of a series of tribal kingdoms (tuaths) stretching from the bottom of Ireland, clockwise, to the northern tip of Scotland. For most of their history these kingdoms were under the often nominal or largely symbolic high-kingships of either Ireland or Scotland. Medieval Scotland had in fact resulted from the ninth-century

5

merger of the Kingdoms of the Scots, or Irishmen from Dal Riada in northeast Ireland (long settled in Argyle on the west coast of Scotland) with the people known as the Cruithne (or Picts), the native people of the rest of what would eventually become Scotland. Much of the subsequent history of these areas centered around the attempts of their chief tribal dynasties to make these "over kingdoms" a political reality.

Meanwhile, geographical factors in Scotland and Ulster, such as mountains and glens, together with the presence of sparser, less diverse population groups, combined to encourage the development of more tightly knit, formalized clan groups, especially toward the sixteenth century. It was precisely these clans and families who were successful in maintaining their group identity beyond the Gaelic period, which ended between 1600 and 1750. The people of these areas could more generally share in the Heroic tradition of Gaelic literature, as members of an Heroic aristocracy, and this is reflected in the number of northern families tracing themselves back to characters in that Heroic literature, particularly the "Ulster Cycle." As a genealogical note however, it should be pointed out that, especially in Scotland, the tribal following of a chief was often encouraged to take the name of the chief, once surnames came into general use in place of clan names. What this means is that not every clansman who bore the name "Robertson" (Mac Raibeirt) was descended from a Robertson chief in the male line, although somehow related either in the female line, or as a male-line branch from before the time of Raibeirt, eponymous ancestor of the Robertson chiefs. This taking of the chief's name was an expression of the old kinship, and was a way for the group to promote their solidarity as a socio-political entity, a phenomenon aided by the relatively late (fourteenth century) general adoption in Scotland of surnames as opposed to clan-names. In Ireland to the south of Ulster, and especially in Munster, society continued to reflect the ancient tribal patterns which emphasized a more limited, numerically inferior warrior aristocracy (the Eoghanacht) in overlord status over an ethnically diverse population.

Nevertheless, Gaelic society in general involved a shared racial-national heritage. This was a time-honored culture which was no more and no less than the lasting expression of its active bearers, the men and women who lived it, made it, and passed it on to their descendants. The culture itself was superimposed over a latticework of tribal divisions; some independent, some semi-independent but owing tribute to another. Central to it was a tribal spirit of patriarchal, extended-family independence. In this spirit, honor was upheld by the working of the clan-lands, and by the demonstrated ability and strength to hold those lands by the sword. A family lost face if it failed to uphold its tribal obligations, for the strength of a tribe was the strength of the honorable commitments made by its constituent kindreds, or basic extended-family units, and was therefore a function of tribal unity.

In spite of inter-tribal political and economic competition, Gaelic society was nonetheless united in culture and language. The bearers of religion, law, literature, history, medicine, music and poetry, as hereditary tradesmen in their fields, enjoyed a special status, and freely practiced their arts among and between such tribal groups. Indeed, far from being merely tolerated by the tribes, these professional classes actually performed the essential functions of the society, maintaining its tribal character of independence and partition. For these professionals, the spoken word held a special and ancient power. Gaelic bards and historians prided themselves in the cultivation of memory for the oral transmission of information and records, a task which they accomplished with the aid of poetic conventions, thematic paraphrase and aphoristic formulas of stock idiomatic cultural meaning (the phrase "be literal" had no meaning prior to the coming of the literate Christians). The spoken ire of a poet would maim a king through sympathetic magic, while his blessing could bring prosperity.

Gaelic tribalism tended to foster a natural aristocracy based on talent. A tribesman's individual talent, and the talent of his immediate ancestors played the major role in determining where one stood within the internal tribal hierarchy. In another sense, the same hierarchy tended to run horizontally rather than vertically, which meant that all members of the tribe, being equally descended from the founding chief or king, shared equally in his royal blood, and therefore counted themselves equal in blood to the king of the tribe. In this way, differences between tribesmen tended to emphasize talent rather than blood, though the tribal king or clan chief himself was "a breed apart."

A chief's personal and family talent played its role in securing him that dignity in the first place, but once inaugurated, a new chief took on a new aspect. As chief, he symbolized the manifestation of the spirit of the tribe, ritualistically reincarnated in each succeeding chief, presumably since the beginning of time. Any man whose father, grandfather or great-grandfather had been chief was generally eligible to be a chief himself as long as he acknowledged the male line and reckoned himself a member of the tribe. However, this system often led to strife between rival nominees and their supporters, especially when the succession was not prearranged by the chief himself (contrast this with the Norman-English custom of primogeniture, wherein the eldest son is automatically the heir).

A chief could appoint his successor by a process known as tanistry, but otherwise the office was filled through election by the tribal council, made up of the heads and elders of the kindred branches of the tribe, though their decision could be influenced greatly by personal combats among the candidates. Indeed, the succession itself was originally carried out by means of a ritual combat between the chief and his successor (or at least challenger) within the kingroup, or "dynastic family." Such ancient practices continued well into the Middle Ages, and among some families (such as the MacCarthys and O'Flahertys) even later. It arose in part from the prudent need to settle such questions

quickly and decisively, for the good of the tribe. The kingship was originally
a sacral (sacred and official), and in a sense, sacrificial position. The king performed a priestly function for the tribe, eliciting due awe from the tribesmen,
and living under religious restrictions ("gessa," or taboos).

There were three pillars of Gaelic polity within the tribal structure: the
Chief, the elders of the kindreds, and the leaders of the church. Where matters
of succession were concerned, there was a rule of thumb in the Brehon law (the
law of the Gael) which specified the criteria for choosing precedence in each
category: "Elder for kin, worth for rulership, wisdom for the church" (Byrne
35). Worth here refers to the eligible candidate with the most kindreds in his
camp. This system helped foster good leadership and keep it closely bound to
the mass of tribesmen, and attuned to their needs and desires. The chief acted
in conjunction with the tribal council of elders, and with the advice of the
church. Although a strictly tribal ruler or dynast could be high-handed with
"alien tuatha" (subservient tribal groups), in keeping with the Indo-European
aristocratic tradition of their earliest ancestors, yet they could also treat them
as respected allies, and raise them to high position. In fact, even in the larger,
more centralized Kingdom of Scots in the late thirteenth century, Alexander
III was known as a highly accessible and personable king. He acted in the
Gaelic tradition of contact with his people, the local constituents of his
kingdom, which was typical of the nobility of the time (this was, of course, long
before the urban population sprawl, and the anonymity and social evils at-
tributable thereto). In this way the Gaelic system came to resemble a sort of
tribal feudalism, in which accountability ran both ways.

Certain kindreds supported such hereditary functions as law, religion, and
the teaching of history and genealogy. Members of these kindreds served as
advisors when matters requiring their expertise were in question. In the Celtic
church, for example, certain kindreds maintained church lands, often as a
branch of the local tribe, and the heads of such kindreds were the bishops and
abbots of the Celtic church. They enjoyed princely status, and often descended from the founding saint of the abbacy as well. They did not observe
celibacy, for this was originally an ascetic rule for certain monastic orders until
its institution (twelfth century) in the Roman church by the Pope as a means
of controlling secular appointments generation by generation. The Celtic
church's lack of celibacy should not be interpreted (as it has been) as an indication that the church was decadent or degenerative, for it judged itself by its
own standards, and never duplicated Latin attitudes on this question. As
Gaelic society was different, so the church organization that emerged within
this tribal infrastructure was also different. Communities of Gaelic ascetics and
hermits continued to seek God in peaceful areas away from men, but their
basic monastic system was from the beginning adapted to the tribal society,
and thus we have the abbey system of the Celtic church. It is worth pointing
out that the Celtic church was the first in Northern Europe, and thus

did not degenerate from a previous and pervasive Roman church, although this assumption has been made (implied here is the vulnerability on the part of the historian to distort history by interpreting it too much in the light of his own age). Irish monasticism was in fact an outgrowth of that of Egypt, not Rome, and its position in Europe was one of antecedence.

At any rate, the tribes, being the focus of Gaelic political power, encompassed virtually the entire Gaelic population. Generally speaking, this meant that anyone with any basic rights at all belonged to a tribe, and usually descended in the male line from one of the ancient Celtic ethno-tribal groups of Ireland and Scotland (the Gaels proper – the tribal sense of the name Gael – and also the Laigin, Erainn and Cruithne), or from one of the Viking or Norman families that came later. The only exceptions of note were those families which had attached themselves wholly to the church or some other hereditary profession, or which became so debased in power that they lost political significance even on the most local scale, and thus lost also their tribal identity (a unique situation arose for the O'Donegans of North Tipperary and O'Duggans of Cork who were tribally isolated and thus became entities unto themselves, while the same can be said for the O'Lynches of County Cavan – see Part II). Some church kindreds, such as the ancestors of the Skenes of Aberdeenshire and the Glenesks of Angus, later became temporal lords of their territories after these abbey lands were secularized in the thirteenth century.

It should be pointed out that families of the Galloway region of southwest Scotland, though of Gaelic origin in many cases, cannot be placed in the larger tribal framework of Gaeldom. The reason for this is their descent from Norse-Gaelic pirates and sea-kings who originally settled the area, whose tribal identity or continuity was lost as that tribalism completely lost its political significance. Thus the families of Kennedy, MacDowell, MacClellan, etc., of the Galloway region, though they form clan groups traceable from about the end of the twelfth century, fall outside the scope of Part II of this book. Other families in the south of Scotland are of Norman origin, but as their ancestors settled in the Lowlands of South Scotland, outside the area of Gaelic influence and cultural assimilation, most of these fall outside the scope of this book. This also applies to some families of the northeastern coastal lowlands of Scotland, and even to the mighty Lowland houses of Douglas and Bruce. The senior branch of the latter inherited and held the Throne of the Scots (in the person of Robert the Bruce) during the critical wars of Scottish independence in the thirteenth and fourteenth centuries, but their male-line failed soon after, and their royal inheritance and representation passed to the House of Stewart.

Tribalism of course influenced Gaelic literature, and the oral tradition is crowded with kings and heroes, often originally of a divine nature, who figure prominently in the genealogies of the tribes. Indeed, if you include descent in the female line, the likelihood was very great that a given Gael might descend, on a regional basis, from an historical king or hero of old. Such likelihoods, together with the pervasiveness of tribalism and the fact that tribal dynasts often had their own pedigree attached to that of the ruling tribe of a province (making them, in a nominal way, honorary members of those tribes), helped reinforce the emergence of a kind of "national family." This is especially true when considering descent within certain geographically defined areas, such as the Scottish Highlands, or one of the provinces of Ireland. This is particularly true in Scotland, where a combination of factors (the intermarriage of Picts and Scots, and the resultant substitution of patrilineal descent for the original matrilineal decent of the Picts) resulted in an unusual homogeneity of patrilineally traced, politically significant tribal/dynastic pedigrees in Scotland. This homogeneity in turn encouraged other tribal branches migrating from Ireland to northern Scotland during the Middle Ages to selectively intermarry in order to acquire dynastic ties to these patrilineal groups, and the same principle applies to the Norman settlers when they came. However, this does not mean that the reality of patrilineally traced ethnic origin ceased to be of importance, for the provincially unifying factors discussed above served only to streamline provincial politics which remained based on ethnic/tribal origin.

The basic dress for men into the seventeenth century included Celtic brogues (black leather shoes not unlike ballerina slippers: a kind of moccasin), knee-length tartan hose of an argyle pattern, a long, saffron dyed linen shirt of ample folds and yardage, and a mantle of wool, which in Scotland evolved into the kilt of today. Originally the kilt was a large, rectangular plaid variously arranged on the body, but generally belted at the waist producing the familiar kilted pleats. District setts grew out of traditional weaving patterns and the local availability of vegetable dyes. In Scotland, the circumscribing geography of mountain and glen encouraged the association of certain district setts with the dominant local clan. However, the modern idea of the Scottish tartan as a kind of "clan uniform" seems to have developed by analogy to the regimental tartans of the 1780s, after the repeal of the ban on Highland dress. Before that time, a poor Highlander wore any wool he could get his hands on, while a rich one traded with other districts or else had a sett of his own made to suit his individual taste. In any case, mixing and matching was the rule, and with the addition of the tartan waistcoat and jacket in the eighteenth century, the Highland squire cut a variegated figure indeed. This was a Celtic society, with individual vanity setting the fashion statement. There was no need then to manifest group identity with a uniform: A person lived all his life with the same clan, in the same place, and with the same leaders. What was needed was a sense of personal identity, always achieved through individual adornment.

Another aspect of the Gaelic tribal culture was its heraldry, the symbolism of which is often of very ancient origin, although it did not develop in its medieval importance until the coming of the Normans in the twelfth and thirteenth centuries. Nevertheless, families often shared common dynastic symbols even though their dynastic connections predated heraldry per se, which indicates that older dynastic traditions were applied to post–Norman heraldry. Occasionally the arms themselves are of truly ancient origin. The arms of the O'Donnells of Tirconnell, for instance, bear the cross of "the kindred of St. Columba," as do the arms of other families of that kindred. The ancestor of the O'Donnells was told to bear this symbol on his shield by the great saint himself, in the sixth century! Other symbols in Gaelic heraldic practice developed out of ancient tribal totems, reminiscent of primitive magic, learned druids, and the pre–Christian religion.

Out of this well of Celtic antiquity comes a heraldic symbol of the great O'Neills and their tribal kin, the sacred salmon, which was originally considered to be the water-borne manifestation of the "otherworld god" and a source of his wisdom. As can be seen in the chart on page 94, the O'Neills traced their descent from Conn Cetchathach ("Conn of the Hundred Battles"). Conn is the otherworld god, and in this manifestation he is considered the "sun-god" (St. Patrick once railed against the Irish practice of worshiping the sun).

"Conn" in Old Irish means "head" in the sense of one's head being the seat of reason. A divine head needs to see, and from its shape and brightness, the sun was regarded as the "divine eye of the heavens." In fact, the Irish word "suil," which etymologically means sun, has acquired the meaning "eye." "The idea of the sun being the eye of the heavens is a very old one. When conceived anthropomorphically, the deity was often regarded as a huge one-eyed being (O'Rahilly 58–59) . . . the deified sun, the heavenly Eye, who has observed the doings of countless generations of men" (O'Rahilly 318).

The "Red Hand of Ulster" is also an O'Neill symbol, recalling a tale about a severed hand, when a sea race was won by the unnatural touch of the "Red Hand" upon the shores of Ulster. In this famous tale, the ancestor of the O'Neills was racing another boat with the object of beating it to and thus claiming a territory for himself. Falling behind at the critical moment, the dauntless O'Neill ancestor lopped off his left hand with an axe, and threw it upon the shore ahead of the other boat, thus winning the land! The royal "lyon" of the Scottish kings, symbol of Dalriadic royal descent, is reminiscent of a time when there were still lions in the forests of Europe, and is quartered in the arms of many famous Scottish families.

For other early examples of heraldry, compare the "proto-heraldic" use of boar-crested helmets, golden banners, etc., as described in the Old English (Anglo-Saxon) epic poem Beowulf, a pre-literate oral composition first written down in the eighth century. The boar was considered to be a magical beast, and was famed for its courage. It appears later on the armorial shields of several Irish families, such as the O'Hanleys and O'Hanlons. The distinctive boar's head arms of the Swintons of Lowland Scotland and their relations, the Gordons and Chisholms, is made more interesting by the knowledge that the

Swintons are an ancient family of royal Anglo-Saxon genesis. Another example of early heraldic practice is the famous raven-banner of the Vikings (the raven was considered in pagan days to be a manifestation of Odin, and was later borne on the banner of the Picto-Norse earls of Caithness and Orkney in Scotland). Another worthy example is the antiquity of the arms of the Scottish family of Murray, derived, like their name, from the province of Moray.

Silver and blue were the ancient livery colors of the Morayshire Picts, and stars are said to have been painted on their bodies, in these colors, as a "warpaint" by which they could be distinguished from other tribes in battle. There was a noticeable tendency toward the use of blue in the original arms of the northeastern mormaerships (Celtic earldoms), the region including Mar, Buchan and Moray. In addition, stars appear in ancient Morayshire cave carvings, a possible indication of their ancient local significance. The heraldic device of "three Moray stars" appears in the arms of the Murrays and most old Morayshire families, including the MacRaes. These colors, silver on blue, also relate to the origin of the Scottish national flag, the cross of St. Andrew (Adam 520, 533).

The heraldic use of the three Moray stars by Murray families in the south of Scotland shows that their significance as a dynastic symbol extended even into preheraldic times, as these families migrated from the province of Moray before formal heraldry developed during the twelfth century. Such preheraldric dynastic affiliations throughout Gaeldom go hand-in-hand with shared heraldic symbology as a proof of the antiquity of pre-formal heraldry.

Such armorial bearings were born in the mists of the unrecorded past. They are a constant reminder of the ancient European origins of the Gaelic race, as indeed, much of what people think and do in their daily lives today is a direct legacy from their earliest ancestors. Many of the assumptions which guide people's lives reflect basic attitudes born of long tradition, and yet they are as common in our day as the Christmas tree (symbol of continuous life in winter) or the Easter egg and Easter bunny (symbolic of fertility in the rites of spring)—all equally survivors from Western civilization's earliest Indo-European roots.

Many such attitudes are so close to us that we scarcely notice them, or else they are held subconsciously. Jungian views on the "collective unconscious" and "racial memory" take on a special aspect when considered in light of our heritage from those distant times. Nightly visitations by a "shee" (faery) prophesying the return of a leader, selfless and heroic (such as Arthur), from an otherworldly sleep (such as on the Isle of Avalon, or within a faery hill or "Sheed") to inspire great loyalty and deliver his people from an enemy (such as the English)—or at least lead them on a great quest (such as for the Grail): These are recurrent archetypal themes, common to the Celtic peoples and their literature. They are an outgrowth of the pre–Christian religion of the Germanic and Celtic peoples (the "dawn religion") which arose out of a mixture of ideas at least partly derived from the pre–Celtic Western-European peoples they conquered and assimilated – peoples of ancient sanctity and impressive temples (e.g., Stonehenge and Newgrange). Thus, one way or another the "dawn religion" seems to ultimately descend from the ancient fertility cults of Neolithic Europe (associated with the famous Cro-Magnon "mother-goddess" or "Venus" figures), and so we have the matrilineality of the Picts (see Chapter IV), and also the nature worship, "second sight," druids, folk-medicine and fertility rites associated with the folk-tradition of historical times. Later, Christians came to associate evil with the horned manifestation of the fertility spirit ("Pan incarnate"), and thus we have the horned devil of today; burning, it seems, with lust. Such ancient fertility cults perceived divinity in the "spark of life" (Moncreiffe 21), and the vitality of this belief is directly expressed in the folklore, music, and dance of Gaelic tradition (Murray 1921). Here faeries are not of the diminutive winged creatures of the traditional English "fairy-tale," but rather are life-sized inhabiters of the otherworld, or of our dreams at any rate.

Gaelic society combined the vitality of its ancient Indo-European tribalism with progressive social institutions, as we shall see in the next chapter. Furthermore, its very existence indicates that the Roman legacy was not the only alternative for Western advancement. Gaeldom long existed in the far west of Europe as a great tribal society never directly touched by the empire of Rome, a society showing its direct links with the most ancient European ethos. It could be brutal and barbaric, yet its church produced a beacon of humanism and civilization that lit the Western world from Aachen to Ravenna, and passed on an uncompromising legacy.

III. The Coming of Gaeldom

The story of Gaeldom begins in the mists of antiquity, and ultimately has its roots in an age when Europe was largely covered with ice. During those early eons only one type of man lived amid the European ice sheet—Neanderthal Man—doing so long enough to develop special physical characteristics beyond strictly *cultural* adaptations. Ample body hair, long noses (to warm the air), fairness (lack of pigment) of eye, hair and skin; such traits are physical manifestations born of long residence in the northern regions, to which all other people were by their very nature foreign. Though other human groups have since mastered the cultural techniques of arctic living, only the Neanderthal was *inherently* a beast of the North, and yet he was a fully modern human (Weaver 577, 612).

Moving quickly ahead in time, Cro-Magnon man came onto the European scene some 30,000 years ago, as the ice retreated; he was the vanguard of other groups which followed in his wake (the term Cro-Magnon can also be applied to all early Homo sapiens of the post–Neanderthal European period, and to their culture). The resultant intermixture of racial elements gave birth to the Indo-European stock, with more blonds, as might be expected, farther north, and a more purely Cro-Magnon admixture on the western fringe.

The last-mentioned stock appears later as the relatively small, dark people who preceded the Celts in the British Isles, and built Stonehenge and other ancient monuments in those western reaches. Red hair, green eyes and freckled skin remain traits hard to place in an original context. They were perhaps indigenous to the southern fringe of the European ice sheet, and may represent early hybridization in central Europe following closely on the heels of the earliest Cro-Magnon influx. It is interesting that the Basques, a relatively small, dark people of ancient provenience in the western mountains between France and Spain, currently have the only native European lanaguage which falls outside the Indo-European language sphere, being of apparently independent origin.

In this Cro-Magnon–Basque connection, it is worth noting that there existed as late as the sixth century, in the northern extremity of the island of Great Britain and beyond the Celtic sphere, a race of "savage" aborigines,

gaeldom
Ethnic Distribution In A.D. 1

speakers of another language possibly related to Basque, and like Basque, unrelated to any of the Indo-European group (see Chapter IV). The Indo-European family of languages itself developed from a pool of dialects in use in the central European sphere before 5000 B.C., and came to form the main stem of European linguistic culture.

As the glaciers retreated, exposing new territory in the interior of Europe, the ocean level rose, and certain coastal regions disappeared beneath the sea. This happened in the case of Great Britain and Ireland, which were both originally connected to the continent, and hence to each other. The lost lands are remembered in folk memory, and many of the magical tales of European folklore are a record of those distant times. They recall a time when vastly different peoples wandered the forests and plains of Europe, and might chance to meet each other only occasionally over thousands of years. In such chance meetings, it might well seem to the people involved that they had come face to face with either giants or leprechauns, depending upon their perspective.

For instance, a group from the open steppe, on coming to a forested region and encountering the men who dwelt there, might well find it "magical" the way such a forest people, especially if relatively small in stature, were able to seemingly disappear as they beat fast tracks into nooks and crannies familiar only to them. Similarly, the leader of a remnant Neanderthal group living, let us say, in forested northern mountains, might well be the origin of the legendary "king of the mountain trolls," and folklore about the elopement of a young prince with the troll king's daughter may well be a record of the very intermixing which guaranteed the disappearance of such separate groups.

In any event, the spreading branches of Indo-European society came to dominate Europe. The Indo-Europeans successfully imposed their languages on the peoples they conquered, and this process brought about the emergence of specific racio-cultural hybrids as the forerunners of the national groups of today.

The Germans (Germanic and Scandinavian tribes) and the Celts were the most closely related of the Indo-European peoples. The ancestors of the Celts emerged on the European scene about 2800 years ago, and lived in tribal kingdoms that spread eventually across Europe east to west, while their Germanic cousins lived above them in the forests of the far north and beyond, to the regions bordering the Baltic Sea. To the south, in the regions bordering the Mediterranean Sea, during the centuries surrounding the time of Christ, came the blossoming of Latin and classical civilization, the result, ultimately, of early Indo-European contact with the east. The Romans had gradually extended their empire northwards at the expense of the Celts, and reached what became their northern boundary during the first century A.D. In the North it was difficult for the Romans to tell who was Germanic and who was Celtic, and as a result they often mistook one group for the other as distinctions generally faded along that hyperborean frontier.

Having reached what was to be its northern limits, the Roman Empire was doomed. Its condition was terminal the moment it stopped advancing, for the economy of the Empire was parasitic and artificial; it fed on expansion. Without the acquisition of new territory by conquest, it had only itself to feed upon, and it was therefore destined to rot from within of its own growing corruption. The end came gradually and painfully during tthe fourth and fifth centuries. The continental Celts were long since Romanized, and it was left to the Germanic tribes to deliver the *coup de grace* that ended an era (Davis 23-33).

The *Pax Romana* was at an end, and the Germanic tribes were in the political driver's seat. A new age of chaos was now upon Europe, and its subsequent history can be characterized as the effort of the various Germanic peoples to recreate the former empire in all its glory. Under the tutelage of the Romano-Celtic Latin clergy, they tirelessly attempted to emulate Roman society, though they never truly understood it. In the process they created something new and lasting, a society forged by the very barbarianism they were trying to deny. For it was the energy and vitality of their Indo-European tribalism that made them different. The fact is that Rome had been a powerful but empty shell. Its stagnation and fall had come about largely because it lacked, for all its culture and civilization, the vitality of the very northern neighbors who were its inheritors.

Meanwhile, in the far North and West, the old Indo-European tribalism continued unimpeded. Its continuous development in Ireland and Scotland contrasted sharply with its decline in the rest of Europe, while its northern expression led directly to the Viking Age. In the British Isles, a series of Celtic tribal invasions had superimposed their members over that insular territory, as we shall see. However, the term "Gaelic" here must be used with caution: The people whose language and culture would come to define the "Gaelic" area which emerged after A.D. 500, that is, the Gaels in the tribal sense of the word, would not arrive until relatively late.

There were three waves of Celtic invasions of the British Isles before the coming of the famous Gaels. The majority of these pre–Gaelic peoples had managed to remain unconquered by the Romans, whose activity in these isles was generally restricted to the broad English plain. A slightly larger area had subsequently remained out of the grasp of the West Germanic peoples who invaded Roman Britain in the wake of the Imperial collapse, as those people sowed the seed of the English nation. The first of the Celtic invaders, the *Cruithne* (from a form of the name "British"), came between 800 and 500 B.C. They assimilated the Cro-Magnon people they encountered, adopting their matrilineal descent system in the process. This was a very un–Indo-European system of inheritance, related to the old Cro-Magnon Mother-Goddess cult, whereby property and royal eligibility were passed through the female line, with sons and brothers providing the actual leaders. The merger of these two peoples, the pre–Celts and the Cruithne, formed the basic population of the British Isles, and this fact, with its attendant matrilineal aspect, is clearly reflected in early Celtic literature (Walton 1-16). While scholars may differ as to its exact nature, matrilineality's traditional existence is born out by historical evidence, despite claims to the contrary (Thompson 226; Smyth 58-68).

In any case, only the traditional matrilineality can explain the non-military possession of the Pictish kingship by sons of foreign kings: It alone can explain the presence of "foreigners" in hereditary positions of power and influence within the Pictish kingdom (these foreigners often simultaneously held patrilineally derived power in the home countries of their fathers as well).

Some time between 500 and 100 B.C. the next Celtic invaders came to the island of Ireland, the *Erainn* ("Erin," or "Eire," Gaelic for "Ireland," is of common linguistic origin). The Erainn were related to the Belgae, who invaded Britain via Armorica (modern Brittany) before the time of Christ, though they originally came from the area now known as Belgium, which recalls their name. As for the Erainn, they were a Germano-Celtic military aristocracy with the material advantage of superior iron weaponry. Though at first a minority population settled in geographically restricted areas, they formed a military overlordship, subjecting most of the Irish Cruithne to tributary status. One Erainnian tribe, the Ulaid, gave their name to Ulster.

The last of the pre–Gaelic Celtic invaders came from the Continent at a relatively late date, just before the coming of the Gaels during the first century B.C., probably as a reaction to Roman pressure in the south of Gaul. These invaders were the Dumnonii, who gave their name to Devon, while their most powerful Irish branch was known as the *Laigin*, and gave their name to Leinster. The Dumnonii (or Domnonii) settled as a distinct tribal population in the south of England and in several areas of Ireland, exercising overlord status over larger regions. A branch from Ireland settled in the area south of Dumbarton in southern Scotland before the arrival of the Romans in the mid-first century A.D., and became the ancestors of the Strathclyde Britons.

Though distinct from each other, all three of these preceding tribal groups spoke similar languages, each originally a dialect of the progressive P–Celtic language of West-Central Europe (as opposed to Q–Celtic, an older language of the Celtic group), and they shared other cultural similarities as well. But there was another branch of the Celts, a great tribal population that had roamed Europe for centuries in search of a suitable home. These were the *Gaels*, and in their search for a Gaelic "Israel," they came to Ireland from the Alpine region of Gaul, sometime during the first century B.C. They brought with them a Q–Celtic tongue distinct from the languages of their P–Celtic predecessors, and this language, Gaelic, would eventually supplant those earlier dialects and become the focal point of the emerging and pervasive Gaelic culture (O'Rahilly 207-208). This original Gaelic was, however, much closer to the P–Celtic dialects than Modern Gaelic is, and the changes which made modern Gaelic what it is occurred entirely within the common Irish and Scottish context.

As for the Milesian scheme of the *Lebor Gabala*, the semiofficial history of the chief Gaelic dynasties, it is pseudo-history of the Middle Ages. The basic story is accurate, recording the arrival of the Q–Celts, or Gaels, who became dominant in Ireland by the end of the fifth century A.D. Gaelic politics of the Middle Ages emphasized genealogy in a particular way, tribal/dynastic ancestry being of central political importance, and even religious significance.

The Middle Ages lasted from about A.D. 500 to about the time of the reformation in Scotland (ca. 1570) and in Ireland to about the time of the English conquest (ca. 1600). The tribal bards and ollavs (scholars) of the early Middle Ages
had developed a whole historical scheme bringing the Gaels to Ireland from
Egypt via the Iberian Peninsula. Inaccuracy was partially a result of Christian
scribes recording and secularizing pagan history and traditions, and partially
deliberate dynastic propaganda, for tribes of all races often tried to have their
own tribal-dynastic genealogy tacked on to the "Milesian stem": the royal
genealogy of the Gaels *per se*. Independent traditions of early genesis in the
local areas of the tribes concerned help tell us the true story.

In this way, after the arrival of the Gaels as an ethno-tribal population,
the essential racio-cultural elements of what would become Gaelic society were
in place, and all later developments would build upon this basic Gaelic
framework. That a warrior aristocracy minority could stand in conquest over
a subject majority and ultimately succeed in imposing its language upon them
is aptly reflected in the emergence of Gaeldom, for by about A.D. 400 the
Gaels had asserted themselves as the dominant group in Ireland. By this time,
however, Ireland's tribal nature was well established, and the Gaels simply
became the overlords of a myriad of once P–Celtic-speaking tribes, though certain of these earlier groups maintained a greater degree of autonomy than the
rest. By the beginning of the historical period (ca. A.D. 500) all of these groups
spoke dialects of Q-Celtic, the prestige language of the dominant Gaels. Thus,
while maintaining its various racial identities, the society as a whole was
streamlining, and the resultant culture can best be described as Gaelic. The
various separate racio-tribal identities were, however, still of central importance in determining inter-tribal political relationships, and would remain so
throughout the Gaelic period (ca. 500–1600 in Ireland, 800–1750 in Scotland).

Throughout the course of their development, the Gaels had remained outside the main European sphere. Although they had been, after the coming of
St. Patrick (ca. 400), fundamental to the conversion (and classical education)
of much of Europe, their Christianity remained more exclusively a matter of
religion and learning, and never became, as it did in Europe, a vehicle for encouraging a revival of Latin culture (Garvin 15).

Outside the realm of Papal conformity, Gaelic society was free to develop
at its own pace and in its own way. Thus were the Gaels able to maintain that
continuity of tribal vitality so important to their Gaelic identity. This identity-
born-of-continuity was itself a vehicle of cultural confidence, and contrasts
sharply with the decline in cultural self-confidence which attended the Europeans' relative break with Indo-European tradition. Europe would eventually
develop a new identity, but there has always been evidence of psychological
ill-health associated, for instance, with religious or moral inhibition initiated
by the European church. The Gaels, for their part, had always accepted such
Latin influences as essentially secondary, in the sense that they had always

adapted them to their existing Gaelic culture (see the discussion of the Christian Celtic church in the preceding chapter).

The differences between the two spheres of Christian influence, the one Celtic (monastic) and the other Roman (episcopalian), is perhaps best summed up by the old Gaelic proverb which simply states: "The Roman Church gave law, the Celtic Church gave love." A good example of these differences can also be found in the nature of the Gaelic conversion to Christianity. The Gaels saw Christianity as the natural outgrowth of their previously existing dawn religion. It was a new magic for the pagan, a sort of next stage toward a truer, fuller religious consciousness. It is significant in this connection that the land for St. Patrick's church at Elphin in County Roscommon was originally donated for that purpose by the Archdruid Ona. The descendants of Ona, the Corca Achlan or Corca Seachlann, of the same stock as the Ciarraighe (see Chapter VIII), branched into several families. The main family here was that of MacBrannan (Mac Branain) or O'Brannan (O Branain), a branch of whom, known as the Ui Branain, later the MacInerneys or Nerneys (Mac an Airchinnigh, literally "son of the Erenagh"), were, interestingly enough, erenaghs (hereditary abbots) of St. Patrick's church at Elphin. A family of O'Brannans served as Erenaghs of Derryvullan in County Fermanagh. Another branch of the Corca Seachlann, the Cineal Mac Erca or O'Monahans (O Manachain) faked a descent from the Ui Briuin, and were called the Ui Briuin na Sionna.

Clerics took over many of the functions of the Druid order, although the lower druidic orders continued as the scholarly class (the bards and ollavs that maintained literature and learning), and both cooperated in running the schools. Outside the Gaelic sphere, Europeans had simply dumped their former religious convictions, at least officially, in favor of the new Roman Christianity. This expressed a severe lack of confidence in their own societal identity and Indo-European cultural roots, perpetuating centuries of withdrawal symptoms, leading ultimately to the Inquisition and the European witch craze at the end of the medieval period.

The differences between the two spheres of influence, the one European and the other Gaelic, were to be very important in determining the types of nationalism that would develop within their respective areas. While the Papacy was attempting to unite the realms of the fallen empire, and with good success, the Gaels were themselves consolidating that western fringe which had never been Roman. They largely assimilated the matrilineal P–Celts of Scotland, the Picts or Albans, and made inroads into Wales and Cornwall as well. All this was accomplished between the fifth and ninth centuries, and in Scotland the first Gaelic-speaking invaders, the Scots from Dal Riada in northeastern Ireland, firmly placed their Gaelic stamp, and eventually their name, on the new territory. The resultant Picto-Scottish Gaelic kingdom came in time to be known as the Kingdom of Scots rather than as the Kingdom of

Scotland, and this epithet was symbolic of the fact that the Scottish kingship was over a national family of related tribes, wherever they might be, and not just over a population arbitrarily residing within a particular territory. The many kingdoms of Ireland were similarly tribal, as were the early Germanic kingdoms of Europe (such as the Kingdom of the Franks), though the Germanic peoples tended to emphasize the ties of chieftain and follower (such as with a band of warriors) along with those of kinship, and this certainly made it easier for them to let go of tribalism in favor of something new. After the high-kingship of the Picto-Scots was finally transformed into a secure central kingdom of Scots under the Stewarts during the fifteenth century, the Gaelic part of that kingdom looked on their king as one who derived his mandate to rule from being the chief of chiefs, i.e., as the chief was to the clan, so the king was to all the clan chiefs themselves. Tribal systems provided for a more personal relationship between king and people, manifest at all levels of society, as discussed in the previous chapter.

It is important not to associate Gaeldom with the general decline of Celtic societies on the Continent, for long after the P–Celts of the European mainland had seen their fortune wane, the Q–Celts of Gaeldom were expanding their territory with all the vitality of their Indo-European cousins and contemporaries, the fifth-century Germanic tribes of Europe. Gaeldom had never bowed its head to the foreigner, and its perspective was one of pride, confident strength, and expansion. This is reflected later in the attitude of the native Irish chiefs of the sixteenth century, as they were (perhaps regrettably) for the most part unrelenting and disdainful of English conquest. Foppish Elizabethan ways certainly elicited a boisterous reaction from members of the O'Neill's heavily armed bodyguard on his historic visit to London in 1562.

Throughout the medieval period, Gaels had been involved in European warfare, primarily as mercenaries. They were also continuously at the heart of European scholarship and monasticism, and continued to send monks or mercenaries as the whim took them, throughout their history, demonstrating in the process the wanderlust so typical to the Indo-European psyche. Here we see mirrored in the Gaelic pilgrimage the wanderings of the early Germanic tribes as they took possession of Europe after Rome, and also the drive that took other Indo-Europeans as far afield as India, Persia and Asia Minor.

The still-pagan Vikings were the last of the great Germanic wanderers from the North, and it is interesting to point out that in their westerly exploration (ninth to twelfth centuries) they found themselves preceded at every turn by the Gaelic lay-monastic settlements: In the Outer Isles of the Hebrides, Iceland and even in North America, where, according to the saga evidence, they found a European community they called Great Ireland, or Whitemen's Land (Anderson 337–338). In Iceland, even today, the Christian church is strikingly similar in its social adaptation to the Celtic original, a situation indicative of both its Celtic antecedent, and the continued social pressures of isolation and self-sufficiency. Both the saga evidence and Gaelic folk-tradition attest to the existence of such far-flung Gaelic settlements, as does the archeological record, and such places are mentioned repeatedly in the sagas.

It is interesting also that the tribalism of the Native Americans in the eastern part of North America was quite similar in many respects to that of Gaeldom, and maintained its independence for about as long (the Ulster Scottish or Scotch-Irish immigrants who settled the territory west of the Appalachians had practiced the techniques of fortifying their farms against hostile tribes during their tenure as settlers in Northern Ireland around 1600). Indications of early contact between the North American Indians and the Indo-Europeans are further suggested by the physical anthropology of the former. Their pre–Columbian physical remains have even been described as being less Oriental and more relatively *European* the more easterly their provenance (Fell, *Bronze Age America*, 84–97). Rousseau's admiration of the "noble savage," seen in this light, may well be a kind of subconscious invective against Europe's own loss of innocence, as the Native Americans themselves may well have been more closely related (and not just in spirit) than previously realized to Europe's own primordial Indo-European self.

Turning from Native American analogues to European ones, I would point out that the supposed mystical Celtic consciousness is really a kind of tendency to superstition characteristic of the early Anglo-Saxons as well, and probably was a shared trait of Indo-European culture. In fact, much of the barbarous, superstitious and tribal aspects of Gaelic society are mirrored in Anglo-Saxon literature (*Beowulf*). These early German cousins appear to have been every bit as ethereal as the Celts, and just as intuitive and sensitive to nuance. The German tribes, originally inhabiting the harsh wilderness of the far North, never had quite the rash, wide-open society enjoyed by their fiery Celtic cousins to the south. In the British Isles, however, proximity, access and considerable compatibility existed between the Gaels and the Anglo-Saxons well into the Middle Ages. Differences here did not really emerge until after the Norman invasion of England, though the machinery was set in motion by the division between the Celtic and English church at the beginning of the medieval period.

Gaeldom was often characterized, especially by the post–Norman English, as barbarous. Yet it was Gaelic scholars who were largely responsible for initiating and sustaining the learned missionary activity which ultimately raised Europe out of the Dark Ages (ca. 500–1000) and resulted in her conversion to Christianity. Such scholars carried on a long tradition of Celtic philosophy, which was famous since ancient times, having been admired by the classical world in the days before the fall of the Celtic kingdoms of Europe. The Celts have always been famous for their love of freedom, wit, and fighting spirit, and these traits are all aptly reflected in the Gaelic psyche. Also important to the Celtic mind is a sense of honor and fairness, and stories of the inherent chivalry of the ancient Gauls in the face of Roman treachery have their Gaelic counterparts in the Gaelic-English struggles of more recent times, which culminated with the destruction of Gaeldom in the seventeenth and eighteenth centuries. These Celtic traits have left their mark on Western man — on his love of freedom — and they provide him a link with the past more direct and lasting than is his nominal connection with Greece and Rome, or even Palestine. It is significant to remember that the flowering of knightly chivalry in Europe during the High Middle Ages drew much of its literary inspiration from Celtic sources (such as Welsh tales about King Arthur and his knights).

In the realm of medieval scholarship, Gaelic vitality and confidence was responsible for much original thought and creativity at a time when virtually everyone else in Europe was simply copying the work of the great classical writers, rather than doing anything innovative themselves. This state of affairs was a symptom of Europe's preoccupation with the backward look to Rome. In any case, such Gaelic creativitiy and independence of thought sometimes provoked a "who do they think they are" form of Papal criticism, for medieval Europeans set a premium on conformity, which mostly came at the expense of creative philosophical inquiry. Rationalism would not become generally popular until much later, though it did make a start during the High Middle Ages, (tenth through thirteenth centuries). The Gaels, for their part, could find Europeans to be both artless and monotonous, and seemingly lacking in nobility or subtlety as well, as they looked on Europeans with a Gaelic perspective.

Such misunderstandings between the two spheres were the inevitable by-product of differences in cultural and moral emphasis and perspective (just as was the later English preoccupation with the "barbarous" elements Gaeldom displayed). As a nation, Gaelic energy was spent either in internal political strife, or in the Gaelic fervor for Christian scholarship, missionary work and monasticism. However, Gaeldom was rich in both human and agricultural resources, and thus constantly had "the wolf at the door," as the foreigner came to forcibly partake of the richness of the land. This unchanging fact sounded the death-knell for Gaeldom, for the Gaelic system was outmoded in this one important sense: Ultimately it could not defend itself against the military, logistical and economic power of the rising European nation-states of the post-Medieval period. Gaelic society was in the end too inward-looking, too absorbed in the living and glorifying of its own archaic culture, and thus failed to move forward with the zeal, for instance, of the searching and farsighted English.

Though the tribes no longer rule in Gaeldom, the Gaelic language is still spoken and still reflected in the accent, idiom and syntax of local English speech in Ireland and Scotland. The *cultural* legacy of Gaeldom, as opposed to political, is still in existence for all to appreciate. It is to this fact that this book is dedicated.

IV. The Kingdom of the Picts: Christianity, Paganism and the Making of Gaelic Scotland

Before there was Scotland, four separate kingdoms existed. The time was the beginning of the seventh century A.D. The kingdom of the Northumbrian Angles occupied the eastern Lowlands southwards starting with Edinburgh: Its northern half was the sub-kingdom of Beornicia. Just west of Beornicia was the British kingdom of Strathclyde, a tribal kingdom of post–Roman genesis, which filled the void left in the northwest of Roman Britain when the Roman legions departed in A.D. 410. Always on the fringe of Romano-Celtic Britain, Strathclyde was further isolated by the Northumbrian conquest of the neighboring British kingdoms of Rheged and Gododdin early in the seventh century. Just north of Strathclyde, in the region now known as Argyle, lay the kingdom of the Scots of Dal Riada, Scots being a generic term for these recent Erainnian immigrants. Dominating the whole region was the kingdom of the Cruithne of Alba. Also known as the Picts, or Caledonians, their kingdom covered the bulk of what is now Scotland.

Society in the north of Britain was tribal. It emphasized kinship bonds and the generosity of the lord as the patron and leader of a band of armed retainers, usually kinsmen, who manned his shield wall in war and his mead bench in peace. The British of Strathclyde and the Scots were Christian, the Picts and the Northumbrians just becoming so. Beyond such differences in religious development, the basic pattern of life appears to have been surprisingly similar: The social fabric, economy, technology and material culture were largely the same between the four Northern "Heroic" kingdoms. But the old pagan institutions were at once a justification for, and a formative influence on, the fabric of Heroic society itself. Because of the interrelationship of these pagan institutions with other aspects of society, their continuation in some form was inevitable unless the society itself was destroyed. Yet because their missionary work was not in the nature of a military conquest, the Christian church was not in a position to alter the basic fabric of society in the Celtic North until

24

the time of the English Civil War in the seventeenth century. This left room for a thousand years of Celtic Christianity. The key ingredients for the making of Gaelic Scotland can be found in the syncretism which occurred between the Gaelic monastic church and Celtic paganism and related social institutions. In the long run, Celtic culture would prove to be relatively tenacious in maintaining its Heroic institutions in the face of outside pressure.

Notwithstanding the unique identity of the Picts and Gaels, a basic Heroic pattern of life was shared by all the Heroic kingdoms in the North. This was partly the result of their common links to late Iron Age Indo-European culture, but more immediately this similarity was the result of mutual cultural leveling after nearly two hundred years of local conflict between these kingdoms. The stakes of war were high, but warfare itself was to some extent conventionalized and even ritualized, with an emphasis on individual combat. The very fact that these four kingdoms were able to remain in "the game" for several hundred years points to similarity in society and military technology. Intermarriage between royal houses and alliances across linguistic boundaries was common, and the evidence from physical anthropology reveals that the people involved basically looked alike, even if they couldn't understand one another. However, other evidence suggests that the leaders were often bilingual. In any case, British and Pictish were both dialects of P–Celtic, while Gaelic, also a Celtic language, could not be too far removed from its P–Celtic cousins.

The Heroic period began with the departure of the Romans, and ended with the coming of the Norse at the beginning of the ninth century. The economy in the Heroic North was pastoral and to some extent agrarian: It was not based upon cities and towns. There was some coinage, of late Roman influence, but the basic unit of exchange was the cow. The king or chief had his dun, or fort, and his drinking hall, but these were not medieval stone castles by any means. Society was "heroic" in that martial valor was regarded as the principal aristocratic virtue. Society was economically, materially and spiritually directed towards the use and maintenance of the warband. Warfare was the major activity.

The typical tribal kingdom in the North consisted of kindreds, stratified hierarchically, but a limited mobility between castes was aided by fosterage and blood-brother relationships between kindreds. The royal kindred was at the top of the social hierarchy, followed respectively by priests, warriors, freeman-farmers and slaves. In the pagan period, society acted within the limited confines of certain sacred gessa or taboos (restrictions), and these applied especially to the sacral king and to the priests (for instance, in Northumbria, priests could not ride horses). Bloodfeud was common in the earlier period between kindreds within the tribe, but especially between kingdoms. Bloodfeud was reduced in the Christian period, especially within the tribe, by the establishment of a "wergild" or "man-price" for each level of the social hierarchy, so that payment would replace a cycle of vengeance.

Warfare was constant and built into the system. The warband was re-
quired for the protection of the king and hence of the kingdom. The king kept
his warband in bread and beer, distributing heirloom swords, gold and silver
rings, and other favors as he was blessed with booty in war. The fame of a king
attracted bold warriors to his hall, but success built upon success, and keeping
an effective warband meant using it to gain more treasure. Treasure in this
Heroic context meant weapons and war gear as much as it meant gold, and
the best heirloom swords were beautifully worked in gold and red enamel, in
addition to being deadly weapons tried and proven on the battlefield.

At the mead bench, the king and warriors were entertained with beer and
impromptu formulaic compositions on traditional themes, such as the Anglo-
Saxon story of *Beowulf* or the British *Y Gododdin*. Such heroic tales set the pattern of Heroic society, for their heroes typically lived richly and died in lasting
fame. In the mead hall, inspired with beer and tales of glory, the king's warriors
pledged themselves to "never desert him in war." This initiated a friendly competition for bolder and more specific pledges of martial action in support of the
king, bringing mirth and comradeship to the mead bench, and treasure to the
warriors involved. A good king was liberal with his gold, while a good warrior
was unrestrained with his pledges. However, such pledges were socially bind-
ing, and the only excuse for not fulfilling one was to die in the attempt; otherwise he lost prestige, reputation, glory, money and even membership at the
bench. A warrior without a lord was a lonely man indeed.

Heroic society in the seventh century was based upon Indo-European continuity with late Iron Age cultures in the North. The tradition giving it its identity was tribal, Heroic, aristocratic, military, preliterate (oral) and pre–Christian (pagan). The pagan aristocracies saw themselves as descended from incarnations of their respective "god of the otherworld." For Anglo-Saxons, this
genealogy would typically include Woden (Odin), the god of wisdom, or Scyld,
as a protective shield and fertility god to his people. Other Celtic and Anglo-
Saxon deities had the power of the muse over various areas of human
endeavor, just as tribal kindreds tended to stay within their hereditary occupa-
tions. Later kindreds had their patron saints, one of the many examples of syncretism and continuity between the old and new religion.

Heroic society was aristocratic, stratified along a caste system similar to
and cognate with that of Aryan (Sanskrit) India. Cognate Indo-European descent accounts for similarities in religion between Hinduism and the pagan cults
of north Britain (and between these and the Persian Mithraism and
Zoroastrianism). Pagan belief in an afterlife was strong and dualistic. However,
Indo-European dualism was fatalistically expressive of the struggle between
good and evil; it did not emphasize a dualism of spirit against flesh as did Judeo-
Christian tradition. The Heroic oral-literary tradition often had events in this
world and in the otherworld of the spirit easily intermixed in a single continuous narrative. The heroes of these are found passing through doorways

into the otherworld at lakes and streams, or else on faerie-hills under cromlechs (dolmans) or inside souterrains (underground chambers).

The otherworld of faerie-maidens (Gaelic "sidhe," pronounced "shee") was part of a dawn or pre-Christian religion that included sacral kings, sun gods and ancestor worship, "gessa" or taboos, moon goddesses, fertility cults, divine heroes, nature worship, druidic oak groves, and goddesses presiding over rivers and lakes. Other aspects included head-hunting and the cult of the head (the Gaelic sun-god, the god of wisdom, is named after the head in its capacity as the seat of reason), ritual triads (things done three times: St. Patrick railed against sun-worship and made use of the three-leaf clover to demonstrate the trinity for his pagan Irish audience), sacred tribal animal totems and shape-changing (werewolves count here, as does the raven, in which form Odin presided over battles), votive offerings in wells (holy wells are still associated with healing and prophecy), burnt offerings and human sacrifice.

For their part, the Picts shared in this common northern tradition, and yet by the seventh century there were differences which made the Picts unique. For one thing, Christianity came later to Pictland, and labored harder in establishing itself there than it had in Ireland or Northumbria. But the real roots of the Pictish difference lay in the continued manifestation among them of elements once common all over the North, and in Ireland as well. Chief among these was the non–Indo-European custom of matrilineal succession (passing royalty through the female line) and the presence of an active pre–Celtic population among the Picts, the last of which were the Atecotti ("very old ones") in the far north. The Picts, as Cruithne in the Gaelic tribal scheme, had followed the pattern of intermarriage with the native pre–Celts as had the Cruithne of Ireland. However, by the first century A.D., none of the other tribal groups of Gaeldom appear in Alba, and the Erainnian Scots did not establish themselves in Argyle until the sixth century. Therefore the Cruithne remained in Alba for hundreds of years essentially as a prototypical [La Tène] warrior aristocracy over an apparently larger pre–Celtic population. In the absence of Celtic reinforcement in the intervening centuries, both the P-Celtic language of the Picts and the non–Indo-European language of the pre–Celtic Atecotti (recorded on ogham stones) survived intact well into historical times. The Cruithne in Alba adopted the matrilineal system of the "very old ones," along with their reverence for the mother-goddess. The system was foregrounded in Pictland, but elements of the cult of the mother-goddess (essentially a neolithic fertility cult) remained in medieval Ireland in the ritual matings of patrilineal Celtic dynasts with white mares symbolizing the land of Ireland: Mother Earth. This symbolic act was the remaking of the original mating of the Celtic male sun-god with the mother-goddess of pre-Celtic Ireland. The Pictish difference was that Pictland maintained the original pattern of matrilineality. Meanwhile, the famous Atecotti merged with the Cruithne about A.D. 600.

The special case of the Picts of Alba can best be understood in terms of their singular material culture, the Pictish symbol stones. There are three types, Classes I, II and III. Class I stones are mostly undressed boulders and free-standing stones, often associated with pre–Celtic religious sites and comprised of incised, stylized zoomorphic figures (animal totems) including snakes, La Tène spirals and interlace, and uniquely Pictish symbols. The Pictish symbols include a moon crescent surmounted by a "v-rod," that is is, a kind of stylized "bent spear" in the shape of a "v," which seems to represent the refraction of moonlight, perhaps in terms of dynamic or sexual energy. Along with the moon crescent appear the matrilineal symbols of the mirror and comb, and a radial La Tène disc which may represent the sun, since two discs are elsewhere linked under a superimposed double v-rod in the shape of a "z," again represented as a bent spear. Sometimes this z-rod is superimposed over an s-shaped snake. Whether as grave-markers or as memorial stones, these symbols are pre–Christian, and may mark sacral dynastic interaction between the Cruithne and the first patrilineal (sun-worshipping) Celts in Scotland, the Erainnian Scots of Dal Riada.

These symbols are also found on Pictish silver jewelry (silver = moon, gold = sun). Jewelry was a formal mark of status in Indo-European society; it is therefore possible that the pagan symbols on Pictish jewelry mark a type of ceremonial bride-price for aristocratic or dynastic marriages. Whatever the case, pagan symbols are combined in the Christian period with the distinctive Pictish cross-slabs of Class II. Class II stones are cut and dressed, with one side supporting a Pictish version of the Celtic Cross, while on the other side appear the Pictish symbols, along with various human processional scenes. This is an overt example of classic syncretism, showing the reconciliation, or at least co-existence, of pagan and Christian belief. Class III stones are cross slabs without symbols, and represent a departure from the distinctively Pictish style.

These three classes of stones match periods in the development of Scotland. The Christian period follows the Class I period about the beginning of the seventh century, inaugurating Class II. In fact, the Pictish expertise with zoomorphic figures in the Christian period indicates direct Pictish influence on "Irish" illuminated gospel manuscripts (this could have been accomplished anywhere in the Celtic church, from Lindisfarne in the south to Iona or even Applecross in the North). In any case, Gaelic penetration of Pictland had begun in the pagan period. This early contact is reflected in Old Irish literature, which records a number of Pictish kings at Tara, the sacred pre–Celtic site of the Irish sacral High-Kingship. Picts also appear early in the Heroic literature and in the royal genealogy of the Eoganacht Gaels in Munster. From the Irish point of view, there was a cultural and tribal continuum between Ireland and Pictland, based upon the common ethnicity of the Cruithne in Ireland and Alba. This continuum was further reinforced by the early fifth century establishment of Gaelic-speaking Erainnians in Argyle ("the coastland of the Gael") on the west coast of what is now Scotland. Atholl, in Perthshire, one of the original Pictish kingdoms (later an earldom), was actually founded as a result of early Gaelic penetration into the heart of Pictish kingdom. Atholl means "New Ireland," and its foundation is connected with the great eight-century Pictish king Oengus (or Angus), who also gave his name to the Pictish kingdom of Angus (later an earldom and now the county of that name below Aberdeen). The Kindred of Oengus in Atholl maintained a patrilineal identity within the Pictish context, and this identity later translated to the Lennox and relates directly to the "Pictish" segment of the genealogy of the Eoganacht Gaels of Munster. It is possible that Celtic patrilineality was the normal kin group organization among the Picts themselves. Matrilineality was special, and may therefore have been reserved for the sacral kingship. This notion is supported by the Pictish king-lists themselves, for they typically list the father, and sometimes even the grandfather, of the Pictish king, notwithstanding matrilineal succession.

The mirror and comb symbols found on Classes I and II symbol stones show up later in medieval Scottish heraldry. A mermaid holding a mirror and a comb, known to local folklore as the "fish-goddess" of Loch Voil in South Perthshire, appears as the heraldic "beast" on the standard of the chief of the MacLarens, and also as one of the crests in the arms of the Murray dukes of Atholl: The MacLarens represent the Picto-Gaelic earls of Strathearn (southern Perthshire) in the male line, as the Murray dukes do in the female. Another Pictish symbol reappears later in medieval Scottish heraldry, the snake. There is evidence of widespread snake-worship in ancient Ireland and Scotland, and the proverb of St. Patrick "banishing the snakes" appears in this light to have pagan significance. The heraldic use of the snake in the arms of the chiefs of the Clan Donnachaidh, the Robertsons, refers to yet a more ancient proverb. The Robertson's shield of "three wolf's heads" is supported by a snake on the left and a dove on the right. This is a symbolic allusion to the proverb which appears in Latin on the privy seal of Alexander III (1249–86): *esto prudens ut serpens et simplex sicut columba*, "be as wise as the serpent and gentle as the dove." The *columba*, or dove, is a play on words, for both Alexander III and the Robertsons belong to the politically important kindred of St. Columba, the great sixth-century saint, who was a prince of the Cineal Conaill in Ireland. The snake is also the heraldic beast of the Rattrays, representatives of the Pictish earls of Mar. They take their name from their barony, Rattray, the seat of which was the now ruinous Castle Rattray (the name is Pictish for "fort dwelling"). Castle Rattray is itself built upon a snake-shaped mound associated by local folklore with pagan snake-worship.

The royal "serpent and dove" proverb above is another classic example of syncretism. It also demonstrates the pragmatic nature of cultural continuity with the Pictish past. Such continuity inevitably gives the lie to any propaganda wherein the later reality of Gaelic instead of Pictish speech in Scotland is anachronistically applied to the past, creating the false impression of long-term Gaelic supremacy. A period of the past must be judged in its own terms, and yet it is a commonplace of Gaelic tradition that Nial, the famous ancestor of the O'Neills of Ulster, was made that way by the success of his descendants, rather than the other way around. This is natural enough, yet as historians we must look beyond such pseudo-history, for it involves politically expedient rationalization, typically anachronistic and simplistic. The most flagrant use of Gaelic dynastic propaganda in Ireland was among the Eoghanacht, but in Scotland it became central to the mystery surrounding the supposed disappearance of the Picts after the ninth century.

The Pictish language died a natural death, as did its sister dialect of Strathclyde British. These dialects of P–Celtic were both isolated and nonliterate. The Picts, like the Gauls and the British of Roman times, preferred to write formal Latin, which was seen correctly as a cousin of Celtic, and considered more suitable for writing than any vernacular whether Celtic or Latin. When written Celtic did come, it was with Irish clerics writing Gaelic. It is unknown how long the P–Celtic dialects continued to be spoken, but vernacular Scottish Gaelic shows the influence of Pictish not only on its vocabulary but on its syntax as well. This difference distinguishes it from the classical (written) Gaelic of medieval Irish and Scottish literature. It is interesting to note that Gaelic itself later underwent the same process of linguistic leveling. For instance, the Gaelic dialect of Atholl (Perthshire) first became clipped, dropping its inflexional endings (in which form it continued into the twentieth century), and then was replaced altogether by English, though again this dialect of English shows marked Gaelic influence. In any case, while Gaelic scholars have always seen through the folksy anachronisms of Gaelic dynastic propaganda in Ireland, such quaint and simplistic stories have often passed as history for those studying the mixed cultural inheritance of Scotland, which includes sources in Old (classical) Irish, vernacular Scottish Gaeic, the Northumbrian dialect of Old English (ancestor of the Scots dialect of Robert Burns), Old Norse, Pictish, Old Welsh, and Latin. Regarding Old Norse, comparisons might prove helpful: The MacLeods are direct descendants of the powerful Norse kings of Dublin, Man and the Isles, and have held their vast lands continuously in right of that descent. There has been no interruption of their power or control, yet their Norse language was eclipsed by Gaelic almost as quickly as Pictish was, though like Pictish it has left its mark on vernacular Scottish Gaelic.

The idea that the union of Picts and Scots under Kenneth MacAlpin in 843 was somehow a Dalriadic takeover itself overlooks the fact that Kenneth, though clearly of Pictish matrilineage, was only of obscure Dalriadic patrilineage, putting the weight of his royalty on the Pictish side. He may have murdered his rival , significantly of a Pictish patrilineage, but even this was a common occurrence. Such dynastic feuding certainly did not carry any nationalistic overtones (the whole concept of Dal Riada and Pictland "rival nation-states" is an anachronism). There was no mass tribal migration or displacement; rather, Kenneth McAlpin represents the ultimate legacy of the Viking terror. Under pressure from the Norwegians, the Picts were forced to give equal dignity to their patrilineal subkingdom as the two peoples were literally pushed together during the Viking takeover of large tracts of the North and West. The Vikings also broke the sacral luxury of matrilineality by forcing on the Picts patrilineal leveling as a warrior expediency. The result was that the High King of the Picts, Ard Ri Albann, was also now the tribal leader, by patrilineal inheritance, of the Cineal nGabrain. As the Picts became patrilineal, the symbol stones cease in their sacral matrilineal aspect, and we move naturally into Class III. The arrival of Class III symbol stones paves the way to modern Scotland, a new entity incorporating all four original Heroic kingdoms: Beornicia, Strathclyde, Dal Riada and Pictland.

The kingdom emerging from the union of Picts and Scots was Gaelic speaking and patrilineal. In the blending of the kingdoms of Dal Riada and Pictland, this continuity of language and patrilineal traditions with the *culture* of Dal Riada tended historically to mask over the generally Pictish context of the whole affair; before the formal annexation of the rest of what is now Scotland in 1124 (i.e., Strathclyde and the Lowlands) the name of the united kingdom remained Alba, the name of the Pictish territory, not Dal Riada, the tribal name of the Scots. The high-kingship was continued from its original Pictish center at Scone (Perthshire), and in its territorial and local administration. In all ways save language and descent system, it remained essentially a Pictish high-kingship. The Pictish royal line—now patrilineal—continued unbroken. The Pictish office of "mormaer" (local sub-king) continued, and these remained in charge of the same provinces, while "thanes" (earlier "toisech") like the barons of later times, continued as the officials—heads of local kindreds—who had charge of territorial/administrative units under the mormaers in the agrarian and pastoral countryside. Kenneth MacAlpin, the first ruler of the united kingdom of Picts and Scots, was styled "rex Pictorum" by the annalists, as are the next three kings in the royal succession. After about 900 A.D. when the style changed, it became king of Alba, (not Scotland or Dal Riada). Moreover, the people of Scotland north of the Forth were after this time known by the collective term "Fir Albann," or "Men of Alba."

The name of Scotland, which comes into use after 1124, was a reference to the reality of Gaelic speech anachronistically applied to the past. Yet at the same time, its use was an acknowledgment of the origin of the kingdom in a Celtic "melting pot" given in the context of rapidly growing Anglo-Norman influence during the twelfth century. The descendants of the Picts by this time spoke Gaelic. This meant that they were now indistinguishable from the descendants of their erstwhile rivals, the Gaelic-speaking Scots of Dal Riada in Argyle, just as they were from the Gaels of the Hebrides, descendants of Viking-Celtic ancestors. In fact, these Hebridian Gaels were still under Norwegian rule, and defended their semi-independent Viking status for another 150 years: Clearly then, to be a Gael was to be a Gaelic-speaker, and as the political situation in the Hebrides and in Ireland itself makes evident, linguistic identity did not infer political unity. Only in the resurrected classical epithet "Caledonia" does any name dignify the separate identity of the Picts, and the limiting of this name to a strictly poetic context may have contributed to romanticizations about the mysterious Picts. The name of Scotland had in any case taken on a political meaning by 1124, which pointedly encouraged the conception of a Scot as a subject of the Scottish royal house, thus taking advantage of the blurred memory of previous political diversity.

The matrilineal system, since it passed hereditary authority through the female line, might seem on the surface to have invited political disaster. For instance, by the time of the merging of the two kingdoms under Kenneth MacAlpin in 843, there had alredy been a long tradition among the Picts of providing their royal women with husbands from powerful tribal dynasties to the West and South. Such exogamy might appear to invite political takeovers by jealous or power hungry sons of "foreigners" unwilling to embrace an inheritance system which disinherited them as soon as their own sisters had children who would be kings by other fathers (in the Pictish system, a son of the princess would rule, but the kingship would pass through his sister to *her* offspring). There is little reason to assume that such an exogamic union was anything more than a sacral marriage to a visiting prince. In any case, the system had its positive side, in that it was less prone to dynastic in-feuding than the Gaelic derb-fine system, since the competition among rival male cousins vying for the throne was effectively bypassed by matrilineality. Also, exogamy had its diplomatic side: It may have been as effective as hostage taking in helping the Picts maintain good relations with the neighboring Heroic kingdoms. Furthermore, the matrilineal system was never in a position to be threatened by outside forces before it was forced into close cooperation with the Dal Riada Scots during the ninth century. At that point, the uniting of the two kingdoms under one king who was heir to both was a natural occurrence. After centuries of royal intermarriage on both sides, and once the union was a political reality, the dynasts of both groups would naturally hasten to cement similar intermarriage arrangements in order to advance their position in the new order. Under Viking pressure, a warlord-dominated society emerged that probably continued to speak Gaelic as a lingua franca for the new kingdom.

The sociolinguistic pressures for a common Celtic tongue had grown stronger with the merger of the royal kindred of the Cineal nGabrain with the royal matrilineage of the Pictish Ard Ri. However, the identification of a Celtic tribal-cultural continuum with Ireland was also growing stronger because tribalism south of Alba and Strathclyde was gradually losing Tits vitality, and any P-Celtic continuum with Wales had been cut off by Northumbrian conquest. The "victory of the Scots" was in reality the pragmatic merger of two closely related peoples, under pressure from outsiders, after centuries of proximity, and with a singular recipe for intermarriage and sometime cooperation: matrilineal succession. This recipe continued to have its effect on the royal succession, which incorporated the Pictish system's nuclear family succession while exchanging its matrilineal aspect. What emerged was a modified form of succession, which served the exigencies of the time by better providing for stability and continuity in the newly merged dynasty. Kenneth MacAlpin's daughter had married Run, king of Strathclyde, and it was her son Eochaid, not either of Kenneth's patrilineal grandsons, who was anointed king in 878. It was a Pictish sense of territorial administration and nuclear family succession that continued in the new kingdom.

There are many examples of the continuity of pagan Celtic instituitions in the Christian kingdom, but the most important single instance of syncretism in Scotland concerns St. Brigid of Kildare in Ireland, also known as St. Bridget or St. Bride. The case of St. Bride also demonstrates the Celtic tribal-cultural continuum with Ireland in action. The story of St. Bride begins in Ireland. According to legend, she was the dughter of Dubhthach, a chieftain of Leinster, and Brocca, a slave girl. Kildare means "church of the oak," and the likelihood of Druidic associations in the name (referring to the sacred oak groves of the Druids) lends support to the tradition that her fifth-century nunnery was built on the site of a pagan cult center. This is far from exotic; it was usual for Christian churches to be associated with former religious centers, just as it was usual for holy days to be associated with pagan festivals as an aid to the establishment of the new religion. As we have already seen in Chapter III, the land for St. Patrick's Church at Elphin in Rosscommon was donated to St. Patrick by the then Archdruid Ona, and the church itself was long administered by his descendants. In any case, St. Brigid's nunnery was associated with her namesake, Brigid, who appears in ancient Irish literature as daughter of the Daghda, or Otherworld god. She is ultimately the mother-goddess of fertility, and was held to preside over learning, literature, craftsmen and especially the healing arts. St. Brigid continued this tradition: As midwife of the Virgin Mary, she is often venerated in her own right. Her nunnery at Kildare was under gessa or taboo: It was forbidden for a man to enter the nunnery or pass through the hedge which surrounded it. Inside, her fire was tended by the virgins of her nunnery, in nightly vigils, and it was said that the fire burned for a thousand years.

Kildare, near Dublin, is not far from Tara, the seat of the ancient High Kings, and site of their inauguration before the "singing stone," which rang out in the sacral presence of the true king. The stone and the place are pre–Celtic, and it is interesting that this, the most sacred spot in Ireland since the dawn of memory, was never surmounted by a Christian church. This may be related to the fact that the "feis," the pagan inauguration ceremony of the High King,

was continued well into Christian times: Diarmait mac Cerbaill celebrated the
feis in A.D. 560. The feis itself involved the ritual marriage of the king with
Tara, the sovereignty of the land of Ireland.

Tradition has it that a century before St. Columba brought the word of
God to the pagan court of the Northern Picts in 564, a previous high king,
Nechtan Morbit, this time of the Southern Picts, had spent part of his exile
as a youth with St. Brigid at Kildare. He later gave her Abernethy, the sacred
site of the Southern Picts, for her church. Thus dedicated to St. Brigid, the
Picts seem to have adopted her name for their kings, many of whom are named
Bridei (as in St. Bride). Of course, since the pagan king ministered to by St.
Columba was himself named Bridei, an association with the pagan Brigid
seems likely to have been the true antecedent, and thus we have another case
of classic syncretism between the pagan and the Christian. The tradition of
St. Brigid of Abernethy may also reflect the fact that St. Boite of Monaster-
boise near Kildare was at work among the southern Picts "with 60 holy men
and virgins" *before* the princely Columba took his largely diplomatic mission
to Inverness. Any "virgins" with St. Boite are likely to have been associated
in some way with Kildare.

The pre-union Pictish kingdom had been made up of seven sub-kingdoms,
and was generally divided north and south by the Grampian Mountains.
While the Kindred of St. Columba ministered to the royalty of the north from
the original Columban foundation at Iona (an island off the coast of Argyll
granted to Columba by the Pictish king), other Irish churchmen, and some
Picts, did the bulk of the missionary work in both the far north, and all along
the eastern coast of Pictland. Apart from the Kindred of St. Columba at Iona,
the foundation of the Pictish church also saw tribal (secular) kindreds
established by St. Maelrubha at Applecross in Ross and by St. Fillan in Glendochart (Perthshire). Other saints include St. Machar, St. Fergus and St.
Nathalan of Aberdeen, St. Drostan of Deer, and St. Blane, founder of
Dunblane (Perthshire), a kinsman of St. Cattan of the Cineal Loairn.

The story of the Pictish church starts with St. Comgall in Northern
Ireland. St. Comgall was the founding abbot of the biggest monastery in
Ireland, Bangor, which he founded in 558 in the territory of the Irish "Picts"
(Cruithne) in the Ards of Ulster (east coast of County Down). Along with St.
Cainech of Aghaboe, St. Comgall had accompanied St. Columba to the Court
of King Bridei at Inverness in 564 in order to translate between the two princes.
St. Comgall himself was the son of Sedna, son of the cruel Trian, the disciple
of St. Patrick who was later cursed by the same saint. They were a princely ec-
clesiastical family of the Erainnian Dal bhFiatach race, kinsmen of Dichuo, the
Ulidian king who first opposed St. Patrick's landing in Ireland, and then was
converted by that saint.

Bangor's mission among the Picts of Alba, begun under St. Comgall, continued under St. Maelrubha, a successor of St. Comgall in the abbacy of

Bangor. St. Maelrubha was of the Cineal Eoghain race, later to be the chief kindred of the Gaels of Ulster. By this time Bangor, by far the largest monastery in Ireland, had become the home of a kind of ecclesiastical tribe in the land of the Irish Picts. The monastery of scholars had become an economic sub-unit as well, serving the needs of thousands of people, body *and* soul. This type of arrangement was to find its parallel in Scotland among the "Culdees" of St. Andrews, Abernethy, Brechin, Lochleven, Monifieth, Monymusk, Muthill, etc., all Pictish foundations. The Culdees were religious communities serving the local church, but without a rule, whose members apparently originated as solitaries.

By the historical period the Irish Picts show no evidence of matrilineal descent among their kings. Yet as St. Maelrubha, himself of the Cineal Eoghan, was connected on his mother's side with St. Comgall, it would appear that the abbacy had passed to him in the Pictish mode, by female line descent. This may indicate a kind of matrilineality in the church of the Irish Picts at this time, itself perhaps indicating a dearth of male heirs among ecclesiastics. In 673 at the age of 29, St. Maelrubha went to the Picts of Alba and founded the monastery of Abercrossan or Applecross, on the coast of western Ross, just opposite Skye. It was here that the patronage of St. Andrew was to be chiefly fostered in a tribal sense.

St. Maelrubha died in 724. In 763, almost one hundred years after the founding of Applecross, a church was erected in Fife to house the relics of St. Andrew, which had been brought to that site, the present St. Andrews in Fife, in 761 by the Irish ecclesiastic St. Regulus (formerly Abbot of Lough Derg on the Clare-Tipperary border). St. Regulus died at St. Andrews in 788, but the cult of St. Andrew flourished, and St. Andrew himself officially became the Patron Saint of Scotland well before the advent of the national flag, the Cross of St. Andrew, in the High Middle Ages.

Tradition has it that the relics of St. Andrew had first been brought to pagan Scotland from Greece in the fourth century. This tradition reflects the early missionary work done in Scotland by St. Ninian in the fourth century, work which was largely forfeit after Ninian's death. It remained to the contemporaries of St. Columba and St. Comgall to establish Pictish Christianity in any strength. Tradition also has it that Angus (Oengus), King of the Picts, attributed a great victory over the Angles of Northumbria in 735 to the intervention of St. Andrew, whose saltire cross appeared in the blue sky. Angus was the king who dedicated St. Andrew's church in Fife, and the story of Angus's vision obviously accounts for the adoption of the cross of St. Andrew, silver saltire on blue, as the national flag. Yet this story is strongly reminiscent of another: The fourth century Roman emperor Constantine is said to have attributed his great victory at Milvan Bridge in 312 to the intervention of Christ. After seeing a cross in the sky, the Emperor determined that the cross should be borne on the shields of his men, in Christ's honor, and this action marked the turning point for the fortunes of Latin Christianity (again, a good story gets recycled: St. Columba gave the O'Donnell a similar command in the sixth century).

The church founded by St. Maelrubha in 673 became the center of a Celtic tribal abbey dedicated to St. Andrew, and administered after the Viking period by a patrilineal kindred with the Irish-style surname "O Beolain." As we have seen, the abbey was located among the Northern Picts, at Applecross on the west coast of Ross. Since the ninth and tenth centuries were transitional between the Pictish and Gaelic systems of descent, we can expect that before that time the abbey had passed to the successors of St. Maelrubha in the Pictish mode of matrilineal descent. Yet such direct Gaelic-Pictish interaction was not forthcoming over much of the North and East, and thus the Pictish matrilineal system was apparently in a position to linger on in the more purely Pictish areas of Ross, Sutherland and Aberdeenshire, away from the direct effects of the centralizing monarchy. We should not be surprised then to find that as late as 1014 the then Earl of Mar (Aberdeenshire) succeeded through an heiress. The fact that this succession did not cause a break in political continuity with the original Picto-Gaelic line indicates a Pictish style succession on the old model.

However, during the period vast areas of Ross, Sutherland, Caithness, Orkney and the Hebrides ("the Isles") were all under Norse rather than Pictish control. In these areas, interaction was Norse-Pictish, and thus matrilineality was faced with an aggressive Indo-European patrilineality of the first order, especially where political control was at issue. We would not expect patrilineal Vikings to pass matrilineally what was acquired in a patrilineal spirit, either by dynastic marriage or masculine sword right. Interaction did occur. Norse sources such as the Icelandic *Landnamabok*, supported by archeology, reveal a very interesting situation: The Norse royalty of the area was already both Christian and half–Celtic by the mid-ninth century (their genealogies show frequent marriages to Celtic princesses).

We should not be surprised, then, to find that Helgi, the son of Ketill Flatnefr, nine-century Norse ruler of the Hebrides, was himself known by the Gaelic nickname of "Bjolan" (Beolain), nicknames being the usual second element in Norse personal names. Nor should we be surprised to find that Helgi Bjolan's relatives brought Christianity to Iceland in the ninth century. The very survival of Applecross as an abbey on the coast of Viking Ross points to fortuitous Norse patronage. Helgi Bjolan is undoubtedly the namesake of the O'Beolains, since his father was ruler of the Hebrides (Applecross faces these) and his nephew was King of Ross. Beolain is certainly not a typical Gaelic name.

The earlier Pictish abbots of Applecross were probably "co-arbs" (blood-related successors) of St. Maelrubha in the Pictish mode of matrilineal descent. Since Applecross, as a Celtic tribal abbey, was continuously active throughout the Viking period, we can infer a similar continuity of co-arbial succession among its abbots. Therefore the O'Beolains, despite a patrilineal connection to Helgi Bjolan (which would have served them well at the time), represent continuity with the old line. Surnames in the earlier "O" form came into use in Ireland in the tenth century: The name of Domnall O'Neill, High King of Ireland, refers to a "Niall" who died fighting against the forces of Helgi Bjolan's kin. In the same way, the name of O Beolain was applied to a tenth-century abbot at Applecross, who despite his Picto-Norse descent, was considered to be connected with Bangor and the Cineal Eoghan, and with the Columban church in Sligo, where a branch of the O'Beolains settled as eranachs (hereditary priests).

The O'Beolains, as hereditary abbots of Applecross, possessed princely authority over the district connected with the abbey, the lands of which spanned the coast of Ross from Glenelg to Lochbroom, extending a considerable distance inland. That they were Pictish co-arbs of St. Maelrubha, with dynastic connections to Norse power in the area, is a natural conclusion, for leadership at the clan level was a tribal office, as was the position of abbot itself. Their connection with the Cineal Eoghan is also suggested by the fact that they did not adopt some form of the Norse galley in their arms.

The O'Beolains of Ross (the name shows up later as "MacBeolain") were also known by the Gaelic epithet *Mac Giolla Aindreis*: "descendants of the servant of St. Andrew." Likewise, the tribe that inhabited their abbey lands in western Ross were known as the Clann Aindreis, or "the race of Andrew." The main line of the co-arbial abbots of Applecross later became vested in the earldom of Ross under the Normanized Scottish kings, and while known by the Anglo-Norman style epithet of "de Ross" (later the surname "Ross"), they were nonetheless known in their native tongue under the Gaelic patronymic of "Mac Giolla Aindreis" or "Giolla Aindreis" (Gillanders). They were the only Gaelic tribal family to be known by such designations, and their significance to the Pictish church is thus aptly implied.

It was Fearchar Mac an tSagairt (significantly, "the son of the priest") who became Earl of Ross about the year 1226. He was the first of the O'Beolain line to become a purely secular ruler (a "Gillanders" does appear with the earls who besieged Malcolm IV at Perth in 1160 because of his northern policies). His career is indicative of the vitality of the Celtic church, for it shows that even as late as the thirteenth century the princely status of the church was secure enough to facilitate the smooth transition of Mac an tSagairt from spiritual to temporal authority, as the old Celtic princely abbacies were discontinued under the Normanizing Robert I.

That the Pictish church eventually became dominant over the influence of the Iona-based Kindred of St. Columba is suggested by the national flag of Scotland, the cross of St. Andrew, which is symbolic of St. Andrew's preeminent position as Patron Saint of Scotland. It is also evident in the great

Christian center and college of St. Andrews in Fife. It is further reflected in
the use, at least from the 1200s, of the cross of St. Andrew on the royal seal,
with its ancient Pictish significance. Thus we see reflected in modern Scotland
evidence of the success of the early Pictish mission initiated by St. Comgall and
St. Maelrubha.

Though the Columban church dominated royal circles in the tenth and
eleventh centuries, the cult of St. Andrew, alive and well among the Culdees
of the east coast, was revived in the national sense early in the twelfth, and
the Columban clerics left Dunkeld (Perthshire), to which they had come under
Kenneth MacAlpin, and went back to Iona. The Columban church had been
banished from Pictland or Alba once before, in A.D. 711, by the Pictish king
Nechtan, in connection with the original rise of the "Cult of St. Andrew."
(This earlier banishment reflects the development of episcopal sees in Pictland
after the synod of Whitby and under Northumbrian influence; the territorial,
bishop-oriented Northumbrian church clashed with the abbey system of the
Celtic tribal church). Some of the twelfth-century Columban monks even
returned to Ireland, taking with them some of the saint's relics. Why all this
happened is probably best explained by several factors. Previous to 1100, the
kings of Albany were high-kings in the Picto-Gaelic sense, and held little local
power outside their own tribal area; they were at best overlords, and war
leaders of the united tribal armies of northern Scotland (Alba) against the Viking sea-kings. Their careers mirrored that of Brian Boru in Ireland (d. 1014) in
this regard. Their secular ecclesiastics were powerful and princely, and were
drawn chiefly from the Kindred of St. Columba, mentioned above. These ecclesiastics were frankly aristocratic, and though sincere, never represented a
grass-roots religious movement, and can hardly be said to represent the old Pictish church, whose true successors were the "Culdees" of especially Fife, Perthshire and Aberdeenshire (the heartland of the old Pictish kingdom).

The Kindred of St. Columba was tied to the Gaelic tribal dynasties. This
would come to have ramifications for the church in the twelfth century, for
under the reforming influence of the Saxon princess St. Margaret, who became
the second wife of Malcolm III (ca. 1090) the church was revived from the grass
roots level by the east-coast Culdees of the original Pictish church. This revival
was facilitated by the fact the bulk of the population was still largely Pictish
in origin, especially outside the West Highland mountain areas (the Pictish
kingdom had always been centered in the coastal lowlands to the east).

The incorporation of the Cineal nGabrain into the Pictish royal house,
with its continued tradition of Pictish nuclear family succession, effectively
disenfranchised the Cineal Loairn, who had previously enjoyed the right to
alternate the kingship of Dal Riada with the Cineal nGabrain. This proves
that the ninth-century union of the royal houses was not an exclusively
Dalriadic one, at least not from the perspective of the Cineal Loairn. The
differences between the old Gaelic and new Picto-Gaelic systems of royal

succession set the stage in the eleventh century for a north-south dichotomy
in the new kingdom, which by this time had incorporated both Beornicia
(Malcolm II) and Strathclyde (Duncan I). The politics of the period reflect the
ambitions of the Cineal Loairn, for as they had traditionally alternated the old
high-kingship of Dal Riada with the Cineal nGabrain, the line which had inherited the Pictish throne, they wished to reassert their ancient rights. Yet even
such Dalriadic awarenesses as these were tempered by the new Picto-Gaelic
style succession, for the seriousness of the claim of the Cineal Loairn depended
on key marriages with factions within the Cineal nGabrain itself during the
eleventh century. There may also be in this a reflection of the more ancient
division of the Pictish kingdom itself into northern and southern parts, for the
Cineal Loairn had migrated northward up the Great Glen into Moray, and
intermarried with Northern Picts.

St. Margaret, the mother of David I, sought to influence the Celtic church
in the North to come into conformity with the Roman church, as the Saxon
church had done. It is not surprising that under her influence the kings of her
line should revive the Church of St. Andrew in Fife from the grass-roots level,
especially since the rival dynasty and revolting tribes of the time were closely
connected with the Kindred of St. Columba (they mainly held sway in the
north and west of the country—Moray and Argyle—where, as we have said,
the more purely Gaelic, as opposed to Pictish, tribal aristocracies were stron-
gest).

While David I and his descendants were attempting to consolidate the
kingdoms of Albany (Picts and Scots), Lothian and Cumbria (Strathclyde) into the Kingdom of Scots after 1124, their chief rivals for power descended from
David's brothers: the MacWilliam claimants from his half-brother Duncan II
(derived from Malcolm III's first wife), and the Moray dynasty from his full-
brother Aethelred, last abbot of the Columban church center of Dunkeld,
who married the Moray "Highland") heiress. Aethelred was, like David I, of the
Kindred of St. Columba, and the interesting thing here is that all of the
claimants of this time descended from royal heiresses of around 1000: As we
have seen, the early Moray dynastic line, associated with Macbeth, whose
representative married the heiress of Clan Duff and about 1000, itself passed
to an heiress who married Aethelred. Meanwhile David and his brothers were
descendants of Crinan, their paternal great-grandfather (d. 1045), who was of
the Kindred of St. Columba and Abbot of Dunkeld, and had married the royal
heiress Bethoc, daughter of Malcolm II.

As alluded to earlier, this state of affairs was a clear departure from the
purely Gaelic, as opposed to Picto-Gaelic, system of succession, and though the
clan and tribal groups would continue to choose their chiefs and dynasts in
the Gaelic way, by male line from among cousins (as the Picts themselves may
have done), the royal succession, including that of the Clan MacDuff, seems
to have blended the Gaelic and Pictish systems to allow for male or secondly

female succession from within the nuclear family alone. This is significantly different from the Irish style "high kingship," and the growing strength of the Scottish royal house at this early date seems clearly to reflect Pictish notions regarding central monarchy, notions for which the Anglo-Normans had a special affinity. This fact, together with their attractiveness as allies because of their martial prowess, may explain why David I's line encouraged their importation as feudal settlers in the border regions after 1124.

There are a number of medieval exceptions to the generally Gaelic-patrilineal norm of tribal succession, showing that Gaelic patrilineality in Picto-Gaelic Scotland was no longer an inflexibile system, if it ever had been. Matrilineal irregularities within the patrilineal norm occur at key points in the history of the Campbells, Rosses, Mackintoshes, Erskines and MacLeods of Raasay. In a similar way, there occurs within the general context of Gaelic patronymic names several which are matronymic in origin though nonetheless following the standard patronymic format. These include O Cnaimhsighe (Kneafsey), O Doirinne (Dorney) and O Grainne (Greany). Yet at the same time it is interesting to note that as late as 1228 the Gaelic earls of Fife, chiefs of the Clan MacDuff (who were the senior representatives of the Kindred of St. Columba in Scotland, descended from a branch which had supported David I), were still passing their earldom exclusively to male heirs, though by this time the Norman feudal laws, which favored daughters over male cousins, were the rule (especially when these feudal laws could aid the king in gaining control of earldoms, property and revenue by marrying his kin to noble heiresses).

Aside from the fate of the Kindred of St. Columba, the Celtic church as a whole began to lose power as early as the twelfth century. This loss of power, indirectly the result of the reforming influence of St. Margaret, directly related to the growing influence at the Scottish court of the Normans, who fostered Roman customs and monastic rules, as well as strict observance of papal authority. Even so, Celtic church practices, though not officially recognized at the Scottish court (sound politics: Religion was the quickest excuse for out-siders to invade in the name of "Holy Church"), nonetheless went on in the Highlands and other more purely Celtic areas for much longer than generally acknowledged, while the original Culdees of Saint Andrew's in Fife continued for a time to fight for their ancient rights against the new and more powerful Norman Augustinians, who had royal patronage. Similarly, the Culdees of Abernethy in Perthshire resisted the Augustinians until about 1272. Abernethy was originally a Pictish foundation (the site of which is still marked by a fine Celtic round-tower from the Viking period). At the time in question, however, Abernethy was administered by the Clan MacDuff, descendants of Aethelred, last Abbot of Dunkeld, a member of the Kindred of St. Columba. More specifically, it was the Abernethy family (named for the abbey); they were the ecclesiastical branch of the Clan MacDuff branch of the successful

Royal House, itself of the Kindred of St. Columba from Duncan I to the death of Alexander III without male heirs in 1286. Nevertheless, the Columban primacy had by then fled back to Iona and Ireland.

Whatever their origins, the centralizing tendencies of the Scottish court during the twelfth century became essentially an Anglo-Norman phenomena. An aggressive Anglo-Norman presence meant that Celtic custom was assailed at the official level, both royal and ecclesiastical. This meant that the privileges of the original Celtic earls were also threatened. The most important of these Celtic earls were the earls of Strathearn, who were descended from the original dynasts of Strathearn ("earl" translated the earlier Picto-Gaelic title of "mormaer," or "great steward," the rank held by dynasts or sub-kings under the Pictish and later Picto-Gaelic high-kingship). As earl of what had been the Pictish province of Fortriu (genitive "Fortrenn"), the Earl of Strathhearn had the most clearly Pictish credentials of any of the royalty in Scotland. Together with the earls of Fife, who originally alternated the kingship of Albany with their cousins of royal house, these earls of Strathearn had a long tradition of being, with the earls of Fife, peers of the kings of Albany and later of the kings of Scots, in the original sense of the word, that of equal. In fact, they were paramount among the seven original Pictish earldoms or sub-kingdoms (Atholl, Angus, Mar, Moray, Caithness, Strathearn and Fife) from Pictish times, whose dynasts were known as "The Seven Earls of Scotland," and who, as late as 1290, still asserted the right to the power of "king-making," as peers, or equals, of the King, as per Celtic custom, thus we have the significance of their direct Pictish links. As earls of Strathearn, they held sway over a territory in the center of the kingdom which included Scone, the inauguration site of the medieval Scottish kings and of their Pictish predecessors.

The Celtic line continued as earls until the destruction of the their local sovereignty in 1344. However, by that time Malise, eighth earl of Strathearn, was also the Viking Earl of Caithness and Orkney by inheritance, and he continued in his northern holdings unopposed until his death. He was all the more a target for royal jealousy because Orkney was still held under the Norwegian king. Close family links had been established between Malise and the Celtic Earl of Ross, and this probably contributed to the forfeiture of the Scottish holdings of both earls in the latter half of the fourteenth century. However, the Celtic earls of Strathearn had fostered a clan in the highland part of their territory: They were descended from Laurence, Abbot of Achtow in Balquhidder, himself a younger son of the House of Strathearn. This kindred held allodial rights to their lands, as kinsfolk of the earl, and came to be known as the Clan Laren, or MacLarens.

The sees of Dunkeld and especially Dunblane were considered to have a direct connection to the earldom of Strathearn, whose Celtic earls enjoyed in them the rights of a king (in the thirteenth-century foundation charter of Inchaffray Abbey in Strathearn the then Earl refers to the bishops of Dunkeld

and Dunblane as "our bishops"). Also in the territory of Strathearn was
Abernethy, the most sacred place of the Southern Picts, and the hill of Creiff,
long associated with the Pictish high-kingship. Abernethy, as we have seen,
was probably dedicated in pagan times to the goddess-spirit Brigid (later St.
Brigid or St. Bride) and a number of Pictish kings bore a form of her name
(Brude or Bridie), apparently as a throne name. The use of the Pictish royal
name "Brude" or "Bridei" was continued, both by the earls of Strathearn and
by the earls of Angus, but under the Gaelic and Christian form of "Gillebride"
(servant of St. Bride). In the twelfth century the name was again changed, as
the area including the earldoms, the fertile east coast lowlands of the old Pictish kingdom, again changed its prestige dialect; after that it appears under the
Anglo-Norman form of "Gilbert." Other Pictish royal names also continued
into the twelfth century. These include "Ferteth" among the earls of
Strathearn, and "Gartnait" among the earls of Mar. These names are far from
quaint or provential: During the Heroic period (fifth–ninth centuries) they occasionally grace the king-lists of Dal Riada and Northumberland, presumably
as a result of dynastic intermarriage.

The earldom of Strathearn was vested in the Crown by David II, who
made his nephew Robert the Stewart Earl of Strathearn in 1357. After his accession to the throne as Robert II, Robert gave the earldom as a palatinate (an
earldom in which the earl has sovereign power within that territory – basically
a small kingdom) to his son David (along with the Earldom of Caithness,
which had also belonged by inheritance to Malise, last Celtic earl of
Strathearn). However, the old traditions of sovereignty within the earldom
became such a political hot potato that it was eventually discontinued.

The earldom passed out of the Stewart family in the early fifteenth century, and devolved upon Malise Graham, grandson of David, Earl of
Strathearn and Caithness by his daughter Euphemia, his only child. In 1427,
however, while Malise Graham was still in his minority and a hostage in
England as well, the acquisitive James I (himself recently returned from a long
captivity in England) flagrantly deprived Malise of the earldom and gave it instead to his uncle, Walter Stewart, Earl of Atholl (during the same period the
insecure and acquisitive Stewarts enhanced their direct power and control
over Scotland by deviously obtaining control of all the most important Scottish earldoms). Subsequently (in 1437) James was murdered, hacked to death
by disgruntled nobles – Stewarts among them – led by Sir Robert Graham, uncle of Malise. After 1437 the title remained in abeyance, and in 1484,
Strathearn was made a "Stewartry" (a sheriffdom of lands held directly by the
Crown) under the Murrays of Tullibardine in Strathearn, descendants of
Malise, Steward of Strathearn through his daughter Ada about 1284. The
office of Steward (or Stewart) was originally that of "first household officer,"
and as such, this Malise undoubtedly descended from a younger son of one
of the earls of Strathearn the office passing with the lands of Tullibardine. The

later sense of the title was that of "Sheriff," and it was in this sense that Sir William Murray of Tullibardine, as a descendant also of the original sheriffs of Perth, became Stewart of Strathearn in 1473, with a lifetime appointment following in 1483. The Tullibardine family continued to rise in power, being made "Earls of Tullibardine" in 1583, and eventually (in 1629) inheriting the Earldom of Atholl, which they hold today. The unusual local power which accrued to the Atholl-Tullibardine family (now dukes of Atholl) is based on a resurgence of traditions of Strathearn/Perthshire regional autonomy together with politico-strategic realities arising in part from the removal of direct royal control over the area after the union of the crowns in 1603.

Old traditions continued to have an effect on the day-to-day life of the kingdom. Below the level of king, churchman and earl, the pattern of life remained surprisingly unchanged. The use of the name "Scotland" was descriptive of the Gaelic-speaking, Celtic power base which carved out the united kingdom between 1130 (the subjection of Moray) and 1266 (the subjection of the Hebrides). The political history, the record of rulers and battles in a kingdom is not the true record of the life of a people. Looking below the level of names and dates, the reigns of kings and the tenure of bishops, we find a Scotland almost humming with elemental Picto-Gaelic energy. It hums like the wind in a grey ruin, sound invading seclusion as sunlight invades shadow and warm life shocks cold stone amid the leafy humus of the past. Even today in the Gaelic-speaking Highlands, one can find venerated cult objects used in a Christian context, such as the "fairy fire stones" used in healing the sick, or blackened in the fire for a more sinister purpose (Thomson 221). The "clay body" used in "working woe" reminds one of sympathetic voodoo magic. Holy wells are still resorted to, and offerings made, and the insane are sometimes dipped in the healing water and then left overnight. Rowan trees are still found planted outside houses, presumably from a continuing belief in black witchcraft, practiced at least as late as the eighteenth century. Some sense of the magical power of iron and of the original semi-devine nature of the blacksmith continues in the practice of nailing horseshoes to walls as talismans against bad luck. On the positive side of witchcraft, healers or "charmers" are still called upon in curing the sick, as are traditional herbal remedies administered in a shamanistic way by country witchdoctors or by hags stooping over cauldrons.

The mind at work here is a Celtic one, a mind still connected to the Gaelic language and to a conservative rural environment. These factors have encouraged the continuation of a Celtic culture which remains linguistically and geographically unremoved from its original context. Christianity, long a part of Gaelic tradition, has maintained in this environment a high level of syncretism with earlier traditions. Politically expedient edicts on religious matters, executed on paper at Edinburgh or Perth, did not necessarily translate into the cultural mind of the people, and the original fusion of Christian and pagan, with its symbolic rationalization in Class II symbol stones, has remained relatively unchanged in the heart of the common people down to the present day (typical of this spirit of syncretism: St. Columba himself is known to have described Christ as "my druid"). Such enduring syncretism reflects the fact that the cultural aesthetic in the North, the Gaelic Heroic ethos, has a direct qualitative link with the seventh century, and this, as much as anything, set Gaeldom apart from the English-speaking Lowlands after 1124.

Oral forms of traditional narrative have long existed side-by-side with textual forms, the later being more static recordings of the same thematic corpus. The common touchstone between the oral and written forms is not an original composition "written in stone" by an author, but rather the collective cultural mind, the same context from which meaning itself derives: Traditional narratives begin in the mind of a speaker, end in the mind of a hearer and create meaning all in the context of the Gaelic Heroic ethos. The cultural mind, the worldview of the Gael, was at once oral, tribal, and born of the original fusion of the Heroic with the Christian. This is true even today. The Heroic worldview had an aesthetic appeal to the Gael that was in part tied to the continuation of a tribal, pastoral way of life: A sense of place or personal identity for the individual was tied to genealogy, to traditions building steam for a thousand years. Such traditions were ultimately based upon the doings of Heroic ancestors after whose stylized, culturally meaningful example it was understood one should try to pattern his life by analogy. Christianity provided an effective articulatory framework for something powerfully mystical and psychologically deep: the Celtic cult of the ancestral dead.

Orality reflected the ancient, preliterate way of processing information for cultural transmission. This involved much more than memory: It was an exploitation of a preliterate patterning in the mind at the conceptual level. Such cognitive patterning was based upon a conceptual framework hierarchically organized by analogy, for instance, to kinship and genealogy. Stock aphoristic knowledge (proverb and gnome), ironic negative understatement (litotes) and formulaic, culturally meaningful descriptive epithets (including metonyms, cognomens, patronymic epithets and kennings): These occupied a certain level of generality within such cognitive relational systems, and could be grouped paratactically, or developed chronologically in the style of oral narrative. As an example of a stock, formulaic epithet from the Heroic period, let us consider that of Conn, traditional ancestor of the Iron Age royal house of Gaels (of which the O'Neills represent the main stem): This is given in Gaelic as "Conn Cetchathach" which means "Conn of the Hundred Battles." The name is stylized and formulaic, an appropriate Heroic nickname not to be taken literally: The meaning both originates and obtains in the closed system of emic cultural knowledge. In other words, the name is an idiomatic label loaded with cultural meaning. "Of the Hundred Battles" is an appropriate epithet for describing the traditional founding-figure of an Heroic-age royal genealogy. Therefore the phrase "of the hundred battles" means that the traditional ancestor so described is of central epic importance to the founding of a Heroic-age kingdom. Thus we have Drust, son of Erp, a traditional, prehistoric king of the Picts (prehistoric in the sense that he flourished before the advent of written records in the sixth century) also described in the Pictish regnal lists as one who "fought a hundred battles." A similar epithet is probably at the root of the traditional "twelve battles of Arthur," and therefore these should not be interpreted literally (as they have been, often at great length) by writers and historians unfamiliar with the oral nature of Heroic society. However, such a stock phrase from oral tradition might be, and probably was, incorporated into a half-literate tradition of dynasic propaganda in the sixth and seventh centuries. The point is that we should avoid the anachronistic assumption by which we apply the modern literate mind's bias towards *literal* history automatically on the oral or half-oral mind of the past.

The political struggles in Scotland between Episcopalianism and Presbyterianism, which culminated in the final defeat of the Stuart kings in 1746, reflect in part the deep cognitive tension between the oral and the literate mind. With the coming of the Scottish Reformation in the sixteenth century, the collective mysticism of a highly syncratic church was replaced by literal interpretations of scripture by individuals. The old Celtic pattern of literate priests serving an oral culture was assailed by the literate mind of the Lowlander—just as the easy cognitive flow of grammatical parataxis, which served the cultural mind, was replaced by the implosive neurosis of complex sentence subordination, which served the individual. The age of reason was attacking the Gothic past, setting the stage for the literary dichotomy between Neoclassical form and Romantic transcendentalism (to the Romantic mind, Shelley's Neo-Platonic prophet was replaced by the minions of a harsh bureaucracy).

In the Gaelic linguistic culture of the Scottish Highlands can be found the last Germano-Celtic bastion of the unrepentant oral mind—a mind once shared by cultures to the south. Thus the mysticism of the Celt is foregrounded to the literate mind. The proud spirit of the Gael, Irish and Scottish, recorded by Samuel Johnson in his *Journey to the Western Islands of Scotland*, is aptly reflected in the dying words of the celebrated Gaelic bard Aodhagan O Rathaille, who, though destitute in the wake of the destruction of Gaelic Ireland, refused to recite his songs to any but the sons of kings.

The Gaelic Heroic ethos comprised an aesthetic principal based on accumulated, orally transmitted cultural knowledge and perspectives. The oral word carried this meaning simultaneously on several levels: the literal level of the cultural present, the symbolic level of art and heraldry, and the archetypal and mythic level of depth psychology. Ultimately, the vitality of the Gaelic Heroic culture was shattered not by the military defeat of the Jacobite clans at Culloden in 1746—but by the introduction of a money economy from England into an agrarian-pastoral society in which the cow had always been the unit of barter. This socio-economic collapse was part of the larger struggle in Britain (and Ireland) reflected in civil wars between 1642 and 1746. This struggle was ostensibly between Episcopalian Royalists (Cavaliers and Tories) on the one hand and Puritan or Presbyterian Parliamentarians (Roundheads and Whigs) on the other, yet at a deeper level it was the traditional rural aristocracy fighting a losing battle against the inevitable rise of an urban mercantile electorate with an epicenter in the English Midlands. In this light the Jacobite rebellion of 1745 forms the midpoint between the beginning of this struggle in 1642, and the final battle, waged in America between 1861 and 1865. Virginia, mother of Presidents, had seen a rush of Cavalier immigration after the English Civil War (Henry "Light-Horse Harry"Lee, 1756-1818, father of Robert E. Lee, was himself the fourth-generation scion of a Cavalier family), while North Carolina received the bulk of Highland immigration to Colonial America (south of Canada) following the last Jacobite rebellion in 1745.

Whether in 650 or 1650, the Gaelic heroic ethos was based upon the doings of the Gaelic aristocratic hero. It involved the élan of a Celtic warrior aristocracy on horseback. The Gaelic hero was a man admired, idealized, and perhaps sacrifical in the eyes of his tribal following. This was the archetypal Highland squire. Educated, perhaps bilingual, he was a man bestriding both eighteenth century and Gaelic values. Quintessentially Celtic in his outlook, he bears strong resemblance to the hero of Y Gododdin. He could sing sweetly at the midwinter feast, or stand grimly with heirloom weapons imbued with magical powers: The basket-hilted broadsword, the dirk, the targe of Picto-Gaelic genesis, the speckled gun with its magic stock: Here is the ideal of the half-naked, well-armed Highlander. A man with two pistols in his belt and a "heart for attachment" to the Stuart kings. Here is the heroic irrationale of the Gaelic mind, at once Scotland's destruction and her saving virtue. It is a mind phallically bent on fulfilling its cultural aesthetic, as related in this translation of the late seventeenth-century vernacular poem "The Day of the Battle at the Head of Loch Fyne" by Alexander Robertson:

> The Laird of Inverslany
> Was standing in the sand
> Having discharged his gun
> In the face of the cavalry.
> He had an embossed shield on his elbow,
> A bloody sword in his right hand,
> A pair of pistols on his hips.
> Going to strike a blow at Archibald [Campbell of Argyle].

Part Two

Tribal Nomenclature

Following is a listing of information on the chief families which made up the tribes and clans of Ireland and Scotland in the mid-sixteenth century. These are the families that had tribal significance, holding some direct political power on the primary, inter-tribal or national level, either as main players, or as constituent support groups of a more local (but nonetheless tribal) nature.

The families are arranged within their respective ethnic groups by tribe, sub-tribe and clan. Implicit here is the understanding that each of the five ethnic groups of Gaeldom fostered related tribal populations, and that these tribal populations comprised the basic political and social structure of Ireland and the Scottish Highlands until the seventeenth and eighteenth centuries.

Every Gaelic tribe originated in one or another of the five ancestral ethno-tribal population groups of Gaeldom, hence the division of Part II into five chapters. The charts which precede each chapter show the relationship of each tribal branch to one of the five euhemerized Celtic ancestor-deities traditionally linking the tribes of that particular ethno-tribal group. Sub-tribal branches of an independent and geographically isolated nature are branched independently on the chart but are linked in the text. The position of the tribes on the chart is generally indicative of their relative locations within Gaeldom.

Sometimes confusion arises in clan and tribal nomenclature, as such names often acquired a double meaning as territorial designations. These names are, in this book, used in their original tribal sense. The tribal and clan names are in Gaelic, the names of the families are given in their translated form, in English. As such, the sept (i.e., clan/family) names given generally represent the main form used with Gaelic prefixes ("O" and "Mac") although there are often a great variety of Anglicized forms extant. "O" and "Mac" denote descent from the person whose name follows, e.g., the forms "MacDonald" (literally "son of Donald") and O'Brien (literally "grandson of Brian") when they are employed as family names, are used in the general sense of marking descent from those individuals. Translations were accomplished in three ways; either by meaning (e.g., "O Sionnaigh" in Gaelic became "Fox" in

49

English), or by phonetic approximation (e.g., "O Cearnaigh" in Gaelic became "O'Carney" in English), or by "attraction," in which case a family's name was translated (by them or for them) by using a common English name of roughly similar sound (e.g., "O hUiginn" – O'Higgin – became "Higgins").

Regarding tribal and clan names, these also indicate descent: "cineal," "clann" and "corca" generally translate as meaning the progeny or kindred of the ancestor whose name follows. Similarly, "dal" means "tribe of," "muintear" means "family of," "siol," seed or progeny, "ui," grandsons or descendants, and so forth. Likewise, terminal affixes such as "-acht," "-na," "-ne," "-raighe" indicate descent from the name which precedes. "Fir" or "feara" means "men of," and is used in clan names which make reference to territories.

As for the families and the area and time covered, with the exception of a few merchant families, and some Anglo-Norman families around Dublin, the entirety of Gaeldom in 1500 was under the political dominance of the families dealt with in Part II. As a genealogical note, it should be stated that descent from these families is a thing to be particularly proud of, for these were the chiefly families whose actions molded the history of Ireland and Scotland. For such families, a code of honor went hand-in-hand with their royal or noble status, and was a major force in the Gaelic ethos, though there were of course exceptions. Family standards of ability and conduct were set generation by generation, and such kin groups were expected, as a matter of blood, to live up to the precedents set by their ancestors and maintain or advance the family's honor and position within the Gaelic tribal aristocracy. Such is the stuff of history.

These Gaelic aristocratic families tended to be very prolific, having large families and often producing children by mistresses as well. As a result, there tends to be a redundancy of patrilineally-traced royal blood in Gaeldom, as men of the commoner sort tended to lose out in the numerical contest of fatherhood, especially over time.

The next five chapters (each beginning with a genealogical chart) provide concise histories of the individual families and of their respective sub-tribal and clan groups. Appendix I lists the coats of arms of the families dealt with in these five chapters, and Appendix II contains a list of comprehensive surnames.

VI. The Cruithne

The Cruithne were the first Celtic racio-tribal group to come to the British Isles, appearing between about 800 and 500 B.C., and coming from the European continent. They were a matrilineal people, tracing royal lineage and inheritance through the female line, and in pagan times had worshiped the mother-goddess of fertility. By historical times they had come to reckon descent patrilineally, by the male line, hence their traditional descent from Conall Cearnach ("Conall of the Victories"), one of the legendary heroes from early Irish literature. Such Gaelic ancestral heroes, being the ultimate ancestors of all the ethnic groups of Gaeldom, are euhemerized deities ("gods made flesh") from the ancient Celtic "Otherworld" of pre-Christian times. Conall Cearnach is ultimately a male-manifestation of Brigid (later St. Brigid), the original mother-goddess of the Cruithne (see Part I, Chapter IV).

The Cruithne of Scotland are the original Albans, or natives of Albany (Scotland north of the Firth of Forth), and are commonly referred to as Picts. The Picts were an equestrian warrior aristocracy of the classic early Celtic type, in overlord status over a more numerous pre-Celtic population (see Part I, Chapter III). They were the last of the Cruithne to lose their matrilineality. This happened during the ninth and tenth centuries (the Cruithne of Ireland had lost theirs centuries earlier), and came as a result of the merger of the Pictish kingdom with that of the patrilineal Erainnian tribe of Dal Riada. This mixing resulted in kin groups being equally of two ethnic groups, one Erainnian and tracing itself in the male line, the other Pictish and at the point of transition from the female line to the male line descent system. The Gaelic-speaking Erainnian half became linguistically dominant at the official level, if only because, in the event of cultural influence from the rest of Gaeldom to the south and west, the Gaelic language was more useful, as a matter of choice, over the relatively isolated P–Celtic tongue of the Picts, especially where bardic literary sharing and political negotiations were concerned (the P-Celtic speech of the Strathclyde British was destined to undergo a similar decline concomitant with the loss of Strathclyde autonomy in the eleventh century).

Gaelic also had obvious *cultural* advantages and prestige, for it was Gaelic-speakers who first brought Christianity, Latin learning and, significantly,

THE CRUITHNE

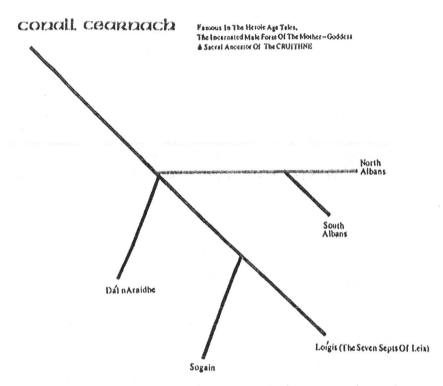

conall cearnach   Famous In The Heroic Age Tales,
The Incarnated Male Form Of The Mother-Goddess
& Sacral Ancestor Of The CRUITHNE

North Albans

South Albans

Dál nAraidhe

Loígis (The Seven Septs Of Leix)

Sogain

writing itself into Pict land or Albany. The fact that Latin orthography was associated with and applied to the Latin and Gaelic languages may explain the relative absence of written records concerning specifically *Pictish* matters—and this state of affairs may well obscure the survival of Pictish as a *spoken* vernacular for some time in the provencial areas away from the Royal Court (Strathclyde British similarly has no written records). Here one may see in operation the always close relationship between language, culture and race, as all three factors became more generally Gaelic with the passage of time, though each influenced the emerging whole (original ethnic tribal affiliations would, however, remain centrally important in the political arena).

It is wrong to think that the Picts were defeated as a group, though no doubt independent bands or kin-groups under certain warlords fell victim to defeat. By the ninth century the cultural distinction between the various Celtic groups was blurring, and in any case such distinctions had never had the nation-state overtones we anachronistically place on them today. Neither were there many players on that ancient landscape, by *modern* standards. From a Gaelic cultural perspective, the ninth-century Pictish aristocracy had long been incorporated into the Gaelic-Irish literary cosmology, and there had been significant cultural inroads into Pictland by Gaelic speakers (the district name "Atholl" in Perthshire means "new Ireland" and predates the union of the Picts and Scots). The Picts were, from the Irish perspective, just another P-Celtic ethno-tribal group, and their aristocracy was probably bilingual from an early period. Yet the individual vitality of their culture is reflected in the distinctively Pictish symbol stones of Scotland, and and in the Pictish P-Celtic borrowings which help distinguish the Scottish dialect of Gaelic.

In any case, the resultant hybridized culture in Scotland produced some clan-families with a particularly strong Gaelic-Erainnian bent, which was especially evident among those linked closely with the emerging Scottish monarchy. Other clan groups emerge which derive their identity more clearly from the original people of the land of the traditionally Pictish areas, and such professed or unprofessed affiliations, when considered in the context of Gaelic society, show fairly clearly how such groups saw themselves or were seen by others in terms of their ethnical affiliations. However, we must realize the hybridized nature of these Picto-Scots, even as we classify them, because of the unique socio-political reality in early Scotland.

Tribes of the Cruithne

The Dal nAraidhe

This tribe is the historical representative of the ancient Picts of Ulster. In the early Middle Ages, the tribe sometimes held the over-kingship of Ulaid, roughly eastern Ulster, alternating it with the chief clan of the Ulster Erainn.

The O'Lynches (O Loingsigh) were a very important family until the Anglo-Norman invasion of the twelfth century. During the eleventh century they were chiefs of Dal nAraidhe in Modern Antrim and Down, and were frequently mentioned in the annals. They were dispossessed by the Normans and their power was broken, but they remain numerous in Antrim and Down.

The Ui Eachach Cobha, a branch of the Dal nAraidhe, gave rise to the Clann Aodha and the Cineal Faghartaigh. The Clan Aodha, or MacGenises (Mag Aonghusa), rose to great power in the twelfth century, and became the chief lords of Ui Eachach, now the baronies of Upper and Lower Iveagh in County Down. Many distinguished chiefs of the name are mentioned in the Irish annals. By the end of the 1500s some of the family had spread southward and westward, into Leinster and Connacht. The Cineal Faghartaigh, or MacCartans (Mac Artain) were lords of the barony of Kinelarty, County Down. They were normally subordinate to the MacGenises, but about 1350 they were for a short time lords of Iveagh, a position usually held by the MacGenises. Both families were tributary to the O'Neill.

The Sogain

The Sogain were the original tribe of the County Galway area, with branches to the north and east, that is, among the Laiginian tribe of Oirghialla in Ulster and also in the Westmeath area (Mide). After the invasion and settlement of their Connacht territory by the Laiginian tribe of Ui Maine (ca. A.D. 400) they became tributary to the Ui Maine king, but held on to a territory in north-central Galway between Galway Bay and the Shannon, which was centered on the barony of Tiaquin. Their chief family in later times was that of O'Mannin.

The O'Mannins, or Mannions (O Mainnin) were the chief family of the Sogain, and their head resided at the castle of Clogher in the barony of Tiaquin, County Galway. They were important tributaries to O'Kelly of Ui Maine, and retained their estates until the confiscations of the seventeenth century. The name is sometimes made into "Manning": Cornet John Manning of O'Neills Dragoons in the Irish army of James II was by descent an O'Mannin.

The Loigis

The Loigis were commonly referred to as the "Seven Septs of Leix." There were several families of this tribe in historical times, including the O'Mores, O'Nolans, O'Dorans, O'Lawlors and O'Dowlings.

The O'Mores (O Mordha) were chief among these families of Leix, and as princes of Leix they were foremost among the chiefs of central Ireland in resisting the English conquest of the sixteenth century. Their main fortress was at Dunamase, near Maryborough, the ruins of which remain to this day. The O'Mores were famous for their conspicuous bravery in defying for several centuries the English conquest and occupation of their territory. Few Gaelic families met with greater cruelty at the hands of the English. In 1609 the remnant of the clan was transplanted to Kerry, where they settled in the neighborhood of Tarbert. However, many subsequently returned to Leix. The O'Mores considered themselves to be under the special protection of St. Fintan.

The O'Nolans or Knowlans (O Nuallain) are a branch of the O'Mores, and were a famous and respected family in Leinster, where their head, as chief of Fothart Feadha, now the barony of Forth, County Carlow, had the privilege of inaugurating MacMurrough as king of Leinster. A branch went to Connacht in the sixteenth century, and became great landowners in Mayo and Galway.

The O'Dorans (O Deorain) were also of the Loigis tribe. They were a great brehon (legal) family in Leinster until their power as a sept was broken by the English. Subsequently the chief family was transplanted to Kerry, and most of the clansmen migrated to Wexford. A branch also went north to Armagh.

The O'Lalors (O Leathlobhair) of Dysart Enos, near the Rock of Dunamase, suffered a similar fate. They were driven from that territory by adherents of the English family of Pigott in the reign of Elizabeth I. The majority as a result of this were dispersed throughout Leinster, and their remnant in Leix were transplanted, with their kinsmen the O'Mores, to Kerry in 1609.

The O'Dowlings (O Dunlaing) were formerly chiefs of Fearann Ua nDunlaing on the west bank of the River Barrow in Leix.

The North Albans

The Picts of historical times were divided into great northern and southern tribal kingdoms. The more ancient Pictish tribal partition described in the second century by Ptolemy is thirteen-fold, and includes the Caledonians themselves as the chief tribe of the North, their territory being roughly equivalent to north-central Scotland above Dunkeld (the fort of the Caledonians) in Perthshire. More recently, in the Middle Ages, there emerged the families of Brodie, MacRae, MacMillan, Buchan, Erskine, Rattray, Forbes, Urquart, MacKenzie, Matheson, and Nicholson.

The Brodies (Brothaigh) take their name from the place called Brodie in Morayshire. They are recorded as being in possession of that place and other lands in Morayshire as early as twelfth century. They received a charter from Robert the Bruce not long before the battle of Bannockburn in 1314, and are described therein as thanes (lords) of the barony of Brodie. They have always been important players in Scottish and Morayshire affairs.

The MacRaes (MacRath) originally came from the province of Moray, as their arms denote. Their arms include the three Moray stars and the colors of blue and silver which are significant to that district (see Chapter II). They were originally an ecclesiastical family closely connected with Beauly Priory under the Bissets in the Lovat district of central Moray. About the time Lovat passed to the Frasers (ca. 1350) through a succession of heiresses, a branch of the MacRaes settled in Kintail on the west coast, and became bodyguards of the MacKenzie chiefs and hereditary constables of the powerful Eilean Donan Castle on Loch Duich. They proved to be powerful and influential allies to the MacKenzies, and became an important factor in their rise to power. The MacRaes of Clunes in Lovat remained close to the Fraser lords there.

The MacMillans (Mac Giolla Mhaolain) originated as an ecclesiastical family, and inhabited the area of Loch Arkaig on the north side of the Great Glen in Lochaber. They later settled in Knapdale in Argyle, which they acquired by marriage with a McNeill heiress, and this became the chief seat of the clan. They were also in Glenmoriston (on the north side of the Great Glen in Moray north of Lochaber) where a branch followed the Grants, while those that remained in Lochaber followed the Camerons. Their arms contain a black lion with three Moray stars in chief (see Chapter II).

The Buchans (Buchan) derive their name from the earldom of Buchan in northwest Scotland, and are the original "tribe of the land" in that province. The heads of the family were the original earls of the province prior to its passage to the Comyn family via an heiress in the thirteenth century. Buchan of Auchmacoy is now considered chief of the name by Lyon Court of Scotland.

The Erskines (Arascain) were originally a Lowland Scottish family of Norman origin. Robert de Erskine, a relative of Robert the Bruce, inherited the Earldom of Mar in 1435 by marriage with the heiress, granddaughter of Lady Elyne of Mar, representative of the Celtic earls. With the earldom came the dignity of the arms and chiefship of the old "tribe of the land" of Mar, and it may be assumed that many of these assumed the name of Erskine. Therefore, though the Lowland branch continues, the Highland Erskines associated with the old Earldom of Mar became chiefs of the Pictish tribe that inhabited that region, in right of their descent from Donald MacEmin, who was himself Mormaer of Mar (ca. 1014) in right of his descent from a Pictish heiress (ordinarily such chiefly inheritance as that of the Highland Erskines, being through the female line, included taking the sept-name of the male-line chief, except in cases likes this of the "tribe of Mar," where no hereditary patronymic was yet in existence). The then Erskine Earl of Mar was forfeited for having served as a leader in the Jacobite rising of 1715, the abortive attempt to reinstate the line of the ancient Kings of Scots, the House of Stewart.

The Rattrays are called after the barony of that name in northwest Perthshire, and appear from their arms to have been a branch of the original House of Mar early in the twelfth century. They played an important role in the history of the district, and in the sixteenth century had a feud with the Stewart earls of Atholl, who were jealous of the Rattray lands in Atholl, which they had inherited from a Stewart heiress. The Earl of Atholl kidnapped the Rattray heiress from Rattray Castle and forced her to marry the third Earl of Atholl. The Rattrays then retired farther up Glen Ericht and built the castle of Craighall-Rattray on a strong promontory above the river Ericht. Rattray itself was recovered in the seventeenth century.

The Forbeses (Foirbeis) and Urquharts (Urchurdan) descend from a thirteenth-century noble family, originally dynastic (i.e., local sub-kings), known as "of the Aird" (southeastern Ross); a family whose earlier branches include the *MacKenzies* (pronounced "MacKingie") and *Mathesons*, and the *Clan Aindreis*, whose leadership was inherited by the ancestor of the O'Beolain earls of Ross. The Forbes clan inhabited the territory on the mid to upper reaches of the Don River in Aberdeenshire. They were confirmed in their ownership of these lands in a charter by Alexander III in the thirteenth century, and had their castle, castle Forbes, in what is now the barony of Forbes on Donside. Beginning in the mid-fifteenth century, their history was dominated by their struggle with the neighboring Gordons, with whom they differed in religion, party, and royalist sympathies (the Gordons were Catholic Jacobites, the Forbeses Protestant Whigs). Theirs was a long history of staunch and honorable service to their cause. They still hold the charter that Robert the Bruce granted to their predecessor, Sir Christian of the Aird, who was active in the Bruce's campaign at Castle Urquhart in 1305, and was later at Halidon Hall. The Urquharts descend from William of Urquart, Constable of Castle Urquhart and Sheriff (agent of royal authority) of Cromarty in the early fourteenth century. This sheriffdom became hereditary in the Urquhart family.

The MacKenzies (Mac Coinnich) lived just west of the Aird in Ross, and descend from Gilleon of the Aird, a dynast of late eleventh or early twelfth century, and the predecessor of Sir Christin of the Aird mentioned above. In medieval times they held their lands of the O'Beolain earls of Ross (later surnamed "Ross"), and on the downfall of that earldom under its later MacDonald earls, the MacKenzies rose to great power in the North, rising against their erstwhile lords, the MacDonalds, at the moment of their need. The MacKenzies were staunch Jacobites.

The Mathesons (Mac Mhathain) remained loyal to the MacDonald earls of Ross to the end, but later adhered to their Mackenzie kinsmen as they rose to preeminence. They lived in western Ross opposite Skye, with early branches in Sutherland as well.

The Nicholsons (Mac Neacail) originally possessed the lands between Loch Maree and Loch Torridon on the west coast of Ross. These lands passed in the early fourteenth century through an heiress to the MacLeods of Lewis. After this the Nicholsons followed the MacLeods of Lewis, and most of them settled by the MacLeods in north-central Skye, where they held for several centuries the lands of Scorrybreac near Portree. Their chief, as "Mac Nichol of Portree," was one of the sixteen members of the Council of the MacDonald Lords of the Isles.

The South Albans

The South Albans descend from the original Pictish tribal population of Stirlingshire, Fife and especially lowland Perthshire and Angus. They were originally known by the tribal designation "the men of Fortrenn" from the province of that name centered around Strathearn. By the seventh century their leading dynasty had monopolized the high-kingship of the Picts. This probably had something to do with the physical proximity of Fortrenn to the English Kingdom of the Northumbrians, who were the main threat to the security of the Picts and Dalriadic Scots as well (see Chapter IV). Out of this Pictish past came the medieval office of mormaer (earl) and the concept of thanage (barony-holding), both hereditary but *territorial* concepts to supplement the strictly *tribal* offices of the Gaels in the kingdom of Albany in the early Middle Ages. The families which emerge in the High Middle Ages include the *Ogilvys*, the *Drummonds*, and those descended from the House of Strathearn.

The House of Strathearn, which fell in the mid-fourteenth century, was made up of the families immediately connected with the earls of Strathearn. These earls were, together with the earls of Fife, foremost among the seven original Celtic earls who were peers of the Kings of Scots under the old high-kingship. They seem clearly to have represented the "tribe of the land" of Fortrenn, the Pictish kingdom on which the Pictish high-kingship had been based before the merging of that kingdom with Dalriada. The earls bore no surname other than the title of Earl of Strathearn, but their various branches throughout the High Middle Ages usually took surnames from their estates during the thirteenth century or later, as per Scottish custom. The only two exceptions to this rule were the *MacLarens* of the *Clan Laurin*, and the *MacLeishes*. The families of the House of Strathearn include the *MacLarens, de Balquhidders, Tyries, Logies, Glencairnies, Duries, Strathearns* and *MacLeishes*.

The *MacLarens* (*Mac Labhruinn*) take their patronymic from Laurence, who was the hereditary Celtic abbot (see Chapter II) of Achtow in Balquhidder in the thirteenth century. This line of abbots, being descended from the earl who founded Achtow, appears to have assumed the leadership of the earl's clan-family following the death of the last earl, who died about 1350. The clan was at that time reduced from being independent owners of their lands to being perpetual tenants under the new overlords, the Murrays of Tullibardine, Lords of Balquhidder and Stewards of Strathearn. These Murrays, with their kinsmen the Morays of Abercairney in Strathearn, both remembered their descent from the Celtic earls through different heiresses in the female line (by whom they acquired their lands). The Clan Laurin, in the plural sense, were probably identical with the "Lavernani" who fought under Malise, Earl of Strathearn at the Battle of the Standard in 1138. They held land in Balquhidder and Strathearn, and spread later, under the Murray earls of Atholl, into that district as well. In the fifteenth and especially the sixteenth century they were constantly at feud with the MacGregors. The MacLarens followed and supported the Stewarts of Appin in their struggles; this as a result of kinship, fosterage and alliance between their respective clans (see under Stewart of Appin in Chapter X). They also followed their Murray kinsmen, the Tullibardine branch of which family became Dukes of Atholl (and we find some MacLaren families holding land in Atholl).

The de Balquhidders, who appear in early records of ca. 1285-1305, were MacLarens (Duncan de Balquhidder appears in 1284, and Conan de Balquhidder in 1296), probably from before the name MacLaren came into general use. The *Tyries* and *Logies* are important younger (cadet) branches of the earls of Strathearn from the latter thirteenth century who founded houses in the lowland part of the earldom. The *Tyries* were closely associated with the Clan Laurin at the end of the thirteenth century, and originally bore as arms a different version of the Strathearn arms, but also variously bore a different version of the original Mentieth arms (see under Drummond, following).

The Glencairnies and Duries are important cadet houses established through the earls' influence in Moray and Fife, respectively. The *Strathearns* themselves probably descend from Robert, second son of Malise, fifth Earl of Strathearn (Robert and Malcolm de Strathearn rendered homage for their lands in 1296). The *MacLeishes (Mac Maol Iosa)* are an ancient Perthshire family, and appear from their name and arms to be the descendants of one of the earls of Strathearn that bore the Royal Strathearn name of Malise (Latin for "Maol Iosa," "tonsured servant of Jesus") in the late thirteenth or early fourteenth century. Some of these MacLeishes settled in Argyle while those in North Perthshire became followers of the MacPhersons of the Clan Chattan.

The Ogilvys derive their name from the barony of Ogilvy in the parish of Glamis in Angus, which had been bestowed on their ancestor Gillebride, second son of Ghillechriost (Gilchrist), Earl of Angus, by William the Lion about 1163. The chief of the name was created Lord Ogilvy of Airlie in 1491, and Earl of Airlie in 1639. While the Earldom of Angus, one of the original seven earldoms of Scotland (see Chapter IV), passed through heiresses to the Stewarts, the Ogilvys bear the arms of the original earls, and represent their male line. Thus they descend from the ancient Pictish dynasts and later mormaers of Angus in the early Middle Ages.

The Drummonds (Drummann) are of the same general stock as the House of Strathearn, being descended from the original Celtic earls of Mentieth (Stirlingshire), which earldom was created out of Strathearn about 1164. After 1230 the Earldom of Mentieth passed from the Celtic earls, through heiresses, first to the Comyns, then to a branch of the Stewarts (who took Mentieth as their surname), and finally to the Grahams, with interruption from about 1380 to 1425. After 1425 it was given back to the Grahams, but was much reduced in authority and extent, being comprised of only the western half of the original earldom. From that point on, the eastern part of the earldom was reserved by the Crown as a "Stewartry" (see Chapter IV). In any case, it is from the original earls that the family of Drummond descends.

The first undoubted Drummond ancestor was Malcolm Beg ("Little Malcolm") of Drummond, who appears as Seneschal (Steward or Stewart) of the Lennox from about 1225. He is probably identical with Malcom de Mentieth who appears on record as a witness in 1237, especially since he is never called "of Drummond" until he is described as such on his son's early fourteenth century tombstone at the High Alter of Inchmahone priory in Mentieth.

The Celtic earls of Mentieth were related by marriage to the Celtic earls of the Lennox, and so it is not surprising to find a cadet of the old Celtic House of Mentieth employed by his relatives in the neighboring earldom, especially when their own family rights of overlordship and land were quickly passing to the Comyns. Thus the Drummonds, who probably represent the male heir of the old Celtic earls of Mentieth, took their name from lands in the Lennox, the lands of Drymen (Dromainn in the Gaelic). However, they also kept their connection with Mentieth, having a feud with the Mentieths (the family of the Stewart earls) which was resolved in 1360, and acquiring Stobhall, their seat in Perthshire, by marriage in about 1345. They rose to high office under the Stewarts, and remained loyal to them through adversity, while at the same time remaining Roman Catholic. As Mentieth had not been a separate political unit from Strathearn before the creation of the earldom during the first half of the twelfth century, the original Celtic earls may have been related to the House of Strathearn, and this thesis is supported by the arms of the Logies (mentioned above under *Strathearn*), two of which are recorded. One is a different version of the arms of the Celtic earls of Strathearn; the other, like the arms of the Drummonds, a different version of the arms of the Celtic earls of Mentieth.

As a note to these armorials, the unique royal livery colors of the Kings of Scots were red on gold, and the King and his two chief peers, the Earl of Fife (see under MacDuff in Chapter IX for the House of Fife's early use of two arms) and the Earl of Strathearn, all used these colors, tincture on metal, expressing their unity in the royal colors of Scotland. These bearings seem to have been officially adopted, as a formal heraldry based on tribal traditions, about the time of the founding of Scone Abbey in 1164 (their arms appear on the Seal of Scone Abbey), just prior to the accession of William the Lion as King of Scots. The other knightly and noble families no doubt followed suit, and thus Scottish heraldry as a formal institution probably dates from this time. It is interesting in this connection that the Drummonds too used these colors in their differencing of the arms of the original House of Mentieth, red wavy bars on gold instead of blue wavy bars on silver.

VII. The Erainn

The Erainn were the second of the Celtic groups to come to Ireland, as discussed in Chapter II. They arrived from the Continent between 500 and 100 B.C., and established their La Tène culture throughout the island as a military aristocracy possessing superior iron weapons technology. They were akin to the Belgae of Southwest Britain, and were generally known as the Ulaid in the North, and as the Erainn or Desi in the South, although all the tribes of this ethnic group were known ultimately to be Erainn. The great Erainnian population groups of around A.D. 600, such as the Muscraige of Munster, gave rise in the Middle Ages to the independently branched tribal groups that follow.

Tribes of the Erainn

The Clann Choinleagain (or MacGilfoyles)

The Clann Choinleagain or MacGilfoyles (Mac Giolla Phoil) were an ancient clan in the territory of the O'Carrolls of Ely, being chiefs of the territory around Shinrone, South Offally.

The Conmhaicne Rein

The Conmhaicne Rein were a clan whose original territory was coextensive with the diocese of Ardagh in County Longford. The chief families of the Conmhaicne Rein included the Muintear Eoluis (MacRannalls and O'Cornyns), O'Farrells, O'Moledys and O'Quins.

The Muintear Eoluis included the families of MacRannall (Mac Raghnaill) and O'Cornyn (O Cuirnin). The MacRannalls were chiefs in the south of County Leitrim, and for years alternated alliance and conflict with their powerful neighbors, the O'Rourkes. The O'Cornyns, on the other hand, became hereditary poets and chroniclers (historians) to the O'Rourke chiefs.

The O'Farrells (O Fearghaill) of Annaly were the ruling race of County Longford, and were seated at the town of Longford, which was known as "O'Farrell's fortress." In later times they divided into two great branches, the heads of which were known as O'Farrell Boy, "the yellow O'Farrell," and

THE ÉRAINN

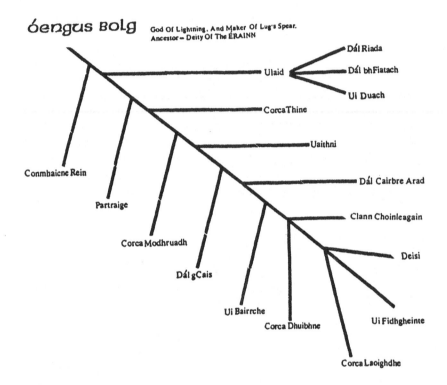

óengus bolg God Of Lightning. And Maker Of Lug's Spear.
Ancestor — Deity Of The ÉRAINN

Dál Riada
Ulaid
Dál bhFiatach
Ui Duach
CorcaThine
Uaithni
Conmhaicne Rein
Dál Cairbre Arad
Partraige
Clann Choinleagain
Corca Modhruadh
Deisi
Dál gCais
Ui Bairrche
Corca Dhuibhne
Ui Fidhgheinte
Corca Laoighdhe

O'Farrell Bane, "the fair O'Farrell." The O'Farrells maintained their in-dependence down to the year 1565, when Annaly was reduced to "shire ground" by Sir Henry Sidney, the English Lord-Deputy. Though they suffered severely under the plantation scheme of James I, the O'Farrells nonetheless were able to take a prominent part in the political and military affairs of the seventeenth century, and afterwards the family was well represented in the French service, providing many distinguished officers to the Irish Brigades. They are now numerous. The *O'Moledys* (*O Maoileidigh*), a branch of the O'Farrells, were settled in Offaly and Westmeath during the sixteenth century, where they were highly respectable.

The Muintear Giollagain or O'Quins (*O Cuinn*) of Annaly were a sept of the Conmhaicne Rien in Longford, known by the clan name of Muintear Giollagain, and were chiefs of an extensive district in Longford until the end of the fourteenth century, when they were supplanted by the O'Farrells. They are now numerous in Longford.

The Corca Dhuibhne

The Corca Dhuibhne were a great clan in West Kerry, the chief families of which were the O'Connells and the O'Sheas.

The O'Connells (O Conaill) of Kerry were formerly chiefs of Magh O gCoin-chin, in the east of County Kerry until dispossessed by the O'Donoghues about the middle of the eleventh century. The O'Connells then followed MacCarthy Mor, for whom they were hereditary castellans of Ballycarbery, near Caherciveen. The head of the family was transplanted to Clare in the time of Cromwell (ca. 1650), and afterwards several of the family became distinguished in the Irish Brigades in the service of France.

The O'Sheas (O Seaghdha) were formerly lords of the present Barony of Iveragh in West Kerry, but were somewhat displaced about the time of the Anglo-Norman invasion in the twelfth century. In the fifteenth century, a branch went to Kilkenny, where they became wealthy merchants, and became foremost among the "Ten tribes of Kilkenny," the otherwise Norman merchant families of that city.

The Corca Laoighdhe

The Corca Laoighdhe were a great clan in the southwest of County Cork. Their territory was coextensive with the Diocese of Ross, and their chief families were those of O'Coffey, O'Dinneen, O'Driscoll, O'Flynn, O'Hea, O'Hennessy and O'Leary.

The O'Coffeys (O Cobhthaigh) were formerly a powerful family of West Cork. They were seated in the barony of Barryroe, where Dun Ui Chobhthaigh, Dunocowhey, marks the site of their residence.

The O'Dinneens or Dennings (O Duinnin) were a literary family, and became hereditary historians to MacCarthy Mor, chief of the MacCarthys, and also to the O'Sullivans.

The O'Driscolls (O hEidirsceoil) were powerful chiefs in West Cork, being originally lords of the whole southwest of that county, the baronies of Carbery, Beare and Bantry. After the Anglo-Norman invasion, their territory was reduced by the encroachments of the O'Donovans, O'Mahonys and O'Sullivans, as a reaction to Norman pressure on those families. From that time the O'Driscolls possessed the seacoast area around the Bay of Baltimore, and were still a considerable power in the area in the seventeenth century, with several strong castles. They took an active part in the Munster wars during the reign of Queen Elizabeth. After the defeat of Irish forces at Kinsale, the property of the O'Driscolls was confiscated and given to Lord Castlehaven.

The O'Flynns (O Floinn) of Ardagh were anciently chiefs of the Barony of
Ibawn, in the south of County Cork. The chief of the family resided at Ardagh
Castle between Skibbereen and Baltimore.

The O'Heas (O hAodha) were sub-chiefs, under the Barrys, of Tuath O
Donnghaile in the southwest of County Cork.

The O'Hennessys (O hAonghusa) of Corca Laoighdhe were chiefs of a territory in southwest Cork near Ross Bay. A scion of this family, Richard Hennessy, was born in 1720, and followed relatives into the French Service, becoming an officer in Dillon's regiment. He rose to high office in the French government, settled in Cognac, and married into the Martell family, afterwards
founding the House of Hennessy cognac.

The O'Learys (O Laoghaire) were originally chiefs of the territory lying
around Rosscarberry in West Cork, but removed from there about the time
of the Anglo-Norman invasion (twelfth century). They had a reputation as a
maritime power from before the 1100s, and later became lords, under the Mac-
Carthys, of the country between Macroom and Inchigeelagh. In 1642, sixteen
leading men of the name were attainted (legally deprived of civil rights), including Connor O'Leary of Carrignacurra and Auliff O'Leary of Cunnowley.
The O'Learys are now numerous throughout Munster.

The Corca Modhruadh

The Corca Modhruadh (Corcomroe) were a great clan in the northwest of
County Clare, where their territory was coextensive with the Diocese of
Kilfenora. The chief families of the Corca Modhruadh were the *O'Connors,
MacCurtins, O'Loghlens, O'Davorens* and the *Corca Thine.*

The O'Connors (O Conchobhair) of Corcomroe derive their name from
Conchobhar, son of Maelseachlainn, Lord of Corcomroe, who was slain in the
year 1002. They were lords of the Barony of Corcomroe, in West Clare, down
to the close of the sixteenth century.

The MacCurtins (Mac Cruitin) are a branch of the O'Connors of Corcomroe, and were originally settled around Ennistymon in Corcomroe. They
were hereditary ollavs (professors/scholars) to the O'Briens of Thomond, and
through many generations distinguished themselves as poets and Gaelic
scholars. After the destruction of the Gaelic order, several of the family were
important antiquarian scholars. One of these, Hugh Buidhe MacCurtin
(Yellow Hugh) who lived from 1680 to 1755, published an Irish Dictionary in
Paris in 1732, and was styled "chief of his sept."

The O'Loughlins (O Lochlainn) descend from Lochlainn, Lord of Corcomroe in the tenth century. Originally one with the O'Connors, in later times
they divided the territory of Corcomroe with their O'Connor kinsmen. Thus
the O'Loughlins became lords of roughly the eastern half of Corcomroe, also
known as "the Burren," and this distinguished family retained their rank as
lords of the Burren down to the reign of Elizabeth I. The family is still

numerous and respectable in Thomond (the majority of County Clare, with adjacent parts of Tipperary and Limerick).

The O'Davorens (O Dabhoireann) or descendants of Dubhdabhoireann, were a distinguished brehon (legal) family, and for many generations they maintained a great literary and legal school at Lisdoonvarna (in the Burren), where the head of the family resided. Duald MacFirbis, the famous Irish antiquary, was once a pupil at this school. The family spread at an early date (before the sixteenth century) into Tipperary, and are now well represented in Thomond (see above).

The Corca Thine or O'Cahills (O Cathail) were chiefs of Templemore, in County Tipperary. They descended from Cathal, brother of Conchobhar (Conor-Na-Luinge Cuaithe), ancestor of the O'Connors of the Corca Modhruadh. The family was numerous at the end of the sixteenth century, and no less than three townlands in Tipperary called Ballycahill are named after them ("Bally" means "townland of").

The Dal Cairbre Arad

The Dal Cairbre Arad dwelt in ancient times in northwest Tipperary and the adjacent part of Limerick south of Lough Derg, as chiefs of that region, the Ara. In the later Middle Ages their descendants are found not far to the south, in Kilnamanagh.

The O'Dwyers (O Dubhuidhir) were chiefs of Kilnamanagh, the mountainous region lying west of Thurles. They were an important sept, though not comparable in power to such neighboring families as the Burkes. The O'Dwyers were intimately associated through the years with resistance to the English. In the Cromwellian act of 1652, Philip and Owen O'Dwyer were exempted from pardon for life and estate. Later, Michael Dwyer (b. 1771), the adventurous 1798 man alluded to by Yeats, evaded the English government for five years, though he was later transported to Australia.

The Dal gCais

The Dal gCais were the great clan of Thomond, or North Munster, an area more especially associated with County Clare (excluding the Burren and Corcomroe on the northwest corner) and adjacent parts of Tipperary and Limerick. They were the axe-wielding footsoldiers who formed the core of the army that defeated the Vikings in 1014, one of the most significant dates in Gaelic history. The chief families of this tribe were above all the O'Briens, but also the MacConsidines, MacDonnells, MacLysaghts, MacMahons, O'Ahernes, O'Kennedys, O'Shanahans, O'Duracks, MacGraths, O'Fogartys, O'Galvins, O'Gradys, O'Hanrahans, O'Hickeys, O'Mearas, O'Molonys, O'Moroneys, O'Hartagans, O'Lonergans, Creaghs, O'Quins, MacNamaras, MacInerneys, O'Deas and O'Griffeys.

The O'Briens (O Briain) were the chief family of the Dal gCais, otherwise known as the Dalcassians, and the heads of the family were kings of Thomond. The O'Briens derive their descent from Brian Boru, High King of Ireland, who was slain at Clontarf in 1014, at the moment of his final decisive victory over the united Viking army. His individual career is remarkable in the history of the Gael, and is so distinguished and outstanding that it cannot be mitigated by faint praise, for among other things he brought a degree of unity and common purpose to the Gael never seen before or since. He came out of virtual obscurity to bring Ireland out of its perpetual chaos just enough to guarantee its existence into the future. Such was his greatness that neither his nobility nor the quality of the seed that produced him can ever be called into question (as a tree bears fruit in kind, so a man's parentage and ancestry were of central social and political importance to the Gael, hence the family names in "O" and "Mac" (see Chapter V). For those interested, the book *Lion of Ireland* by Morgan Llywelyn gives his life story with remarkable accuracy and human interest.

In any case, it was Brian who raised his clan, the Ui Toirdealbhaigh, to preeminence among the Dalcassians, although there is evidence that the Ui Toirdealbhaigh were originally from Connacht (see Chapter IX). He laid the foundation for his progeny's future greatness, just as the guerrilla tactics of the Ui Tordealbhaigh, under Brian's leadership, laid the foundation of Brian's later reputation and success as a "Viking-stopper." The O'Briens became not only the ruling family in Thomond, but some of them were over-kings of Munster and some High-Kings of Ireland as well. Their own possessions included the whole of County Clare, and large parts of Tipperary, Limerick, and Waterford as well.

The O'Briens divided into several branches, the most important of which were the O'Briens of Ara, in northwest Tipperary, the chief of which was known as Mac I Bhriain Ara; those of Coonagh in the east of County Limerick; those of Pobelbrien, now the barony of that name in County Limerick (their chief stronghold was Carrigogonnell, on the Shannon); those of Aherlow, in Tipperary, and finally those of Cumaragh, in County Waterford, who had extensive possessions along the Cummeragh Mountains, that is, the valley between Dungarvan and the Suir. Other families of the Ui Toirdealbhaigh, whose original territory was in the east of County Clare, include the *MacConsidines, MacLysaghts, MacDonnells* and *MacMahons*.

The *MacConsidines (Mac Consaidin)* are a branch of the O'Briens, being descended from Domhnall Mor O Briain, King of Munster, who died in 1194.

The *MacLysaghts (Mac Giolla Iasachta)* are also descended from Domhnall Mor O Briain (Great Donal O'Brien), who lived from 1163 to 1194. They formed a sub-sept of the O'Briens, being originally settled around Ennistymon, County Clare, and spread afterwards throughout Clare and Limerick, with a branch also going to County Cork.

The MacDonnells (Mac Domnaill) descend from Domhnall, son of Murtagh Mor O'Brien, High-King of Ireland, who died in 1119. They were hereditary bards to their O'Brien kinsmen. A branch of these Thomond MacDonnells settled in Connacht.

The MacMahons (Mac Mathghamhna) descend from Mahon, another son of Murtagh Mor O'Brien, mentioned above, who lived from 1094 to 1119. Their patrimony consisted of the territory comprising the present baronies of Moyarta and Clonderlaw in the southwest of County Clare. The famous Marshall of France, Patrick MacMahon, later president of the French Republic, was of these Clare MacMahons, being the grandson of John MacMahon, himself a French marquis (d'Eguilly).

The Ui Bloid were a branch of the Ui Toirdealbhaigh whose territory originally lay around the deanery of Omulled in the east of County Clare. Besides the *O'Shanahans* and *O'Duracks*, the Ui Bloid comprised the chiefly families of *O'Aherne* and *O'Kennedy*. The *Ui Cearnaigh*, of which the *O'Ahernes (O Eachtigheama)* were the chief family, inhabited the territory around Six-mile-bridge until they were driven out about 1318 by the MacNamaras. Afterwards they are found chiefly in Limerick and Cork, but also in Waterford. The *O'Kennedys (O Cinnide)* derive their descent from Cinneidigh, son of Donnchuan, brother of Brian Boru (see under O'Brien above). They were originally seated at Glenomra, where their territory was coextensive with the present parish of Killokennedy, in the east of County Clare. On being driven from that territory by the O'Briens and MacNamaras, they afterwards settled in north-central Tipperary, in the baronies of Upper and Lower Ormond, where they became numerous and far more powerful than they had ever been before. From the twelfth to sixteenth centuries they ranked as Lords of Ormond, and were divided into three great branches, O Cinneide Fionn (The Fair O'Kennedy), O Cinneide Donn (The Brown O'Kennedy) and O Cinneide Ruadh (The Red O'Kennedy). They are said by Keating to have considered themselves to be under the special protection of St. Ruadhan of Lorrha. A branch of the family settled in Antrim about 1600. The existence of the *Clann Cearnaigh* O'Kennedys of the Laiginian tribe of Ui Maine in Galway probably indicate the pre-Dalcassian origin of the collateral kinsmen of Brian Boru (see Chapter IX), and thus of the great Brian himself.

The MacGraths (Mag Raith) or *MacCrays (Mac Raith)* were hereditary poets and chroniclers to their O'Brien kinsmen, and spread with them into Tipperary and Waterford. They ran a bardic school at Cahir and the ruins of their castle in Waterford are still to be seen.

The O'Fogartys (O Fogartaigh) were a Dalcassian sept in County Tipperary, and were formerly the chiefs of Eile Ui Fhogartaigh, now the barony of Elyogarty in east-central Tipperary.

The O'Galvins, or Gallivans (O Gealbhain) were a prominent Dalcassian sept in the early fourteenth century, and representatives of the family have remained in the original Clare homeland, with branches also settling in Kerry and Roscommon.

The *O'Gradys (O Grada)* were an important Dalcassian family in County Clare. They were originally seated in the parish of Killonasoolagh, near the River Fergus in South Clare, but after 1318 they obtained a wide territory around Tomgraney in the north of that county, from their O'Brien kinsmen and patrons. This territory embraced several parishes in Clare and Galway. In 1543, Donogh O'Grady, "captain of his nation," was knighted by Henry VIII, and formally granted the lands of his clan. After him, the heads of the O'Gradys served the English interests, and some Anglicized their name as "Brady," though this was an alias and usually the form "O'Grady" was resumed. A branch of the family settled in Connacht, while the chief family settled in Limerick several centuries ago.

The *O'Hanrahans or Harhans (O hAnradhain)* are a Dalcassian family of County Clare. After rising to some importance in Limerick under the O'Briens, they are chiefly associated with Clare and Limerick.

The *O'Hickeys (O hIcidhe)* were a great medical family in Thomond, and were hereditary physicians to their kinsmen the O'Brien rulers of Thomond. Their original seat was at Ballyhickey in County Clare.

The *O'Mearas or Maras (O Meadhra)* were a Dalcassian family in Tipperary. They were chiefs of a district called Rosarguid, in the barony of Upper Ormond, in north-central Tipperary, and their chief, The O'Meara, had his seat at Toomyvara (Tuaim Ui Mheadhra). The O'Mearas retained a considerable property down to the revolution of 1690.

The *O'Molonys (O Maoldhomhnaigh)* are a Dalcassian family who were formerly chiefs in the barony of Tulla in the east of County Clare.

The *O'Moroneys (O Murruanaidh)* are another family of the Dalcassians still numerous in Thomond.

The *Cineal mBaoith* were one of the original Dalcassian clans from the time of Brian Boru. Their representatives in historical times were the *O'Hartagans* and the *O'Lonergans.* The O'Hartagans *(hArtagain)* are a Dalcassian sept of Limerick, and are descended from Dunlaing O'Hartigan, one of the heroes of the battle of Clontarf, who fought against the Vikings in 1014 (see under O'Brien, above). The O'Lonergans *(O Longargain)* are a Dalcassian sept that was originally settled in County Clare in the earlier Middle Ages, but after 1318 they settled in Tipperary after being driven from their original patrimony by the O'Briens and MacNamaras. The family produced a number of great ecclesiastics during the Middle Ages.

The *Clann Dealbhaoith* anciently inhabited the Barony of Bunratty, in the south of County Clare. The main stem of the clan was the ancient family of *O'Neill* of Thomond, but this family is now represented by its two modern branches, *O'Nihills* of Limerick (from the Norse form of O'Neill) and the *Creaghs* of Bunratty. The Creaghs *(Craobhach)* derive their cognomen of

Creagh from one of their ancestors who carried a green branch in a battle against the Limerick Vikings (called Danes though of Norwegian origin). They subsequently became a respectable merchant family in Limerick, and later also in Cork, while keeping up their connection with Clare as well. The family provided several distinguished churchmen in the fifteenth century.

The *Muintear Ifearnain* or *O'Quins (O Cuinn)* descend from Conn, Lord of Muinntear Ifearnain, who flourished in the latter part of the tenth century. They were originally seated at Inchiquin, and their territory, which was designated Muinntear Ifearnain from their clan name, comprised the country around Corofin, in County Clare.

The *MacNamaras (Mac Conmara)* were the chief family of the *Ui Caisin* or *Clann Chuileain*. They were, next to the O'Briens, the most powerful of the Dalcassian families, and were hereditary marshalls (military commanders) to the O'Brien kings of Thomond. It was their privilege to inaugurate the O'Brien. Their original territory was called Ui Caisin, which corresponded to the present deanery of Ogashin, including nine parishes, in the east of County Clare. In later times, however, they ruled over a greatly enlarged territory which comprised the whole of Upper and Lower Tulla, the entire eastern quarter of County Clare. This territory was known, from their other clan name, as Clann Chuileain. In the sixteenth century a branch of the family settled in County Down.

The *MacInerneys (Mac an Airchinnigh)* are of the same stock as the Mac-Namaras, and formerly held considerable property around Ballycally, in the parish of Kilconry and Barony of Bunratty (South Clare), which they lost in the Cromwellian confiscations. The family is now numerous in Clare and Limerick. Their name denotes descent from an erenagh, or hereditary ecclesiastic (Chapter II).

The *O'Deas (O Deaghaidh)* were the chief family of the *Ui Fearmaic*, being the lords of the territory of that name in northwest County Clare, which comprised the greater part of the present Barony of Inchiquin. They had their chief strongholds at Tullyodea and Dyserttola; a branch where chiefs of Slewardagh in East Tipperary.

The *O'Griffeys (O Griobhta)* were the chief family of the *Cineal Cuallachta* in the southeast of what is now the barony of Inchiquin (the northwest quarter of County Clare, just east of the coastal baronies of Corcomroe and the Burren). They followed the O'Deas, and had their castle at Ballygriffy in the parish of Dysert, near Ennis. The name is usually Anglicized as *Griffin*.

The Deisi

The *Deisi* were an Erainnian race. The main group so called settled in Waterford and south Tipperary at a very early date as vassal-allies of the Eoganacht Gaels of Cashel, after driving out the earlier inhabitants. The chief family of these Southern Deisi was that of O'Phelan.

The O'Phelans (O Faolain) are the chiefly family of the Deisis, and were lords of that people and territory prior to the twelfth century Anglo-Norman invasion. They are still a numerous family in this original territory; while a branch also became established (probably as a result of the Anglo-Norman invasion) at Magh Lacha, a plain in the barony of Kells, County Kilkenny, where they also became numerous.

The Partraige

The Partraige were the ancient and remote people who inhabited the wastelands of Iar Connacht (literally, "west of Connacht," i.e., beyond Connacht proper) between Loch Corrib and Loch Mask. Little is heard of them besides their existence until the emergence in historical times of the *O'Malleys*, who later disguised their origin by the assertion of kinship with the Ui Briuin Gaels (which was probably founded on intermarriage).

The O'Malleys (O Maille) were a great sea-power around Clew Bay in County Mayo. Their territory was coextensive with the baronies of Burrishoole and Murresk on the west coast of County Mayo. Their leading men were often famous as naval commanders, and the clan always had a considerable fleet under their power, an unusual occurrence in Ireland, even among coastal families. The O'Malleys were known to literature as the Manannans, or "sea-gods" of the Western Ocean, and many tales tell of their prowess. There appears to have been a branch of the family settled before the sixteenth century in the Limerick area, as lords of Tuath Luimnigh.

The Uaithni

The Uaithni were located in County Galway in prehistoric times, but later came to inhabit the northeast of County Limerick and the adjoining part of County Tipperary. In historical times the tribe is represented by the *O'Heffernans*.

The O'Heffernans (O hIfearnain) were anciently the chiefs of Uaithne-Cliach, now the barony of Owneybeg, in the east of County Limerick. They were dispossessed by the O'Mulryans in the fourteenth century, but families of the name are still very numerous in Limerick and Tipperary.

The Ui Bairrche

The Ui Bairrche were originally from South Wexford, in the baronies of Forth and Bargy, but they were driven from this territory by the Laigin of Ui Ceinnsealaigh, and the main body settled among their allies among the northern Laigin, mainly in the area of the barony of Slievemargy in the southeastern corner of Leix and the adjoining portions of Carlow and Kilkenny. Their chief representatives in historical times are the *O'Tracys* and *MacGormans*.

The MacGormans (Mac Gormain) were, prior to the Anglo-Norman invasion, lords of Ui Bairrche. Soon afterwards, however, they were driven from this territory and settled in Monaghan and Clare. The Clare branch became very numerous, and their chiefs became marshalls (military commanders) under the O'Briens. The form O'Gorman is now used by some who have resumed the use of Gaelic prefixes, however, MacGorman is the proper form.

The Ui Fidhgheinte

The Ui Fidhgheinte were originally located in the west of County Limerick, where they were settled as allies of the Eoghanacht, coming later to be regarded as a branch of that tribe, of whom they were twice kings (in 796 and 909). Their chief septs in the later Middle Ages were the O'Cullanes, O'Kinneallys, O'Donovans and MacEnerys.

The Ui Conaill Gabhra were a clan anciently residing in the south Limerick baronies of Upper and Lower Connelloe, Shanid and Glenquin. Their modern representatives are the O'Cullanes and O'Kinneallys. The O'Cullanes (O Cuileain), originally lords of Connelloe, were driven out of this territory and settled in southwest Cork near their O'Donovan kinsmen. The O'Kinneallys (O Cinnfhaolaidh) were originally settled in the present baronies of Upper and Lower Connelloe in south Limerick, but soon after the Anglo-Norman invasion, they were dispossessed of their lands by the Fitzgeralds and others, and are afterwards found settled in West Limerick and Kerry.

The O'Donovans (O Donnabhain) were the chiefs of the Ui Cairbre Aedhbha, a clan which included as well the MacEnerys. The principal stronghold of the O'Donovans was at Bruree. About 1178 they were driven from this territory and subsequently settled in southwest Cork, where they wrested a territory from the O'Driscolls of Corca Laoighdhe with the aid of their old allies, the Eoghanacht O'Mahonys. To this territory they gave their clan name of Ui Cairbre, retaining considerable power and land in this new quarter down to the close of the Jacobite wars in the late seventeenth century. Branches settled in Wexford and Kilkenny. The MacEnerys (Mac Inneirghe) were anciently chiefs of Corcomohid, in the barony of Upper Connelloe, in the south of County Limerick. They had a castle at Castletown MacEniry, the ruins of which remain to this day. Although their territory was eroded by the encroachment of the Anglo-Normans after the twelfth century, the MacEnerys retained a considerable portion of their patrimony down to the revolution of 1688.

The Ulaid

The Ulaid were the great Erainnian people who gave their name to Ulster, and it is they who are celebrated in the Ulster Cycle. Their direct royal representatives in historical times were the Dal bhFiatach of County Down, but they also encompassed the Ui Duach and Dal Riada as well.

The Dal bhFiatach or MacDonlevys (Mac Duinnshleibhe) were a warlike clan that held great power in County Down and South Antrim until 1177, when they met and were defeated by the Norman army under John de Courcy, though only after brave resistance. The battle occurred near Downpatrick. After this defeat the MacDonlevys were reduced in power, although as late as 1273 they were referred to as kings of Ulidia (Uladh), the name of their original territory. Afterwards branches of the clan sought new homes as far away as Scotland. The main line became hereditary physicians to the O'Donnells, and had their new patrimony in Tirconnell (County Donegal). The MacDonlevys are also known as *MacNultys or Ultachs (Mac an Ultaigh)*, which literally means "Son of the Ulidian." The *MacNallys (Mac Con Ultaigh)* of the Armagh-Monaghan border, whose name means "son of the hound of Ulidia," are also of Dal bhFiatach stock.

The *Dal Riada* were originally a tribe of North Antrim in Ireland, but from as early as the third century, and especially during the late fifth century there had been a steady settlement of the adjacent coastal and island areas of Scotland by these Dal Riada Scots. This area, which became the Scottish part of the greater tribal kingdom of Dal Riada, was separated from the rest of Scotland by mountains. The Scottish part of the tribal kingdom of Dal Riada was known as Argyll which means "coastland of the Gaels," for by this time the population of Ireland had long been Gaelic-speaking, and the Dal Riada considered themselves to be Gaels in the general sense, though nonetheless Erainn in the context of ethno-dynastic politics. About A.D. 500 the kings of Dal Riada took up permanent residence in the Argyle, and with the coming of the Vikings in the ninth century, the tribe, by then centered in Argyle, was cut off from their Irish collateral kinsmen in Antrim, the *O'Quins* of Antrim, who declined in power after the Anglo-Norman invasion. The chief kindreds of the Dal Riada of Argyle, the *Cineal Loairn* and the *Cineal nGabrain*, soon spread into much of Scotland with the uniting of their kingdom and the Kingdom of the Picts (Chapter IV).

The *Cineal Loairn* derive their descent from Loarn, son of Erc, a king of Dal Riada in the fifth century. They originally inhabited the present districts of Lorn (named for them) and Mull, with the adjacent mainland and island territory to the north and west. This territory comprised the northern part of Scottish Dal Riada, and when the time came for expansion, the Cineal Loairn migrated up the Great Glen. The chief kindred branches of the Cineal Loairn were the *Clann Duibhne*, or *Campbells*, the *MacGillivrays* and *MacInneses*, the *Cineal Baodan*, or *MacLeans*, the *MacNaughtens*, the *MacNabs*, the *Clan Chattan*, and the *Camerons, MacGillonies, MacMartins* and *MacSorleys*.

The *Clann Duibhne* or *Campbells (Caimbeul)*, the most powerful clan in Argyle and one of the most powerful in Scotland, descend from the issue of the thirteenth century marriage between Sir Gillespic Campbell and the heiress of Duncan Mac Duibhne of Lochawe. Thus did the Campbells inherit the leadership of the Clann Duibhne, whose name they retained notwithstanding the fact that they, like the Galbraiths of Loch Lomond, were by origin Strathclyde Britons from around Dunbarton, where they were still important to the end of the thirteenth century. Ethnically these Strathclyde Britons were Laiginian, being descended from a Dumnonian influx from Ireland (see Chapter III). The senior line of the Campbells, descended from Sir Gillespic's older brother Duncan, were the MacArthurs (Clann Artair) of Loch Fyne and Lochawe. The MacArthurs lost power after their chief, Iain MacArthur, "a great prince among his own people and leader of a thousand men," was beheaded by the Stewart King James I in 1427. Afterwards they lived under the protection of their Campbell kinsmen. As for the Campbells themselves, they rose to preeminence in Argyle under royal patronage following the downfall of the MacDonalds' Lordship of the Isles. The chief of the Lochawe line, the main stem of the family, was created Duke of Argyle in 1457. The Campbells of Glenorchy, later Earls of Breadalbane (1681), descend from the grandson of Sir Gillespic, while those who inherited Cawdor (in Moray) descend from the third son of the second Earl of Argyle. The Campbells became infamous for their political pragmatism, which led them to commit acts of brutality and treachery against neighboring clans, notably the MacGregors and the MacDonalds of Glencoe.

The MacGillivrays (Mac Giolla Bhratha) and MacInneses (Mac Aonghuis) are of the same stock, and akin to the Clann Duibhne. The original territory of the MacGillivrays was in Morven and Lochaber, in the north of the original Cineal Loairn territory. In the thirteenth century, after political upheavals weakened the power of the Lords of the Isles in the area, most of the MacGillivrays joined the Clan Chattan confederacy, and by 1500 had moved into Strathnairn. Those that remained in Morven followed the MacLeans, the Mull branch being principal among these. The MacInneses seem to have traditionally been the constables of the castle of Kinlochaline, originally under the MacDonalds, but later, about 1600, under the MacKenzies. However, they usually followed their kinsmen, the Campbells.

The Cineal Baodan, or MacLeans (Mac Giolla Eoin) descend from Baodan, great-grandson of Loarn, king of Dal Riada. The clan was originally settled in Morvern, where they gave their name to a district, and one of their early ancestors was abbot of the nearby Isle of Lismore. In later times they migrated up the Great Glen into Moray, and later still, about 1160, they were one of several clans transferred to the Scone area (Tayside in Perthshire) by Malcolm IV. Their eponymous ancestor was Gillean (Giolla Eoin) of the Battleaxe, who lived during the reign of Alexander III (1249-1283), and fought at the Battle of Largs in 1263. Gillemoir MacLyn of Perthshire, son of Gillean, settled in Lorn, and his son, a supporter of Robert Bruce, was named "Malise," which was the favorite name of the earls of Strathearn (Perthshire) at that time, and almost unique to them. Malise's grandson, Ian Dhu MacLean, settled in Mull, and was the father of Lachlan Lubanach, progenitor of the MacLeans of Duart, the chief family of the clan. He was also father of Eachin Reganach, progenitor of the MacLaines of Lochbuie, and the MacLaines disputed the chiefship with the Duart branch on the claim that Eachin was elder to Lachlan, though the chiefship was settled on the Duart branch by tanistry. Both of these brothers lived in the reign of Robert II. The clan held wide power in the Hebrides, as allies of the MacDonalds, under the Lord of the Isles. One of Eachin's sons, Charles MacLean, settled in Glen Urquhart, in Moray, and was the founder of the Clann Thearlaich, also known as the MacLeans of the North. The Clann Thearlaich joined the Clan Chattan confederacy (see below) about 1460, but nonetheless appealed to MacLean of Duart, as their hereditary chief, for protection against harassment by the Chisholms. The Duart chief recognized their rights as clansmen, and forced the Chisholms to desist.

The MacNaughtons (Mac Neachdainn), like the MacLeans, were one of the clans transplanted from Moray about 1160 by Malcolm IV to the Crown lands in Perthshire, where they became thanes of Loch Tay. However, by 1247 they were back in Argyle, and held the upper part of Lochawe, Glenara, Glenshira, and Loch Fyne. The strongholds of the clan were in the latter two places, at the castles of Dubh-Loch in Glenshira and Dunderave on Loch Fyne. Since the clan had resided in the region of Strathearn (Perthshire) for the previous several generations, it is not surprising that in 1247 the then chief, Gillecrist MacNachtan, son of Malcolm MacNachtan, granted the church of Kelmurkhe (Kilmorich) at the head of Loch Fyne to the Abbey of Inchaffray (a foundation of the original earls of Strathearn, and continued under their special patronage). In 1267 this Gillecrist (Gilchrist) was appointed hereditary keeper of the Castle of Fraoch Eilean on Loch Awe, thenceforward to be held for the King of Scots by the Clan MacNachtan. A branch of the clan returned to Loch Tay and Glen Lyon, and was connected with the bishopric of Dunkeld.

The MacNabs (Mac an Aba) of Strathfillan and Glendochart in Perthshire descend from the hereditary abbots of Glendochart, who were, before the secularization and discontinuance of Celtic abbacies around 1300, of equal status with the local medieval earls of Atholl and Menteith. Afterwards, the MacNabs became important chiefs in the western part of the old abbey lands. The original line of abbots were the co-arbs of St. Fillan, a prince of the Cineal Loairn, and descended from the Saint's brother. The chiefs of the MacNabs were known by the proverbial title of "The MacNab."

The Clan Chattan (Clann Chatain) was a confederation of clans in the Moray areas of Lochaber, Strathnairn and Badenoch. The main stem of the clan included the MacPhersons, Davidsons, MacBeans or MacBains, Cattanachs, and by inheritance, the MacKintoshes. These clans were joined by others, of different origin, who at various times applied for protection of the MacKintosh chiefs, who were also captains, or high chiefs, of the Clan Chattan confederation. These included the MacGillivrays, MacIntyres, MacLeans, MacQueens, MacAndrews, and others.

The MacKintoshes (Mac an Toisich) are paternally an offshoot of the Clan MacDuff of Fife, whose chiefs, the earls of Fife, held vast territory in Moray during the thirteenth century. Rothiemurchus, the earliest known territory of the Mackintoshes, was surrounded by this territory. In 1291, Angus, sixth chief of the MacKintoshes, married Eva, daughter and only child of Dougal Dall, sixth chief of the Clan Chattan. The Clan Chattan line stretched back to the first chief, Gillechattan Mor, heir of the co-arbs of the abbey of Kilchattan on the Isle of Bute, the special abbey of the Cineal Loairn. The line of this Gillechattan Mor, whose name means "great servant of St. Cattan" (the patron saint of the Abbey of Kilchattan) acquired land in Lochaber and Badenoch, probably by Pictish succession. This may explain the use of the wildcat as the heraldic beast of the Clan Chattan, informally referred to as the Clan of the Cats: St. Cattan's name means "little cat," and the Northern Picts had an ancient totemistic connection to the cat (hence the name of the province of Caithness in northern Scotland – see under "Sutherland" in Chapter X). As for the MacKintoshes, since no surname was associated with the Clan Chattan chiefship in these virtually pre-surname days in Scotland, the new line of Mac-Kintoshes kept their name, but continued as captains of the Clan Chattan.

The Clann Fhionnlaigh or *Farquharsons* (Mac Fhearchair) of Invercauld in Aberdeenshire are descended from the *Shaws* of Rothiemurchus, cadets of the MacKintoshes. They inherited Invercauld from the MacHardys.

The MacPhersons (Mac an Phearsoin) descend from Ewan Ban, son of Muriach, "Macgilliechattan Clearach," Celtic Prior (or "Parson") of Kingussie, and fourth chief of the Clan Chattan. With the passing of the chiefship to the MacKintoshes through Eva, daughter of the sixth chief, the MacPherson chiefs represented the male-heir of the Clann Chattan, and thus disputed, with the MacKintoshes, the high-chiefship of the Clan Chattan, and with the *Clann Dhai*, or *Davidsons*, the leadership of the right wing (the position of honor) of the Clan Chattan's 2000-man army.

The Davidsons (Mac Dhaibhidh) descended from David Dhu, another son of Muriach, ancestor of the MacPhersons. In order to hamper the unity of the powerful Clan Chattan, the early Stewart kings played off the MacPhersons against the Davidsons by fomenting the continuance of their dispute. This action led to the famous Battle of the Clans at Perth in 1396, a "legal battle" before the king, contested to the death between a limited number of clansmen of the MacPhersons and the Clan Dhai (the identity of the Davidsons as the latter party, although likely, has not been proven absolutely).

The Clan Vean, or *MacBeans (MacBheathain)*, alias MacBain or MacBeath, originally came north from Lochaber in the train of Eva, heiress of Clann Chattan, and appear from the sword in their arms, to have held the office of swordbearer under the original Clan Chattan chiefs. They then settled in Inverness, and had their chief seat at Kinchyle, in eastern Inverness-shire. Other branches were settled in Strathnairn and Strathdearn.

The *Camerons (Camshron)* derive their name from a place in Fife, where the original knightly family settled as cadets of the earls of Fife. The Cameron arms are a different version of one of the two distinct coats of arms used by the Mac-Duff chiefs, earls of Fife (the Fife practice of bearing two arms probably arose to forstall confusion in the official and military use of the main Fife arms, which are very similar to the Royal Arms, being the "undifferenced" version of those arms, a reflection of ultimate seniority of the House of Fife in Scotland—see under MacDuff). A scion of this house, Sir Robert Cambron, was sheriff of Atholl in 1296 under the earls of Atholl, who were at that time themselves a branch of the earls of Fife. Thus the male-line ancestor of the Clan Cameron was brought to the border of Lochaber, which would become the home of the clan. By the end of the fourteenth century, the southern estates of the Camerons had passed out of the family through heiresses, but soon afterwards the Camerons themselves inherited the chiefship of a clan in western Lochaber, of the same stock as the Clan Chattan, whose chief families were the *MacGillonies (Mac Giolla Onfhaidh)* of Strone, *MacMartins (Mac Mairtin)* of Letterfinlay (who have almost entirely adopted the name of Cameron), and the *MacSorleys (Mac Somhairle)* of Glen Nevis. By about 1411 their first traceable chief, "Black Donald" Cameron, was already chief of the MacGillonie branch of the clan when he married the heiress of MacMartin of Letterfinlay, who brought to him the captaincy of the Clan Cameron. He was ancestor of the Camerons, alias MacGillonies, of Strone and Lochiel, the latter being the chief family, and deriving the designation of Lochiel from the name of the barony erected from the lands of the Captain of Clan Cameron in 1528. The name Cameron, from the original Fife family, does survive in the south, though rare, and was common in Edinburgh in the seventeenth century.

The *Cineal nGabrain* originally dwelt south of the Cineal Loairn in the island districts of Jura, Bute, and Arran, and the mainland districts of Cowal and Kintyre. They derive their descent from Gabhran, King of Dal Riada in the sixth century. They were the chief clan of the Dal Riada, and merged with the Pictish Royal House in the ninth century. Their chief descendants include the *Fergusons, MacKerseys, MacFies, MacGregors, MacKinnons* and *MacQuarries*.

The *Fergusons (Mac Fhearghuis)* of Strachur on Loch Fyne, and their kinsmen the *MacKerseys (Mac Fhearghuis)* of Kintyre are not connected with the several clans of the name in other parts of the Highlands, with the possible exception of the Fergusons of Balquhidder. The Strachur Fergusons stronghold was the "Black Castle" on Beinn Bheula. The Lowland family of the name in Ayrshire, the Fergusons of Kilkerrin, were originally of the Kintyre branch, as suggested by their arms, and by the similarity of the name of their original lands, Kilkerrin (dedicated to St. Ciaran) to the name of the place called Kilkerrin (now Campbelltown) in Kintyre (the Fergusons of Kilkerrin may originally have been hereditary keepers of the cross of St. Ciaran).

The Siol Alpin is the name of a group of clans traditionally connected by their mutual *traditional* descent from Kenneth Mac Alpin (first king of the united kingdom of Picts and Scots in the ninth century – see Chapter IV), a tradition which simply indicates that they were all of generally "South Argyle" Dalriadic stock. These families include the *MacGregors (Mac Grioghair)*, an "outlaw" clan of the Argyle-Perthshire border, many of whom were forced to assume aliases, and to which clan belonged the famous eighteenth century adventurer "Rob Roy" MacGregor (alias Campbell); The *MacFies* or *MacPhies (Mac Dhuibhshithe)* of Colonsay; the *MacKinnons (Mac Fhionghuin)* of Mull, Skye and Iona (the last abbot of Iona in 1550 was a MacKinnon), and the *MacQuarries (Mac Guadhre)* of Ulva and Mull in the Hebrides, who followed the MacLeans after the downfall of the MacDonald lords of the Isles. The *MacFies* lost Colonsay after joining in the rebellion of Sir James MacDonald in 1615, after which some followed the MacDonalds, while others settled in Lochaber and followed the Camerons. The MacKinnons and MacFies were closely connected with the Abbey of Iona, being the local clan-stock of the Iona area. The MacKinnons became erenaghs, or hereditary abbots, of Iona after the failure of the original Cineal Conaill line around 1200. The MacFies may descend from the "Dubhsidhe" who was lector of Iona in 1164. The MacFies held part of the Isle of Jura, and sat on the Council of the Isles advising the MacDonald lords thereof. After the downfall of the Lordship of the Isles in the late fifteenth century, the main branch of the MacFies followed the MacDonalds of Islay, and a sixteenth-century branch settled in Ulster.

The Osraighe (including the *Ui Duach* and the *MacGilpatricks*) were of the same stock as the Ulaid, being descended from Oengus Osraigh, ancestor of the Dal bhFiatach. The Osraighe migrated to Ossory (County Kilkenny), which they gave their name to, in very early times. For the purpose of incorporating the separate territory of Ossory within over-kingdom of Leinster, the Osraighe were later given a fake but transparent descent from the Laigin. The Osraige gave rise to the medieval dynasty of Ossory, the *MacGilpatricks* or *Fitzpatricks (Mac Giolla Phadraig)*, and to their collateral kinsmen the *Ui Duach* or *O'Brennans (O Braonain)*. The *MacGilpatricks* descend from Giolla Phadraig, son of Donnchadh, lord of Ossory in the tenth century. They originally ruled over all Kilkenney and part of Leix as well, but after the Anglo-Norman invasion their territory was greatly encroached upon by the Butlers and others, and afterwards they held a greatly reduced territory in the very north of County Kilkenny, alongside their kinsmen the O'Brennans.

VIII. The Laigin

The Laigin, or Dumnonii, were the third ethno-tribal group to come to Ireland, coming from Gaul shortly before the Gaels themselves, sometime during the first century B.C. Branches of the Dumnonii settled first in the Devon-Cornwall area before others moved on to Ireland (Chapter III).

In southern Britain their kingdom gave its name to Devon (Dumnonia). In the time of King Arthur (ca. A.D. 500), as the tribe most closely associated with that great Pendragon, these Devon Domnonii established a dual kingdom which included the north coast of Brittany (Domnonie), from whose royal house eventually sprang the House of Stewart (which house inherited the crown of the Scots in 1371 and that of England in 1603). The Stewarts are covered under the chapter on the Normans, having come to Scotland in the wake of Norman conquest of England, in which they served as allies of the dukes of Normandy.

In Ireland the Dumnonii were generally known as the Laigin, and originally became overlords in the southeastern and central regions, and in Connacht. From there they later spread to other parts of Gaeldom, as we shall see.

Tribes of the Laigin

The Cianacht

The Cianacht encompassed the O'Connors (O Conchobhair) of Keenaght, and the Luighne. The O'Connors were lords of Keenaght, County Derry, until dispossessed by the O'Kanes shortly before the Anglo-Norman invasion in the twelfth century. The Luighne were of County Sligo, where they had settled as fighting men to the Northern Gaels in the early centuries A.D. The Cianacht were closely related to the Dealbhna and Saithne.

The Luighne or "race of Lugh," included the families of O'Hara (O hEaghra) and O'Gara (O Gadhra). The O'Haras descend from Eaghra, Lord of Luighne (now the Barony of Leyney) in South Sligo, who died in 926. In the fourteenth century the O'Haras divided into two branches, the heads of which were

78

THE LAIGIN

Labraíd Loingsech King Of The Otherworld. And Father Of Nuadu. Ancestor–Deity Of The LAIGIN

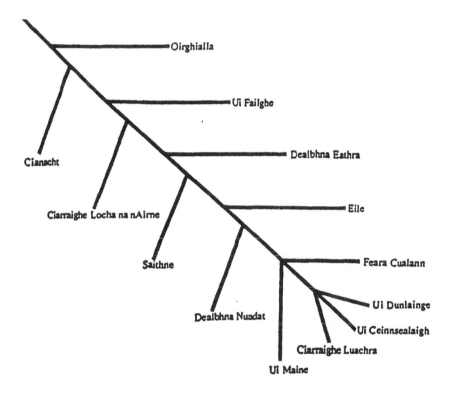

known as O'Hara Boy (Buidhe), the Yellow O'Hara, and O'Hara Reagh (Riabhach), the Speckled or Brindled O'Hara. A branch of the family settled early in County Antrim, and became very important there.

The O'Garas were once one clan with the O'Haras, and together their territory, Luighne, included the modern baronies of Corran and Leyney in South Sligo, and Gallen and North Costello (Sliabh Lugha) in Mayo. About the end of the tenth century the two families separated, and divided the territory between them, the O'Garas taking the Mayo portion. They were driven from their territory by the Jordans, Costellos and other Anglo-Norman settlers, and resettled in Greagraidhe, in Sligo, now the Barony of Coolavin, and were later known as lords of Coolavin. They built their stronghold, Moygara, at the northeastern extremity of Lough Gara. Branches went to Munster before the end of the sixteenth century, and are known as Geary or Guiry. The O'*Duanys* or *Devanys* of Sligo are a branch of the O'Garas.

The Dealbhna Eathra and Dealbhna Nuadat

The Dealbhna Eathra and Dealbhna Nuadat were closely related to the Cianacht and Saithne. They originally comprised a single tribal kingdom in the Roscommon-Offaly area, but in course of time the various branches of the *Dealbhna* became separated under different overlordships, just as the Ui Maine became separated from their collateral kinsmen to the northeast of the Shannon, the Oirghialla, by the growing apart of the North Gaels which itself resulted in the ultimate overkingdoms of the Connachta and Ui Neill. The *Dealbhna Eathra* were situated to the east of the Shannon around Clonmacnoise, as a semiindependent tribal kingdom nominally subject to the Southern Ui Niell. Their chief families in medieval times were the *MacCoghlans* and O'*Conrahys*.

The *MacCoghlans (Mac Cochlain)* descend from Cochlan, lord of Dealbhna Eathra in 1053. The heads of the family were for centuries the lords of Dealbhna Eathra, and the territory of their tribal kingdom was in later times called after them "Delvin (Dealbhna) MacCoghlane." Their territory comprised the modern barony of Garrycastle, in County Offaly. They were once very powerful, and had ten strong castles in the Garrycastle area. The O'*Conrahys (O Conratha)* are a branch of the MacCoghlans.

The *Dealbhna Nuadat* were centered on the other side of the Shannon, between it and the River Suck in County Roscommon, and were tributary to the Ui Maine. Their later representatives are the O'*Hanlys* of Connacht.

The O'*Hanlys (O hAinle)* were chiefs of Cinel Dobhtha, called in later times Tuaohanly and Doohy Hanly, being a district along the River Shannon north of Lough Ree. The O'*Hanleys* held this territory as late as the seventeenth century as tributaries of the O'Connor Don of Ui Maine. In the late sixteenth century several related gentlemen of the name were given in succession the office of "Seneschal" ("Royal Officer") of "Tohahohanly" under Queen Elizabeth I.

The Saithne

The Saithne were closely related to the Cianacht and Dealbhna. They originally inhabited a territory in the southern part of the kingdom of Brega, the kingship of which they in ancient times had shared with kindred groups. Their lands in Brega lay southeasterly, midway between the River Boyne and the River Liffey. Their later representatives were the O'*Caseys*.

The O'Caseys (O Cathasaigh) were originally lords of Saithne, in the north of the present County Dublin, until they were dispossessed by the Normans under Sir Hugh de Lacy soon after the Anglo-Norman invasion (twelfth century). Afterwards they became an important Erenagh (church) family, being hereditary keepers of Kilarduff and Dunfeeny in County Mayo, Cloondara and Tisrara in County Roscommon, and Devinish in County Fermanagh.

The Ciarraighe Locha na nAirne

The Ciarraighe Locha na nAirne were originally part of a greater kingdom, the tribal kingdom of Ciarraighe, centered at Cruachu (the ancient capital of Connacht). This kingdom was fragmented by the Ui Briuin of the North Gaels during the late eighth century or early ninth century. They may have been, in more ancient times, closely related to the ancestors of the Oirghialla, the allies of the North Gaels (in the Heroic Age tales of the North, the "Ulster Cycle," Cruachu is the center of the Gaelic-Laiginian alliance). The Ciarraighe were indigenous to Connacht. Their main representatives in the Middle Ages were the O'Kierans (O Ceirin) of northwest County Mayo. The native territory of the O'Kierans was in the south of the barony of Costello, but they were reduced in power there by the Anglo-Norman encroachment, and branches in Donegal and Clare became more important.

The Ciarraighe Luachra

The Ciarraighe Luachra were the original tribe of North Kerry, a branch of the Ciarraighe. Before the Anglo-Norman invasion had had a semiindependent kingdom between Tralee and the Shannon. Their chief family was that of O'Connor (O Conchobhair) of Kerry, whose stronghold was at Carrigafoyle, near Ballylongford. They held the Barony of Iraghticonor in the extreme north of County Kerry after the southern part of their territory was encroached upon by the Fitzmaurices of Clanmaurice and other Norman settlers. The O'Connors held Iraghticonor down to the reign of Elizabeth, when it was confiscated by the English and given to Trinity College.

The Eile

The Eile were originally a tribe of western King's County (Offaly), where place-names recall their early residence in that region. After the battle of Druim Derge (A.D. 516), at which battle they were decisively defeated by the expanding southern Ui Neill, they migrated to the area known after them as "Ely" in the south of Offaly and including northeast Tipperary. Their chief families in later times were the O'Carrolls of Ely, the O'Mahers, the O'Riordans and the O'Flanagans.

The O'Carrolls (O Cearbhaill) descend from Cearbhaill, Lord of Ely, who was one of the leaders at the famous battle of Clontarf in 1014. The head of the O'Carrolls was originally lord of all Ely, but after the Anglo-Norman invasion their power was restricted to South Offaly, which was subsequently called Ely O'Carroll.

The Ui Cairin or O'Mahers (O Meachair) are of the same stock as the O'Carrolls, and were lords of Ui Cairin, now the Barony of Ikerrin, in the old Ely territory in Tipperary. After the Anglo-Norman invasion, Ikerrin was added to Ormond, but The O'Maher (chief of the sept) was left in control of the territory as tributary to the Butlers, the Anglo-Norman earls of Ormond, under whom they flourished.

The O'Riordans (O Rioghbhardain) are a branch of the O'Carrolls of Ely, and probably descend from Rioghbhardan, son of Cucoirne O Cearbhaill, Lord of Ely, who fell at the battle of Sliabh gCrot in 1058. As late as 1576 a "Gaven O Rewrdane" was a "freeholder" in Ely O'Carroll, and one of the most important followers of Sir William O'Carroll. By this time branches had spread into Leix and Kilkenny, but even earlier the greater portion of the sept had removed to Cork and Limerick. In 1597 Maurice O'Riordan of Croome was attainted by the English, his lands being given to a George Sherlocke.

The O'Flanagans (O Flannachain) are of the same stock as the O'Carrolls of Ely, and were chiefs of a territory known as Cineal Arga, now the barony of Ballybrit, in southeast Offaly.

The Ui Failghe

The Ui Failghe, closely related to the Eile, had probably separated from them by A.D. 516, the year of the defeat of the Eile at Druim Derge by the Southern Ui Niell. The Ui Failge descend from Failge Berraide, who a few years earlier had won the battle of Fremainn Mide (A.D. 510). This victory probably accounts for their being able to remain in the more northerly portion of Offaly while their cousins, the Eile, were forced to migrate south. The chief families of the Ui Failghe include the *O'Connors* of Offaly, the *O'Mooneys*, *MacColgans*, *O'Hennesseys*, *O'Holohans*, *O'Dempseys* and *O'Dunnes*.

The O'Connors (O Conchobhair) of Offaly were a powerful and warlike sept of the northeast of what is now County Offaly. They descend from Conchobhar, son of Fionn, Lord of Offaly, who died in A.D. 979. From their stronghold at Dangan, now Philipstown, they successfully defended their territory from the English of the Pale (i.e. County Dublin) for more than 300 years. They were finally dispossessed by the English about 1550. The *O'Mooneys (O Maonaigh)* of around Ballymooney in County Offaly are a branch of the O'Connors.

The Clann Cholgan included the families of *MacColgan*, *O'Hennessy* and *O'Holohan*. The *MacColgans (Mac Colgan)* were chiefs of the territory around Kilcolgan in the extreme northeast of County Offaly. The O'Hennessys (O hAonghusa) shared the lordship of Clann Cholgan (i.e., their clan-name was applied to the territory they possessed) with their kinsmen the O'Holohans (O hUallachain). Their territory comprised the present barony of Lower

Philipstown, a district adjoining the hill of Croghan, near Kilbeggan, and lying just east of the O'Connors in northeast Offaly. A branch of the O'Hennessys were chiefs of Gailenga Beg, the district between Dublin and Tara, until they were dispersed into Offaly as a result of the Anglo-Norman invasion. Some of the O'Hennessys spread early into Tipperary and Clare. In County Clare they are now known as Henchy or Hensey.

The Clann Mhaolughra or O'Dempseys (O Diomasaigh) were chiefs of the territory known after them as Clann Mhaolughra on the River Barrow, which comprised the baronies of Portnahinch in Leix and Upper Philipstown in Offaly. They were very powerful, and owing to the friendly terms they had with the English during the reign of Elizabeth I (ca. 1590), their lands escaped confiscation until after the fall of James II (ca. 1690). Their patron saint was St. Evin, who established the church at Monasterevan.

The Ui Riagain or O'Dunnes (O Duinn) were chiefs of Ui Riagain in the northwestern corner of County Leix. They were, along with their kinsmen the O'Connors and O'Dempseys, one of the chief families of Leinster. A branch of the family possessed a territory around Tara until dispersed about the same time as the O'Hennesseys of that area (see above). The clan-name Ui Riagain, Anglicized Iregan, may reflect some relation to the sept of O'Regan (O Riagain) of the Southern Ui Neill, one of the Tribes of Tara, which settled in Leix after the Anglo-Norman invasion.

The Feara Cualann

The Feara Cualann, or "Men of Cuala," originally inhabited the territory of that name, Cuala, which included a large portion of the present counties of Dublin and Wicklow. Their chief representatives in later times were the O'Cullens and O'Mulryans.

The O'Cullens (O Cuilinn) were chiefs around Glencullen in County Wicklow, in which area they have dwelt to this day. Though they were overshadowed as a power in the area by the O'Byrnes and O'Tooles about 1300, Cullen of Cullenstown was counted as one of the leading gentry of County Wexford as late as 1598, and they appear to have retained considerable influence. Kilcullen, on the Wicklow border of County Kildare, is named for them.

The O'Mulryans (O Maoilriain) originated in Leinster, but settled around the north Tipperary-Limerick border sometime during the thirteenth or fourteenth century. They became very numerous and powerful in their new home, the territory which is now the baronies of Owney in Tipperary and Owneybeg in Limerick. In the year 1610, William Ryan surrendered to the King of England all his rights to the lands of "Owney O Mulrian," in order to receive them back as a royal grant, by letters of patent. These land were later lost, however, in the mass confiscations of the seventeenth century. The name is numerous and respectable in Limerick and Tipperary.

The Ui Ceinnsealaigh

The Ui Ceinnsealaigh were the most powerful tribe of Leinster, and usually held the provincial overkingship until the time of the Anglo-Norman invasion (which their representative, King Dermot MacMurrough of Leinster, helped bring about). The center of their power lay around the Diocese of Ferns, in northern Wexford. Their chief families were the *Kavanaghs, Kinsellas, O'Murphys* and *O'Morchoes.*

The *Kavanaghs (Caomhanach)* descend from Domhnall (Donal) Caomhanach, son of Diarmaid Mac Murchadha (Dermot MacMurrough), King of Leinster at the time of the Anglo-Norman invasion (died 1171). He was called "Caomhanach" as a result of his having been fostered by the Co-arb (blood-related successor) of St. Caomhan at Kilcavan near Gorey. The adoption by his descendants of Kavanagh (i.e., "belonging to St. Caomhan") as a family name is unusual: It is, like Kinsella below, one of the very few non-patronymic names used among the pre-Norman Gaelic population. The patrimony of the family included extensive districts in counties Carlow and Wexford, where the name is very common.

The *Kinsellas (Cinnsealach,)* descend from Enna Cinnsealach, brother of Domhnall Caomhanach (Kavanagh) and son of Dermot MacMurrogh. They possessed most of the barony of Gorey in the north of County Wexford, where they remain to this day, but they remained much less numerous than their kinsmen, the Kavanaghs. Their lands were formerly referred to as "the Kinsellaghs." A branch of the Kinsellas, the *O'Murphys (O Murchadha)* of Muskerry, settled early in County Cork, where they became connected with the barony of Muskerry in the west-central part of that county.

The *O'Morchoes,* or *O'Murphys (O Murchadha)* were chiefs of Ui Feilme, now the Barony of Ballaghkeen in the northeast of County Wexford, all along the coast. They maintained their independence and identity as a clan down to the first part of the seventeenth century, and are now very numerous throughout Leinster.

The Ui Dunlainge

The *Ui Dunlainge* anciently inhabited the Liffey Plain, the territory around the River Liffey, just to the northwest of the Wicklow Mountains. They were very important in north Leinster, and held the provincial overkingship of Leinster itself from 738 to 1042, alternating it between their chief clans, the *Ui Dunchada, Ui Faelain* and *Ui Muiredaig.* Their representatives in later times were the *O'Byrnes* and *O'Tooles.*

The *Ui Faelain* included the *O'Byrnes (O Broin)* and their kinsmen the *MacKeoghs* or *Kehoes (Mac Eochaidh)* of Leinster. The O'Byrnes descend from Bran, son of Maolmordha, King of Leinster in 1014. Maolmordha died fighting on the side of Earl Sigurd of Orkney against Brian Boru, High-King of Ireland, at the battle of Clontarf in 1014).

The O'Byrnes originally possessed what is now the northern half of County Kildare, which was called after the Ui Faelain. They were driven from this territory by the Normans, soon after the Anglo-Norman invasion, after which they retired to the fastness of the nearby Wicklow Mountains. Here they became very powerful, and at the head of the Wicklow clans they terrorized the invaders, first the Anglo-Normans, and later the English, both of whom they defeated in many a fierce engagement. Their territory in these times was known as Criochbhranach, and included the Barony of Newcastle with parts of the baronies of Ballinacor and Arklow.

The Ui Muireadhaigh or O'Tooles (O Tuathail) descend from Ughaire, King of Leinster (died 956), and were chiefs of what is now the southern half of County Kildare, which bore the designation of Ui Muireadhaigh after their clan-name. They were driven from this territory by Walter de Riddlesford soon after the Anglo-Norman invasion, afterwards retiring to the mountain fastness of Wicklow, like their O'Byrne kinsmen. Here their new territory comprised first Ui Mail on the western slope of the mountains, and later Feara Cualann, in the north. Here, in alliance with their kinsmen the O'Byrnes, they carried on incessant warfare with the invaders, Anglo-Normans and later English, which continued over more than 400 years. They maintained their independence as a clan down to the close of the reign of Elizabeth I (ca. 1600), after which the whole of Fercuolen was confiscated by the English. The O'Tooles however retained considerable property for a time, and a branch of the family settled as well in west Connacht, where they became numerous.

The Ui Maine

The Ui Maine were the great Laiginian tribe whose original territory comprised adjoining parts of what are now the counties of Galway, Roscommon, Clare and Offally. The Ui Maine were closely related to the Oirghialla, for their ancestors were the same as those of the Oirghialla, being the ancient Laiginian allies of the great tribe of the North Gaels (the names of three of their respective original sub-tribal groups duplicate each other—the Clann Bhreasail, or Ui Breasail (Macha); the Ui Fiachrach Finn, or Ui Fiachrach Arda Stratha, and the Clann Chearnaigh. The Ui Maine separated from the Oirghialla at the same time that the Ui Neill differentiated from their North-Gaelic kinsmen, the Connachta (see Chapter IX). As the Ui Neill and their Oirghialla allies moved eastward into the rest of Ulster, the Connachta moved southwards into the rest of Connacht, and thus did their Laiginian allies, the Ui Maine, acquire what would become their tribal patrimony.

The O'Kellys (O Ceallaigh) were chiefs of the Ui Maine, and as such ruled over a large area in Galway and Roscommon down to the reign of Elizabeth I, at the end of the sixteenth century. They came to be regarded as one of the "Three Connachts" along with the North-Gaelic tribes of Ui Fiachrach and

Ui Briuin, although they were Laiginian (the original "Three Connachts" in-cluded the Ui Neill, who branched eastwards and started a new and separate dynasty in the early 5th century A.D.). The *MacKeoghs (Mac Eochadha)* are a branch of the O'Kellys, and were formerly chiefs of Moyfinn in the Barony of Athlone in County Roscommon.

The *O'Fahys (O Fathaigh)* were chiefs of a territory known as Poblewinter-fahy (Pobal Mhuintir Ui Fhathaigh), which lay in the Barony of Loughrea in south-central Galway. They remained in possession of these lands down to the Cromwellian confiscations of the mid-seventeenth century. Fahysvillage, in Loughrea, recalls their presence there.

The *O'Horans (O hUghroin;* later *O hOghrain)* are a branch of the Ui Maine, and were originally seated around Clonrush in the south of County Galway, where they remained numerous and held large estates down to the Cromwellian confiscations of the mid seventeenth century. A branch migrated early to County Mayo, where they became co-arbs (hereditary successors) of St. Mochua at the abbey of Balla.

The *O'Sheehans (O Siodhachain)* are a Ui Maine sept of Galway that in the High Middle Ages (tenth–thirteenth centuries) were hereditary trumpeters to The O'Kelly. They later spread into neighboring County Clare, and became attached to the ruling dynasty there, under the Ui Toirdealbhaigh or O'Briens, and as a result came to be regarded as Dalcassian.

The *Clann Bhreasail* were settled in southeastern County Galway between Lochrea and Ballinasloe. Their chief family was that of *O'Donnellan (O Domhnallain)*, the head of which family resided at his castle at Ballydonnellan in the clan territory. The family was famous as ollavs (professors), and pro-duced several famous poets, mentioned in the *Annals*.

The *Clann Uadach or O'Fallons (O Fallamhain)* were lords of a territory in the barony of Athlone which comprised the parishes of Camma and Dysart, in the south of what is now County Roscommon. The ruins of their castle are at Milltown, in the parish of Dysart.

The *Siol nAnmchadha or O'Maddens (O Madain)* were of the same stock as the O'Kellys, from whom they separated and became independent about 1050. They descend from Madadhan (slain A.D. 1008), son of Gadhra Mor, chief of the Ui Maine from 1014 to 1027. The clan-lands, called after them Siol nAnmchadha, comprised the modern barony of Longford in the southeast of County Galway, and also the parish of Lusnagh in County Offaly, on the other side of the Shannon. They held these lands under the Burke overlord-ship and remained in possession down to the Cromwellian confiscations of the mid seventeenth century (some of their confiscated estates were restored to them under the Act of Settlement in 1677). In 1612, Donal O'Madden, "captain of his nation," settled all of his estates, including his manor and castle of Longford, on his son and heir, Anmchadh, or Ambrose, O'Madden, in tail male.

The *Ui Diarmada* included the O'Concannons (O *Concheanainn*) and O'Mullens (O *Maolain*). The O'Concannons were chiefs of Corca Mogha (Corcamoe) in the northeast of County Galway. Their chief resided at Kiltullagh, in the parish of Kilkerrin, which is also called Corcamoe after their territory. The O'Mullens are of the same stock as the O'Concannons, and their territory bordered on that of O'Concannon, in northeast County Galway.

The *Ui Fiachrach Finn* included the O'Mullallys (O *Maolalaidh*)—"grandson of the speckled chief") and O'Naghtens (O *Neachtain*). The Ui Fiachrach Finn originally inhabited the fertile plain of Maonmhagh, being the area surrounding Loughrea in south-central Galway, but were dispossessed by the Burkes soon after the Anglo-Norman invasion, and forced to seek territory elsewhere.

The O'Mullallys settled in the parish of Tuam in northern Galway, their new territory comprising the lands known as Tulach na Dala (Tullaghnadaly), or Tolendal, four miles north of the town of Tuam. The O'Mullallys were ardent Jacobites, adhering to the Stewart cause in the wars of the seventeenth century. James Lally of Tullindaly sat as representative of Tuam in King James's parliament of 1689. After the Jacobite defeat he retired to France with his brother Gerald. Gerald married a noble French lady, and their son and grandson became famous in Europe under the title Count Lally de Tollendal. The O'Naghtens were chiefs of Maonmhagh before the Anglo-Norman invasion, after which they removed to the Feadha, or Fews, of Athlone in South Roscommon, where they formed a distinct clan down to the reign of Elizabeth I (ca. 1580).

The Oirghialla

The *Oirghialla* were closely related to the Ui Maine, as mentioned above. They were the Laiginian allies of the North-Gaelic tribe of Ui Neill, which virtually monopolized the high-kingship of Ireland during the post-fifth century historical period. The Oirghialla helped the Ui Neill effect the conquest of most of Northern Ireland from the Ulster Erainn, and later they settled a vast territory there including the counties of Louth, Armagh, Monaghan and Fermanagh, a territory which is called after them, Oriel. so important were they in the Ui Neill political sphere that they were given an honorary traditional descent (which was nonetheless fake and thinly disguised) from the great-grandfather of Nial of the Nine Hostages, ancestor of the O'Neills of the line of Conn. Their representatives in the later Middle Ages include the Mac-Bradys, O'Boylans, O'Flanagans, O'Mulroonys or Moroneys, Maguires, MacKernans, MacAuleys, O'Cassidys, O'Corrigans, MacManuses, MacMahons, Mac-Canns, O'Hanraghtys, O'Hanlons, O'Lynns, MacEvoys, MacDonalds, MacDonells, MacAlisters, MacIans, MacSheehys, MacIntyres, MacDougals, and Conns.

The MacBradys (Mac *Bradaigh*) were a powerful family of Breffny (Cavan and West Leitrim), being chiefs of Cuil Bhrighed or Cuil Bhrighdein, which

comprised the district around Stradone in County Cavan, a few miles to the
east of Cavan town. They are traditionally a branch of the O'Carrolls of
Leitrim, which family had been lords of all Oriel until the twelfth century
Anglo-Norman invasion. The MacBradys are now numerous throughout
Ulster.

The *Ui Chremthainn* anciently inhabited the territory between Lough Erne
and the River Blackwater, in what is now County Fermanagh and the north
of County Monaghan. The chief branches of the Ui Chremthainn include the
Clann Lugain, and also the *O'Mulroonys* or *Moroneys* and the *O'Boylans*.

The *O'Boylans* (*O Baoigheallain*) were of the same stock as the *O'Flanagans*
(*O Flannagain*) of northwest Fermanagh. The O'Boylans were, after the Anglo-
Norman invasion, lords of all Oriel, a widespread territory stretching from
Fermanagh to Louth. Later, in the thirteenth century, their power in Oriel was
subdued by the MacMahons, and their territory was reduced to what is
now the barony of Dartry in the west of County Monaghan, an area
then known as Dartraighe. They did, however, remain powerful, and in
O'Dugan's fourteenth-century "Topographical Poem" they are called "the bold
kings of Dartry," and are praised for their horsemanship and their blue
eyes.

The *O'Mulroonys* (*O Maolruanaidh*) were the leading clan of Fermanagh
before the rise of the Maguires, who subjugated them about 1300. A branch
of the O'Mulroonys afterwards settled in the northeast of County Galway,
where they were chiefs of Crumhthan (Cruffan), a district comprising the
modern barony of Killyan and part of the adjoining barony of Ballimoe. For
the Galway branch, the name has changed to Moroney.

The *Clann Lugain* included the *Maguires*, *MacKernans*, *MacAuleys*,
O'Cassidys, *O'Corrigans* and *MacManuses*. The Maguires (Mag Uidhir) are first
mentioned in the *Annals* in A.D. 956. They rose to great power in the later
part of the thirteenth century, and became lords of Fermanagh, where the
town and castle at Maguiresbridge recalls their importance there. They were
long one of the most powerful and influential families in Ulster, and produced
many great soldiers and ecclesiastics. During the reign of James I, in the first
part of the seventeenth century, much of the territory of the Maguires was included in the vast confiscation of Ulster which followed the English conquest
of the north. More land loss followed in the Cromwellian and Williamite confiscations, for the Maguires were ardent Jacobites, and later they were prominent among the "Wild Geese" in the service of France and Austria. As barons
of Enniskillen their chiefs were accepted as nobility at the Court of France until the title became extinct about 1795.

The *MacManuses* (*Mac Maghnuis*) descend from Maghnus, son of Donn
Maguire, chief of Fermanagh, who died in A.D. 1302. The head of this family
resided at Senadh Mic Maghnusa, now Bell Isle, on Lough Erne. The
O'Cassidys (*O Caiside*) were a distinguished medical family, being the

hereditary physicians to the Maguires. They also provided ollavs (professors or learned men) to the Maguires, and one, Rory O'Cassidy, Archdeacon of Clogher, is said to have participated in the compilation of the *Annals of Ulster* under Cathal Maguire in the fifteenth century. The first literary figure of the name was Giolla Moduda O Caiside, who died in 1143, and whose Gaelic poetry is still preserved. Before the end of the sixteenth century, branches of the family had settled in the Midlands around County Westmeath.

The *O'Corrigans (O Corragain)* were an ecclesiastical sept closely related to the Maguires, and men of the name long filled abbacies and other church offices in County Fermanagh. By the sixteenth century the name had already spread into Connacht and the Midlands. Other branches of the Maguires include the *Clann Fearghaile* or *MacKernans (Mac Thighearnain)*, chiefs of the territory called Clann Fearghaile in central Fermanagh, and the *MacAuleys (Mac Amhlaoibh)*, who gave their name to the barony of Clanawley in west-central Fermanagh. A branch of the latter settled in Connacht under the form Gawley (Mag Amhlaoibh).

The *MacMahons (Mac Mathghamhna)* were one of the most powerful and influential families in Ulster. They rose to preeminence in Oriel on the decline of the O'Carrolls of Leitrim in the thirteenth century, having subdued the O'Boylans in the process. They maintained their rank as lords of Oriel down to the reign of Elizabeth I in the late sixteenth century, and retained considerable property in County Monaghan as late as the Cromwellian wars of the mid-seventeenth century. Their last chief, Hugh MacMahon, was betrayed and arrested for complicity in the plot to seize Dublin Castle in 1641, and sent to the Tower of London. Three years later he was beheaded at Tyburn. Besides many distinguished chiefs, the family produced many eminent ecclesiastics as well.

The *Ui Breasail Macha or Clann Bhreasail* were originally seated in what is now the barony of Oneilland East, in the extreme northeast of County Armagh. Their chief clan, the *Cineal Aonghusa*, of which the *MacCanns (Mac Anna)* were the chief family, inhabited the south shore of lough Neagh in County Armagh.

The *Ui Meath Macha*, of which the O'Hanraghtys *(O hAnrachtaigh)* were the chief family, originally inhabited the north of County Louth, the O'Hanraghtys being lords of North Louth. They were pushed as a result of the Anglo-Norman invasion into County Monaghan, where they settled in the modern barony of that name, Monaghan, County Monaghan.

The *Ui Niallain*, of which the O'Hanlons *(O hAnluain)* were the chief family, inhabited the territory of that name, Ui Niallain, now the baronies of Oneilland in the northeast of County Armagh, and at one time also the territory of Oirthear (now the baronies of Orier), in the east and southeast of the same county. The O'Hanlons were long known as lords of Oirthear. They were a powerful clan, and had many valiant chiefs mentioned in the *Annals*.

They maintained their independence as a clan down to the year 1587, when the then chief, Sir Oghie O'Hanlon, surrendered his lands to the English Crown, in order to have them re-granted by letters of patent in tail male (to be held of the Crown), thus abolishing the chieftaincy. The O'Hanlon was afterwards hereditary royal standard bearer north of the River Boyne, and owing to his loyalty to the English, retained most of the clan-lands down to the Cromwellian confiscations of the mid seventeenth century.

The Ui Tuirtre of South Derry moved eastward across the River Bann as their lands were absorbed into the expanding Ui Neill over-kingdom of Cineal Eoghain in the eighth century. They kept their western lands (the present barony of Loughinsholin) as a tributary kingdom to the Cineal Eoghain, but resided in Lough Beg, which lay strategically between their new and old territories. East of the Bann they were allies of the Dal nAraidi, though they profited by their decline. They were also sometimes overkings of Ulidia. The medieval representatives of the Ui Tuirtre were the O'Lynns (O Floinn or O Loinn) of South Antrim, who defeated the Norman John de Courcy when he attempted to invade their territory in 1177. They maintained their independence until about 1368.

The Ui Macc Uais Mide were a branch of the Ui Macc Uais of what is now the Barony of Upper Strabane in the northeast of County Tyrone. They settled in Mide (what is now County Westmeath with part of Offaly) and came very early to be treated as a sub-kingdom of the Southern Ui Neill (North Gaels), just as the Ui Macc Uais of Tyrone were treated as a sub-kingdom of the Cineal Eogain clan of the Northern Ui Neill.

The chief family of the Ui Macc Uais Mide was that of MacEvoy (Mac Fhiodhbhuidhe), who were anciently lords of Ui Macc Uais in County Westmeath, now the barony of Moygoish. Later, at some time before 1563, they settled in what is now Leix (formerly Queen's County). Here they were known as Muintear (or Tuath) Fhiodhbhuidhe, being lords of a territory in what is now the barony of Stradbally which comprised the parishes of Mountrath and Raheen. They came to be regarded as one of the Seven Septs of Leix. In 1609 the chief men of the family were transplanted by the English to County Kerry as were the leading members of the other Leix Septs. The rest of the clan remained in the home territory, however, where they remain to this day.

The Cineal nAlbanaich were a branch of the Oirghialla that settled in the northwest Highlands and Islands in very early times. Their chief clans descend from Godfraidh Mac Ferghusa (i.e., "Fergus"), a prince of the Oirghialla in Northern Ireland who came to Scotland, or Albany, in the ninth century as an ally of Kenneth MacAlpin, first king of the united kingdom of Picts and Scots. The Cineal nAlbanaich settled north of Argyle in the Hebrides, in the area of Skye, where they acquired Pictish and later Norse connections. The chief clans which branched from the Cineal nAlbanaich are the Clann Dhomhnuill and the Clann Dubhghaill.

The *Clann Dhomhnuill* or *MacDonalds* (*Mac Dhomhnuill*) descend from Dhomnuill, or Donald, son of Reginald (or Ranald) mac Somerled, King of the Isles and Lord of Argyle and Kintyre (1164–1207). Ranald's mother was the daughter of Olav, Norse King of Man and the Isles. It was from her that he derived his titles in the Isles, his paternal grandfather Somerled being already Lord of Argyle (the Lordship of the Isles was under the control of the King of Norway until 1266).

The *Clann Dhomhnuill* includes the families of *MacDonald* of *Clan Donald* and Islay, the *MacDonells* of Keppoch and *MacDonnells* of Antrim, the *MacIans*, *MacAlisters*, *MacSheehys*, and the *Clan Ranald*. The MacDonalds of Clan Donald, or *Clann Uistein*, the chief family of the clan (now represented by MacDonald of MacDonald, and his cadet, MacDonald of Sleat, both of Skye), were the leaders of the most powerful tribal organization in Scotland, and were long vested in the Lordship of the Isles (the last Lord of the Isles died in 1503, the title being taken over by a jealous, House of Stewart, see Chapter IV). They descend from Donald, son of John, first Lord of the Isles (from 1354) and his second wife, a daughter of Robert II of the House of Stewart.

The *MacDonalds* of Islay and *MacDonnells* of the Glens of Antrim, the *Clan Ian Vor*, descend from Iain Mor, or "Big John" the Tanist, a younger full brother of Donald, second lord of the Isles who married the MacEoin or Bissett heiress of Antrim about 1400, thus inheriting lands in Antrim, which were settled by them in ernest during the first part of the sixteenth century. The *Clan Ranald* of Lochaber, or *MacDonells* of Keppoch, (between Loch Lochy and Loch Spean in Lochaber, or southern Inverness-shire) descend from Alasdair, another younger full brother of Donald.

The *Conns*, an old Aberdeenshire family, traditionally descend from William Con, son of Donald of the Isles, chief of Clan Donald in the first part of the sixteenth century. They took the name of Conn from the traditional ancestor of the Clan Donald (see above under Oirghialla). The Conns appear under the appellation "of Auchry" before 1539, and appear in the district from 1522. They were a prominent Roman Catholic family in the sixteenth and seventeenth centuries, but were driven into exile soon after 1642 (George Con was the Pope's agent at the court of the Queen of Charles I).

The *MacDonalds* of Clanranald, captains of the great Clan Ranald "proper," descend from Ranald, son of John, first Lord of the Isles and his first wife, the heiress of the MacRuaris of Uist Isle and Garmoran, the mainland district between Skye and Argyle (from Loch Hourn to Loch Sunart), both of which they inherited (the MacRuaris descended from another son of Reginald mac Somerled). Their younger branch, the *MacDonells* of Glengarry (just east of Garmoran) descend from Donald, himself the son of Ranald, ancestor of the Clan Ranald.

The *Clann an tSaoir*, or *MacIntyres* (*Mac an tSaoir*) are also a branch of the Clan Ranald. They settled in Lorn, or North Argyle, sometime during the fourteenth century, having come from the Hebrides in a galley "with a white cow," to settle in Glen Oe (or Noe) just south of Loch Etive. There they were hereditary foresters to the Stewart lords of Lorn. A branch settled in Badenoch under MacKintosh protection in the fifteenth century, and became members of the Clan Chattan Confederacy.

The MacIans (Mac Iain), or MacDonalds of Glencoe (just east of Appin in the north of Argyle), also known as the Clan Ian Abrach, descend from John Og, son of Angus Og, Chief of Clan Donald in the time of Robert the Bruce (early fourteenth century). The MacIans (MacDonalds) or Clan Ian of Ardnamurchan (the peninsula just west of Garmoran) descend from Angus MacIan, one of the relations of John, first Lord of the Isles, who was granted Ardnamurchan by King David II. The Clan Alister, or MacAlisters (Mac Alasdair) of the Loup in Kintyre descend from Alasdair, or Alexander, younger son of Donald mac Reginald mac Somerled, King of the Isles and eponymus ancestor, or name-founder, of the Clan Donald.

The MacSheehys (Mac Sithigh) descend from Sitheach, great-grandson of the same Donald. They were a famous gallowglass family (galowglasses were heavily armed foot-soldiers) employed as hired bodyguards by various tribal kings in Ireland, as per Gaelic aristocratic custom. They are first mentioned in the Annals in 1367, having taken part in a battle that year between two factions of the Royal O'Connors of Ui Briuin in Connacht. In 1420 they settled County Limerick as constables to the Earl of Desmond, and built their castle of Lisnacolla, or Woodfort, located in the parish of Clonagh, about four miles west of Rathkeale in north-central Limerick.

The Clann Dubhghaill or MacDougals (Mac Dubhghaill) descend from Dubhghaill, King of the Hebrides and Lord of Lorn (North Argyle) who was the son of the great Somerled and brother of Reginald (or Ranald), ancestor of the Clann Dhomnuill, or MacDonalds. Lorn was held by Dubhghaill under the Scottish crown, while the Hebridian islands under his control were held of the King of Norway. Dunollie Castle in Oban Bay was the principal stronghold of the MacDougal chiefs, whose power declined after their defeat at the hands of King Robert I the Bruce in the Pass of Brander in 1309. The MacDougals were related by marriage to the Bruce's rivals, the Cummins, and thus backed them during the period leading up to the battle of Bannockburn in 1314. As a result, the MacDougals were forfeited and lost their vast island territories, although they were later restored to the mainland Lordship of Lorn by King David II (after their seventh chief married a granddaughter of Robert I). Eventually the MacDougalls lost the lordship of Lorn, which (like many other old Scottish Dignities) passed almost inevitably to the covetous House of Stewart. The family further suffered as a result of their support for the Jacobite cause during the seventeenth and eighteenth centuries. Nevertheless, based upon their proverbial connection with Lorn, the family has ever been known, both officially and informally, as the MacDougalls of Lorn.

IX. The Gaels

The original ethno-tribal invaders known as the Gaels were the last of a series of Celtic invaders that would come to be considered native to the Emerald Isle after the beginning of the historical period (about A.D. 500 – see Chapter III.) They arrived in Ireland sometime during the first century B.C., and brought a distinctive language, the ancestor of modern Gaelic, which would come to dominate the hybridized Gaelic culture that emerged from the prehistoric melting pot of Ireland (hence the later general appellation "Gaels" which was applied to all Gaelic-speaking people of Ireland – and later Scotland). Two great tribal nations of Gaels emerged in the light of the historical period: The North Gaels and the South Gaels or Eoghanach. Between about A.D. 1 and 400 the North Gaels expanded their foothold in the northwest of Ireland and established themselves as Sacral ("totemistically" sacred) High-Kings at the ancient site of Tara near Dublin with the aid of their allies, the Laiginian tribe of Oirghialla. These events are enshrined in the heroic tales of the *Ulster Cycle* of literature or *Red Branch*, one of the three great collections of early Irish literature along with the *Finn Cycle* and the later (medieval) *Cycles of the Kings* (as opposed to ordinary folk-tales). Because of the royal tribal preeminence of the North Gaels, clans representative of other ethno-tribal groups sometimes tried to affect genealogical connection to their sacred ancestral tribal stem as a kind of "social climbing," but only the unstudied were fooled by these generally half-hearted attempts. Similar circumstances prevailed in the South, among the long dominant Eoghanacht.

The North Gaels

Connachta

The North Gaels divided into two great branches in the mid-fifth century A.D.: the *Connachta* and the *Ui Neill*. Afterwards the tribal leadership of the Connachta itself divided into three great dynasties, known as "the three Connachts." These soon spread over the entire western region of Ireland, which they gave their name to: The province of Connacht. After the decline of the

93

THE GAELS

conn cétchathach = roaín ruaío

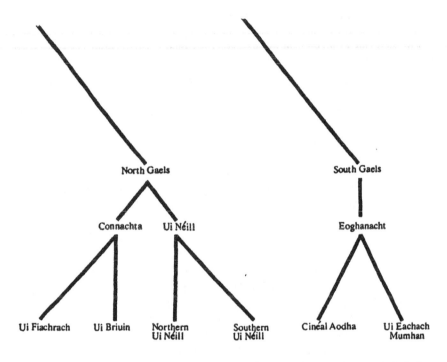

The Sun-God Incarnate. Source Of Wisdom
And 'Great Traveler' Of The Heavens.
Ancestor-Deity Of The GAELS

Ui Ailello in the eighth century, the remaining two Connachts included the tribes of *Ui Fiachrach* and *Ui Briuin*, notwithstanding the fact that the Laiginian tribe of *Ui Maine* came, with its rise to power in the southeast of County Galway, to be regarded as filling the remaining traditional "third" of Connacht (the Ui Maine originated as allies of the Ui Briuin akin to the Oirghialla, and thus were of relatively late introduction in Connacht. (See Chapter VIII).

The *Ui Fiachrach* descend from Fiachra, brother of Nial of the Nine Hostages, ancestor of the Ui Niell. Fiachra's son and grandson were both High-Kings in the second half of the fifth century, though after that the High Kingship of Tara was vested in the Ui Neill. Afterwards the Ui Fiachrach were the royal tribe of Connacht, although in the early seventh century they began alternating the rather nominal provencial kingship of Connacht with their Ui Briuin kinsmen until about A.D. 700. After this time the Ui Briuin monopolized the kingship of Connacht, and in time molded it into an effective over-kingdom. The Ui Fiachrach, however, continued as the most influential Connacht family until the middle of the eighth century; then they divided into two great branches, the *Ui Fiachrach Muaidhe* (of the Moy) or *Northern Ui Fiachrach*, and the *Ui Fiachrach Aidhne* or *Southern Ui Fiachrach*.

The *Northern Ui Fiachrach* were seated in what are now the counties of Mayo and Sligo. The chief family of the tribe was that of *O'Dowd (O Dubhda)*, whose chiefs were known as "Kings of the Moy" from their dominance of the Moy estuary in north Mayo. Before the Anglo-Norman invasion of Connacht in 1237 the O'Dowds were the ruling family in all lower Connacht, including the greater part of counties Mayo and Sligo. They were also a great seapower, like the O'Malleys of Iar Connacht, which was unusual among native Irish families, for seapower was generally given over to the Viking clans of the Irish Sea. In the fourteenth century the O'Dowds had a series of able chiefs in immediate succession, and drove the Anglo-Norman settlers out of their territory, though they never regained quite the regal preeminence they had formerly held. The family suffered in the confiscations of the seventeenth century. Branches of the family settled in Kerry before the end of the sixteenth century, and are now known as Doody.

The O'Finnegans (O Fionnagain) were chiefs in the area of the Galway-Roscommon border, where two places called Bally-Finnegan recall their presence in the baronies of Ballymoe and Castlereagh. *The O'Keevans (O Caomhain)* of Sligo and Mayo were an important family among the Ui Fiachrach Muaidhe, and it was the privilege of their chief to inaugurate The O'Dowd in the chiefship of Ui Fiachrach. The *O'Bolans (O Beollain)* were seated at Doonaltan, in what is now the barony of Tireragh in West Sligo.

A branch of the Ui Fiachrach Muaidhe, the *Fir Ceara* of central Mayo, included the *O'Kearneys (O Cearnaigh)* and *O'Quigleys (O Coigligh)*. The O'Kearneys held extensive tracts of land around Balla and Manulla in central Mayo, and a branch of them became leading ecclesiastics among the Dalcaisians, while another became established as erenaghs of Derry. The O'Quigleys were anciently lords of the barony of Carra (from Fir Ceara) in central Mayo. After the Anglo-Norman encroachment they were dispersed throughout Ireland, and are later to be found mostly in western Ulster, but also as far away as Wexford where the name is spelled Cogley (Kegley is used in Meath).

The Southern Ui Fiachrach, or *Ui Fiachrach Aidhne* were settled in the district of Aidhne in the extreme southwestern part of County Galway, on the border of County Clare. This district was co-extensive with the diocese of Kilmacduagh. They had been pushed into this more restricted area by the expansion of the Ui Briuin Ai into central Connacht, an action which divided them from their northern cousins, and at the same time forced the Ui Maine of west-central Galway to encroach upon their territory. The O'Shaughnessys (O Seachnasaigh) were the chief family of Cinel Aodha in the district of that name (Kinelea), being the territory around Gort in southern Galway. They alternated the kingship of the southern Ui Fiachrach with the O'Heynes, and became famous in the wars of the seventeenth century, but lost their lands as a result of the confiscations following the last Jacobite war towards the end of that century.

The Cineal Guaire included the families of O'Heyne (O hEidhin) and O'Cleary (O Cleirigh). The O'Heynes descend from Maolruanaidh O hEidhin, lord of Aidhne, who fell (as co-commander of the Connacht army with The O'Kelly of Ui Maine) at Clontarf in 1014. He was the first to bear the name of O'Heyne. The O'Heynes' illustrious seventh-century ancestor was Guaire Aidhne (hence their clan-name of Cineal Guaire), last Ui Fiachrach King of Connacht, celebrated for his hospitality. The O'Heynes shared the lordship of Aidhne and the chiefship of the Southern Ui Fiachrach with their O'Shaughnessy kinsmen, being themselves chiefs of a territory in the north of the present barony of Kiltartan, around Kinvara (where the fortress of Dunguire recalls the name of their illustrious ancestor). The Abbey of Kilmacduagh is known as O'Heyne's Abbey. The O'Shaughnessys and O'Heynes have kept possession of large tracts of their respective original patrimonies in South Galway.

The O'Clearys descend from Cleireach, who flourished about A.D. 850 and was seventh in descent from the celebrated Guaire the Hospitable, king of Connacht mentioned above. The O'Clearys were originally the chief family of the Cineal Guaire, but lost power early in the eleventh century, and by the thirteenth century they were driven out of Aidhne altogether. After that they are found chiefly in Mayo, Kilkenny, and Cavan. The Mayo branch was settled in Tirawley just west of the Moy estuary. From there they spread to Donegal, where they succeeded the famous O'Scingins as poets and chroniclers to the O'Donnells by marriage to the daughter of the last O'Scingin ollav (professor) towards the end of the fourteenth century. That family of ollavs being extinct, the O'Clearys inherited their patrimony and were granted other lands besides by their O'Donnell patrons, and had their chief seat near Ballyshannon, the castle of Kilbarron. The O'Clearys won lasting fame as the compilers of the Annals of the Four Masters and other invaluable works on Gaelic history, the former being the most distinguished work of its kind.

The O'Houlihans (O hUallachain) were originally chiefs in County Clare, where their arms and their proximity to Aidhne suggest a clan affiliation with the O'Shaughnessys (both the O'Shaughnessys and the O'Heynes had important medieval branches settled in just over the Clare border in Limerick). The O'Houlihans were in any case pushed by Cromwell into Connacht, though some were dispersed southward to County Cork, where they adopted the form

"Holland," by which name they are still known. In Roscommon and Mayo the name became Nuallachain, and was Anglicized as Nolan. The O'Scanlans (O Scannlain) of south Galway and Clare are kinsmen to the O'Shaughnessys and O'Heynes, and a branch of them spread southward as an ecclesiastical sept, being formerly erenaghs of Cloyne in County Cork.

Ui Briuin

The Ui Briuin descend from Brion, who was the brother of Fiachra, ancestor of the Ui Fiachrach, and of Nial, ancestor of the Ui Neill; all mentioned above. The Ui Briuin divided into several branches, including the Ui Briuin Ai, Ui Briuin Breifne, and the Ui Briuin Seola. These tribes, or more accurately their respective tribal dynasties, alternated the kingship of Connacht, much as their ancestors had formerly done with the Ui Fiachrach (this had not been a regular alternation: Sometimes the kingship would alternate between branches of the Ui Briuin or Ui Fiachrach themselves in immediate succession before going over to the other tribe). The real expansion of the Ui Briuin dates from about the middle of the eighth century, from which time they began to extend their power beyond their various sub-tribal centers in central and northeastern Connacht.

The Ui Briuin Ai rose in the late eighth century to firmly take possession of Cruachu and the overlordship of the subject tribes, or "alien tuatha" of Connacht. This they accomplished from their relatively narrow strip of original patrimony, which lay south of Cruachu in north-central Roscommon, and extended over the upper reaches of the River Suck into central Connacht. Their chief dynastic family, which was also the chief dynastic clan of the whole Ui Briuin, were the Siol Muireadhaigh (Silmurray), who derived their name from their ancestor Muiredach Muillethan, King of Connacht, who died in 702.

The Siol Muireadhaigh included a number of very important families, chief amongst them the O'Connors (O Conchobhair). The O'Connors descend from Conchobhair, king of Connacht, who died in 882 (their name is more directly taken from a namesake of Conchobhair's in the late tenth century). They separated into three great branches, the O'Connors of Sligo; the O'Connors of central Roscommon, the head of which family was known as O'Connor Roe (the Red O'Connor); and the Royal O'Connors themselves, kings of Connacht, the head of whom is still known as the O'Connor Don (the Brown O'Connor). Tairrdelbach Ua Conchobair, the first to take the family name, was High King of Ireland in the mid twelfth century.

The O'Malones (O Maoileoin) are a branch of the O'Connors, and were long a distinguished ecclesiastical family at Clonmacnoise, of which several were abbots and bishops. Several of the family were prominent Jacobites in the wars of the seventeenth century. The O'Mulconrys (O Maolchonair) also are a branch of the O'Connors. They were a great literary family, and served as hereditary poets and chroniclers to their clan, the Siol Muireadhaigh. Their chief seat was at Clonahee, near Strokestown, County Roscommon, where they had considerable land holdings in right of their profession. A branch settled in Clare, and became famous for their learned teaching in history, one of them being described as the "chief teacher in history of all the men of Erin in his own time." The family also produced a number of eminent ecclesiastics.

The *O'Beirnes* (*O Birn*) first appear as stewards to their kinsmen the Royal O'Connors, and later, after driving the O'Monaghans out of Tir Bhriuin in north-central Roscommon (a rich territory lying between Elphin and Jamestown) about the middle of the 13th century, they ruled that territory for over 300 years. The *O'Sheridans* (*O Sirideain*) were an ecclesiastical family who were erenaghs (hereditary abbots) of Granard in County Longford before becoming devoted followers of the O'Reillys. Still later, in the seventeenth century, the family rose to eminence on the literary fame of its members. One of them, Thomas Sheridan, was secretary of state under James II.

The *Clann Chathail*, a branch of the Siol Muireadhaigh that gave two kings to Connacht during the ninth century, included the families of O'Carry and O'Flanagan. The *O'Carrys* (*O Carthaigh*) were a literary family of Roscommon, three of whom attained the distinction "chief poet of Ireland," being described as such in the *Annals* during the eleventh and twelfth centuries. The family later spread into Longford, Sligo and Donegal. The *O'Flanagans* (*O Flannagain*) were the chief family of the Clann Chathail, and long served as hereditary stewards to the kings of Connacht. They were chiefs of a territory called after them Clann Chathail, which lay near Elphin in northeastern Roscommon.

The *Clann Mhaolruanaidh* included the *MacDermots* (*Mac Diarmada*) and their branch-families, the *MacDonoghs* and *O'Crowleys*. The MacDermots were the second most powerful family of the Siol Muireadhaigh next to the O'Connors, and derived their clan-name of Clann Mhaolruanaidh from Maolruanaidh, son of Tadhg O'Connor, king of Connacht who died in 1097. From Diarmaid, the grandson of Maolruanaidh, who died in 1159, they took the family name of Mac Diarmada. About the middle of the fourteenth century they divided into three branches, each with a chief of its own, namely: MacDermot of Moylurg, overlord of the MacDermots, who had his fortress at the Rock of Lough Key near Boyle; MacDermotroe, or the Red MacDermot, who was chief of Tir-Thuthail (the parish of Kilronan centered at Alderford) in County Galway, and MacDermot Gall, (the Anglicized MacDermot) who early fell in with the English. The MacDermots of Moylurg retained their rank as lords of the territory of Moylurg, now represented by the parishes of Frenchpark and Boyle in northwest County Roscommon, down to the end of the sixteenth century, after which time they continued to hold considerable property as princes of the adjoining Sligo territory of Coolavin.

The *MacDonaghs* or *MacDonoughs* (*Mac Donnchadha*) are a branch of the MacDermots of Moylurg, and were chiefs of Tirerrill and Corran in County

Sligo and had their chief seat at Ballymote in the center of that county. The O'Crowleys (O'Cruadhlaoich) are also a branch of the MacDermots of Moylurg in County Roscommon, Connacht. They settled in County Cork as fighting men, or gallowglasses, to the MacCarthys.

The MacCarthys were the leading family of the Eoghanacht and were thus the chief family of the Cork-Kerry area. Gallowglasses, being heavily armed soldiers (as opposed to kerns, the lightly armed and armored soldiers from the clan-lands, whose usual occupation was farming), were commonly imported as chiefs' bodyguards (and to provide a nucleus of professional soldiers), especially from the western Highlands of Scotland (the name gallowglass means "foreign youth").

The O'Mulvihills (O Maoilmhichil) are an early branch of the Siol Muireadhaigh, being descended from Maolmhichil, chief of Siol Muireadhaigh in 866. They were originally chiefs of the district of Corca Sheachlainn in the east of County Roscommon, but lost power at some time prior to the fifteenth century, though the remained common in the area. Branches settled in counties Clare and Galway in the sixteenth century, where they are known as Mulville or Melville. The O'Duigenans (O Duibhgeannain) were a distinguished literary family seated at Kilronan, County Roscommon. They were hereditary chroniclers or historians to their MacDermot kinsmen, and also to the O'Farrells and MacRannells.

Finally among the Siol Muireadhaigh were the Muintear Rodhuibh, or MacGeraghtys (Mag Oireachtaigh), who descend from Oireachtach O Roduibh, one of the "four royal chiefs" under the Royal O'Connors in the latter part of the twelfth century ("Oireachtach" means "a member of the court, or assembly"). The MacGeraghtys were originally of County Roscommon, where they were important chiefs over a territory in the barony of Athlone named from their clan-name "Muintear Rodhuibh." About the middle of the six-teenth century they were dispossessed as a result of the first stages of the English conquest. However, they still formed a distinct clan in neighboring County Galway as late as 1585.

The Ui Briuin Seola originally inhabited the plains around Tuam in central Galway until pushed from that area in the eleventh century by the expansion of the royal ancestors of the O'Connors. Their chief clan was the Muintear Mhurchadha or O'Flahertys (O Flaithbhearthaigh) who after the expulsion from the Tuam area settled on the east side of Lough Corrib in what is now the barony of Clare, but which was known after their clan-name as Munter-morroghoe. They were pushed from this territory by the Anglo-Normans in the thirteenth century, and afterwards became lords of Iar-Connacht, the western part of Connacht on the other side of Lough Corrib and Galway City (the mostly Norman inhabitants of that city had an inscription on one of the city gates: "From the fury of the O'Flahertys, Lord-God deliver us" – a prayer originally used by churchmen against the Vikings of earlier times). A branch of the O'Flahertys, the *Clann Choscraigh*, included the families of *MacGarry* (*Mag Fhearadhaigh*) and also the *MacHughs* (*MacAodha*). The MacGarrys or Garrihys were seated at Moygarry in County Sligo as late as 1585. The name spread into Roscommon and Leitrim as well, and in some cases became O'Garriga (*O Gearaga* or *O Giorraighe*), and was mistranslated from this form into English as *Hare*. The MacHughs were seated in the old O'Flaherty territory in the barony of Clare, County Galway.

Another branch of the Ui Briuin Seola, of which the O'Lees (*O Laoidigh*) were chiefs, also settled in western Connacht. The O'Lees were erenaghs, or hereditary abbots, of Annaghdown, and produced a number of distinguished ecclesiastics. They are better known as a medical family, and were for many centuries hereditary physicians to the O'Flahertys, and sometimes to the Royal O'Connors as well. As early as the fifteenth century the family had produced a complete course in medicine, written in Latin and Gaelic. They were widely disbursed towards the end of the sixteenth century, and in north Connacht used the form MacLee.

The *Ui Briuin Breifne* carved out a territory for themselves between Lough Allan and the river Erne in central Fermanagh in the late eighth century. They expanded east of the Shannon and into the wastelands of Cavan in the ninth and tenth centuries, and afterwards played an ever-increasing role in the politics of the midlands. Their chief families were the O'Rourkes (*O Ruairc*), kings of West Breffny (County Leitrim), and the *Muintear Mhaolmordha* or O'Reillys (*O Raghailligh*), lords of East Breffny (County Cavan). The O'Rourkes were, prior to the twelfth-century Anglo-Norman invasion, overlords of the Ui Briuin Breifne in Leitrim and Cavan, and ruled over a territory which at its widest extent stretched all the way from Drumcliff in Sligo to Kells in Meath. Three of their chiefs, in the tenth and eleventh centuries, were kings of Connacht as well. After the Anglo-Norman invasion, their cousins the O'Reillys became lords of East Breffny, which became known as Breffny O'Reilly, while the O'Rourkes were lords of West Breffny, thenceforward known as "Breffny O'Rourke." The O'Rourke kings took a leading part in the wars against Elizabeth I in the late sixteenth century, from which wars they suffered severely. They did, however, retain considerable property down to the Cromwellian confiscations of the mid-seventeenth century, after which many of them rose to distinction in the military service of continental powers, especially Poland and Russia.

The *Teallach Dhunchadha* (*Household of Dunchadh*) or *MacTernans* (*Mac Tighearnain*), also known as *Tiernans* or *MacKiernans* (*Mac Thighearnain*) descend from Dunchadh, eighth-century ancestor of the O'Rourkes. Their clan name was given to their territory, now the Barony of Tullyhunco in the west of County Cavan. The *Teallach Eachach* or *MacGoverns* (*Mag Shamhradhain*, also known as *Magaurans*, descend from Eochaidh, son of Maonach (Maonach was a brother of the Dunchadh mentioned above). The patrimony of the

MacGoverns lay in the northwest of County Cavan, and was called after them "Tellach Eachach," now the Barony of Tullyhaw, where there is a townland called Ballymagauran.

The MacShanlys (Mac Seanlaoich), long allied with the Royal O'Connors, are of the same stock as the MacGoverns, and were seated in Corca Achlann, also called Corca Seachlan, in the east of County Roscommon, and also at Ballymacshanly in the south of County Leitrim, where their chief was known as MacShanley of Dromod. In Leitrim they were often at feud with their neighbors the MacRannalls. The MacClancys (Mac Fhlannchadha) are an ancient family in the north of of County Leitrim. They appear from their arms, traditional Milisian descent (see Chapter III) and long identification with Leitrim, to be collateral kinsmen to the O'Rourkes of the Ui Briuin Breifne.

The O'Reillys were lords of Cavan, and in the thirteenth and fourteenth centuries they extended their dominion into parts of Meath and Westmeath, being sometimes lords of all Breffny as well. They maintained their independence as a clan down to the time of James I in the early seventeenth century, though they suffered heavily under the Cromwellian confiscations. Many O'Reillys rose to high ecclesiastical rank, and five of them were primates of Armagh.

Ui Neill

The Ui Neill were the great royal tribal dynasty of the North Gaels. Having separated from the royal kinsmen, the Connachta, shortly after the career of their illustrious fifth century ancestor Niall of the Nine Hostages, they set out from a base in Sligo and soon (by the beginning of the sixth century) monopolized the Sacral High-Kingship of Tara, which for hundreds of years they alternated between their own two illustrious branches, the *Northern Ui Neill* and the *Southern Ui Neill*. The Northern Ui Neill divided into three great clans, the *Cineal Eoghain*, *Cineal Conaill* and *Cineal Cairbre*.

Northern Ui Neill

The Cineal Eoghan were the Royal Clan of the North Gaels, associated with the High-Kingship of Tara. Though in the early period they alternated the overkingship of the north with their Cineal Conaill cousins, by the end of the eighth century they had monopolized the overkingship of Ulster and with it the northern representation in the High-Kingship, aided by the fact that they had, with their centrally dominant fortress of Aliech in northeast Donegal, the strategic advantage, together with the energy and will to exploit it. Their original patrimony included the modern baronies of Raphoe and Inishowen in Donegal, but from their center at the great fort of Ailech in Inishowen, they soon spread throughout Derry and much of Tyrone as well (Tyrone, Gaelic "Tir Eoghain," the land of Eoghain, is named for them).

Until the mid-thirteenth century the leading family of the Cineal Eoghain was *MacLoughlin (Mac Lochlainn)* of Inishowen; in 1241 they lost a decisive battle to their kinsmen the O'Neills, and afterwards they declined in power, though a branch became established in County Leitrim under the O'Rourkes.

The great *O'Neills (O Neill)* themselves descend from Niall Glundubh, High-King of Ireland, who fell fighting against the Vikings near Dublin in 919. His grandson Domhnall, who flourished about 943, was the first to bear the dynastic name of O'Neill. They were the chief family of the Cineal Eoghain from 1241, and as overlords of Tir Eoghain (which included the modern counties of Tyrone, Derry and those northeastern parts of Donegal), and kings of Ulster they make a very distinguished group in history from the eleventh to the seventeenth century. Such O'Neill magnates as Conn, Shane the Proud, Sir Phelim and Owen Roe are all outstanding figures. A powerful branch of the family settled in Antrim and Down in the fourteenth century, where they were known as Clann Aodha Bhuidhe, or the *O'Neills* of Claneboy. Other branches of the O'Neills include the *O'Branigans (O Branagain)* of Derry, who provided eranachs (hereditary abbots) to the churches of Derry in County Derry and Derryvullan in County Fermanagh; the *O'Rahillys (O Raithile)* of Kerry, a literary family that settled early in County Kerry near Killarney, and the *MacMartins (Mac Mairtin)* of County Tyrone.

The *O'Cahans (O Cathain)* were a great family in County Derry, sub-kings of the Cineal Eoghain, whose heads were privileged to be one of the hereditary inaugurators of the O'Neill. They rose to great power during the twelfth century, and were lords of Keenaght, being possessed of the greater part of what is now County Derry until their lands were confiscated by the English in the Ulster Plantation of the sixteenth century. A branch settled in Thomond (northeast Munster). There is a sixteenth-century O'Cahan knight's effigy at Dungiven in County Derry. The *Monros (Mac an Rothaich)*, derive their name from a place at the foot of the River Roe in Derry, and according to the Clan Donald tradition, they came into Scotland in the train of a daughter of the O'Cahan that became a MacDonald princess. They possessed the vast district of Foulis on the Cromarty Firth in Ross, and also lands in Strathoykell.

The *Roses (Rois, Ros)* take their name from the district of Ross in northern Scotland, and are connected with the O'Cahans by the Clan Donald seanachies (historians). Hugh Rose of Geddes witnessed the foundation charter of Beauly Priory by the Bissets. They acquired their principal holdings, the Barony of Kilvarnock in Nairnshire, by marriage with an heiress. They may have acquired their O'Cahan connection win the same way, by marriage, and may originally have been of Norman origin.

The *Siol Gillivray* included the families of *MacLachlan (Mac Lachlainn)*, *Lamont (Mac Laomainn)*, *MacSorley (Mac Somhairle)*, *MacNeil (Mac Neill)* and *MacEwen*, and also the *MacSweeneys* of Ireland and *MacSweens* of Skye. They descend from Anrothan O'Neill, the Ulster prince who in the first half of the eleventh century married the joint heiress of the Cineal Comhgall (after whom Cowall is named) and their collateral kinsmen the Cineal nGabrain of Knapdale. His two grandsons, Donnshleibhe (Dunsleve) and Domhnall (Donald) O Neill are the ancestors of the branches of the clan. From Dunsleve, lord of Knapdale in the early thirteenth century are descended the MacLachlans, Lamonts, MacSorleys, MacSweeneys, MacQueens or Mac-Sweens and the MacEwens. The MacLachlans inhabited Strathlachlan in Argyle, and had their stronghold, Castle Lachlan, on the south shore of Loch Fyne. In 1230 the then chief Gilpatrick, son of Gilchrist (ancestor of the MacGilchrist branch of the family, lords of Glassary—see under Scrymgeour) witnessed a charter granted to Paisley Abbey by Laomainn, his cousin, ancestor of the Lamonts.

The Lamont territory was in Cowall, where they were the most powerful family until the great massacre of several hundred of their men, women and children by the Campbells in 1646, an act of revenge for the Lamonts' complicity in the murder of several Campbells by MacDonnells from Antrim a few years earlier. After foolishly surrendering their castles of Toward and Ascog (on the southern extremity of the eastern and western peninsulas of Cowall, respectively) the garrisons, now at the mercy of the Campbells, were cruelly tortured and put to death, and the castles burnt and razed. The grandfather of Laomainn was the brother of Gilchrist, ancestor of the MacLachlans.

This grandfather, Ferchar, had two sons, Malcolm, father of Laomainn, and Duncan, ancestor of the MacSorleys (Mac Somhairle) of Glassary in West Cowall, the majority of whom later assumed what became the mutual clan-family name of Lamont. The Lyons of Glamis in the Strathmore district of Angus descend, according to tradition, from a scion of the Lamonts of Cowall. John the son of Lyon (Johannes filius Leonis) and Hugo the son of Lyon (Hugo filius Leonis) were members of an inquest on the lands of Rostinot in 1321-1322. John Lyon had a charter of lands in Perthshire ca. 1342-43 from David II. Another John Lyon (or "Lyoun") appears, possibly the son of the former, as clerk and secretary to David II. He was known as the "White Lyon," which suggests an epithetic allusion to the "White Lyon on Blue" of the arms of the Lamonts, his own arms being a reversal of those colors. He was later granted the thanage of Glamis as a free barony by King Robert II ca. 1371-72, and soon afterwards married the king's daughter. This family later became barons of Glamis (1445) and earls of Strathmore. Some small broken clans in Angus are recorded as petitioning to "be allowed to take the name of Lyon, and be counted clansmen of the Strathmores."

The MacSweeneys (Mac Suibhne) of Donegal and MacQueens or MacSweens (Mac Shuibhne) descend from Suibhne, son of Dunsleve O'Neill, Lord of Knapdale. His grandson Murchadh was a captain of Gallowglasses, or West-Highland mercenary guards (see above under Ui Briuin Ai), and was active in Ireland by 1267. Early in the fourteenth century the MacSweeneys made a permanent settlement in Tirconnell (County Donegal) where they served as Gallowglasses to the ruling O'Donnells. There were three great branches of the MacSweeneys: MacSweeney of Fanad who had the castle of Rathmullin on a large tract of land in the northeast of the barony of Kilmacrenan, itself in the northwest of County Donegal; MacSweeney of Baghnagh, now the barony of Banagh in the west of County Donegal, and MacSweeney, Lord of Tuatha Toraighe, or Tory Island. A branch of the first mentioned family settled in the barony of Muskerry in central County Cork, where they served as captains of Gallowglasses for the MacCarthys. They had several castles in this area, and were known for their hospitality. There is a sixteenth-century MacSweeney knight's effigy at Killebegs, County Donegal, and another at Sligo, County Sligo dated 1577, but under the variant form of O'Sweeney (O Suibhne), which is rare. Branches of the family remained in Knapdale around Castle Sween (probably founded by their ancestor Suibhne), and later also appear at Garafad in Skye, which they held for the nominal annual price of a salmon as trusted vassals of the MacDonalds of Clanranald.

The "Clan Revan" MacQueens of the Clan Chattan Confederacy were pro-prietors of lands in Strathdearn, where they held Corybrough, and also in Strathfindhorn. They descend from Revan MacQueen, who accompanied Mora MacDonald of Moidart when she went to the Clan Chattan country to wed the tenth chief of the MacKintoshes in the early fifteenth century. Revan later fought under The MacKintosh at the battle of Harlow in 1411.

The MacEwens (Mac Eoghainn) and MacLeays or Livingstones (Mac Donn-shleibhe) both represent early branches of the line of Suibhne; the former were allied with the MacLachlans, while the latter were followers of the Stewarts of Appin. A branch of latter family was important hereditary ecclesiastics as keepers of the pastoral staff of St. Moluag and the Castle of Achandan on the Isle of Lismore off the coast of Appin. Their adoption of the English name of Livingstone during the mid-seventeenth century was influenced by the fact that the Isle of Lismore was at the time under the authority of a branch of the Lowland House of Livingston (see Chapter X). The difference in spelling is now significant to family identification, though in earlier times Livingstone was synonymous with Livingston.

The MacNeills descend from Domhnall O'Neill, mentioned above. They eventually separated into two great branches, the MacNeils of Barra and the McNeills of Gigha (both islands off the west coast of Scotland, the latter lies just off the coast of Cowall). Both families were originally followers of the Mac-Donalds as vassals of the lords of the Isles (from whose Clanranald branch the MacNeils inherited the Island of Barra in the Outer Hebrides about 1400), but after the downfall of the MacDonald lords in the late fifteenth century, the Barra branch followed the MacLeans of Duart, while the Gigha branch, who also held lands in northwest Cowall, subsequently followed the MacDonalds of Islay. The two branches were afterwards found fighting on opposing sides in the clan-wars between the MacLeans and MacDonalds. A fourteenth-century branch of the MacNeills settled in Antrim and Derry.

The *O'Creans (O Croidheagain)* of the Cineal Eoghain, also known as the *Creghans* or *Crehans*, originally inhabited the Cineal Eoghain lands in Donegal, but later removed to Sligo, where they became wealthy merchants and landowners. They were one of the few early merchant families of native (pre–Viking-and-Norman) stock. The *O'Donnellys (O Donnghaile)* are descended from Donnghal, fourth in descent from Domhnall, King of Ailech, who was himself the brother of Niall Glundubh, eponymous ancestor of the O'Neills. The O'Donnellys were originally seated at Drumleen, north of Lifford in County Donegal; but were expelled from there by the Cineal Connell, and afterwards settled at Ballydonnelly, now called Castle Caufield, west of Dungannon in County Tyrone. Here the famous Shane O'Neill was fostered by the O'Donnellys, who were hereditary marshalls of The O'Neill's forces.

The *O'Hegartys (O hEighceartaigh)* of the Cineal Eoghain were chiefs in the present barony of Loughinsholin in the south of County Derry, and by about the beginning of the seventeenth century some of them settled in the baronies of Barrymore and Carbery West in County Cork. The family was numerous in the Irish Brigades of France, and several O'Hegartys were, during the eighteenth century, particularly distinguished in that service.

The *Cineal Moen* or *O'Gormleys (O Goirmleaghaigh)* were a sub-clan of the Cineal Eoghain originally seated in what is now the barony of Raphoe, County Donegal. They were expelled from Donegal, as were their kinsmen the O'Donnellys, in the thirteenth century, and afterwards settled on the opposite side of Lough Foyle, between Strabane and Derry. They held considerable property until the confiscations attendant to the Plantation of Ulster in 1608.

The *O'Hagans (O hAgain)* of the Cineal Eoghain descend from Tighearnach, who was a son of Muireadhach mac Eoghain, and thus a grandson of Eoghain, the eponymous ancestor of the clan. They were divided into two groups: The main being chiefs of Cineal Fearghusa, a territory around Tullaghoge or Tullahogue in County Tyrone (Tir Eoghain), and the other being chiefs of Cineal Tighearnaigh in County Derry, where their presence is recalled by the place called Ballyagan (there is another Ballyhagan in Antrim). It was the hereditary privilege of the O'Hagans to inaugurate The O'Neill at their seat of Tullahogue (along with the O'Cahans).

The *O'Beolains (O Beollain)* or *Gillanders (Giolla Aindreas)* of the Cineal Eoghain were co-arbs (hereditary abbots) of St. Maelrubha at Applecross in Ross-shire, as discussed in Chapter IV. They were a powerful princely family, and became earls of Ross in the early thirteenth century. Towards the end of the fourteenth century they inherited the chiefship of the *Clann Aindreas*, or *Clann Giolla Aindreas* (Clan Gillanders), a native Pictish tribe related to the MacKenzies and Mathesons and among whom they had long been ecclesiastical and secular leaders. At about the same time they were artificially dispossessed of the Earldom of Ross by the King of Scots, and afterwards the family adopted as a surname what had for some time been the descriptive epithet of (de) *Ross*. They are also known by the patronymic of *MacAndrew* (*Mac Gille Aindreas*) from the clan name, while the original family name of O *Beollain* survives as MacBeolain, following Scottish prefix usage. A branch of the O'Beolains became hereditary abbots (erenaghs) of the Columban church at Drumcliffe in Sligo, and were famous for their hospitality. Some of the MacAndrews settled in the Clan Chattan country, and sought the protection of the MacKintosh about 1400. The MacBeolains occupied Glenshiel and the south side of Loch Duich as far as Kylerhea. Fearcher MacTaggart (Mac an tSagairt – "the son of the priest") of Applecross was created Earl of Ross in 1234.

It is interesting that the "three lions rampant" in the arms of the O'Beolain earls of Ross are unique in Scotland, and in Ireland occur only in the arms of families with *ecclesiastical* affiliations with the Connacht area (witness the arms of the O'Scanlans, O'Horans, O'Garas and O'Kearneys). Even the "three lions *passant*" of the Dalcassian O'Briens may reflect a Connacht connection. We need only consider the short genealogy of the Ui Toirdealbhaigh, their late acquisition of Dalcassian leadership (which was based on the success of the Ui Toirdealbhaigh against the Vikings), and also the fact that a number of Connacht families spread south as either ecclesiastical (O'Scanlan) or temporal (O'Heyne and O'Cahill) families. A number of medieval families considered "Dalcassian" are known to have origins in Connacht, including the O'Heaneys, O'Hehirs, O'Markahans and O'Kearneys. Though their primary identification was with Cashel in Munster, the O'Kearneys also had connections with the Columban foundations at Derry and Drumcliffe.

The Cairneys or *Cairdeneys* (*Cardanaigh*) of Foss in Perthshire descend from Sir John de Ross, son of the Earl of Ross, who came south in the train of Euphemia de Ross in anticipation of her marriage to Robert The Stewart in 1355. Not long after the accession of Robert and Euphemia as King and Queen of Scots in 1371, John de Ross received a grant from the King of the barony of Cardeney near Dunkeld, in which charter he is styled *dilectus consanguineus noster*. He assumed the epithet "de Cardeney" to replace that of "de Ross" (Ross was not yet a surname), and it was apparently his son William who married Rinald MacNair (Mac an Oighre), the heiress of Foss in nearby Rannoch. Another son, Robert de Cardeney, was bishop of Dunkeld in the early fifteenth century, and a daughter, Mariota, was mistress to Robert II. Mariota gave the King a number of natural children (Alexander Stewart of Inverlunan, James Stewart of Kinfaus, and John Stewart of Cardeney) and also had natural issue by Alexander MacNaughton, chief of the MacNachtans. This last was Dr. Donald MacNaughton, dean of Dunkeld during the tenure of his uncle (Robert de Cardeney) whom he succeeded as bishop.

Foss was in the Appin (abbey land) of Dull which was granted about 1200 to the Priory of St. Andrews by the then bishop of Dunkeld. The MacNairs are the first family found in possession of Foss after the abbey lands were secularized in the early fourteenth century. The name *Mac an Oighre* has a co-arbial ring to it (like *Mac an tSagairt* above and *Mac an Aba Oighre*—"the son of the heir of the abbot"—the Gaelic style of the MacNabs of Inchewin in Glendochart, the old senior line of the MacNabs dispossessed by Robert I), and probably refers to the heir of the abbey lands of Dull, centered at the mouth of Glen Lyon and the north end of Loch Tay (see page 9). As the MacNaughtons were also settled here before they were set up as keepers of the King's castle on Loch Awe about 1250 (their collaterals the MacLeans, who share with them the armorial quartering of the "hand holding a blue cross" of the Lismore co-arbial kindred, also returned to Lorn under royal patronage about this time), the MacNairs may represent a twelfth-century ecclesiastical branch of the clan. In this case, William Cardeney's connection with Foss may have precipitated Mariota's liaison with the chief of the MacNaughtons. The MacNairs remained in Rannoch until the time of the reformation, by which time Foss had passed from the Cairdeney lairds to the Stewarts. After that the MacNairs are found with the MacNaughtons in Argyle. The Cairdeneys held Inchewan (by Dunkeld) and other lands in Perthshire, remained Roman Catholic, and adhered to the Stewarts, as did the MacNaughtons, who were forfeited for their Jacobite sympathies in 1691. John Cairny, son of Robert Cairny of Tulcho in Perthshire, appears in the 1678 muster roll of the King's Life Guard of Horse under (the younger) Murray of Atholl.

The *Cineal Cairbre* or *Clann Chairbre* descend from Cairbre, son of Niall of the Nine Hostages. Their patrimony was in what is now the barony of Carbury, in the north of County Sligo. One of their line, Tuathal Maelgarb, was High-King of Tara in 544. But their main representative in later times was the family of *O'Brolan (O Breollain)*, descended from Ainmire, brother of King Tuathal, being the son of Cormac Caoch, son of Cairbre, eponymous ancestor of the clan.

The *Cineal Conaill* descend from Conall Gulban, son of Nial of the Nine Hostages and were possessed of the territory of Tir-conaill (the land of Conall), now County Donegal. They provided High-Kings of Tara alternately with their Cineal Eoghain cousins until the end of the eighth century, the Cineal Eoghain being dominant as overlords of the Northern Ui Niell from the end of the eighth century onward. This state of affairs was contributed to by the geographical disposition of the Cineal Conaill in mountainous and remote west Ulster. In this relatively isolated position, the Cineal Conaill in Donegal lacked the strategic geographical advantage enjoyed by the Cineal Eoghain at Ailech and in County Derry.

The *Clan Dalaigh* or *O'Donnells (O'Domhnaill)* of Tir-conaill originally possessed the patrimony of Cineal Luighdheach (the descendants of Lugaid, son of Setnae, uncle of St. Columba), their original clan-name, it having been applied to the mountainous district between the River Swilly and the River

Dobhar in north-central Donegal: The territory around Kilmacrenan. They
derive their clan-name from their ancestor Dalach, Lord of Tir-conaill, who
died in 868, and who was the first of their immediate ancestors to become Lord
of Tir-conaill, a dignity continued by his son Eigheachan, father of their
eponymous ancestor Domhnall. They did not, however, again become chiefs
of the Cineal Conaill until the thirteenth century, when they rose on the
downfall of some of their Cineal Conaill kinsmen, the O'Canannains or O'Can-
nons (O Canannain) and O'Muldorys or O'Mulderrys (O Maoldoraidh). Both of
these families are now very rare.

Afterwards the O'Donnells established themselves as the ruling family of
the Cineal Conaill and all Donegal, and continued as such for centuries, until
the final submergence of the Gaelic order in the seventeenth century. The
O'Donnells, as princes of Donegal, were consistently one of the most able
families in the Gaelic aristocracy, and not only successfully defended their territory against both the English and native adversaries alike, but they also made
their power respected throughout the north and west of Ireland. Their most
famous chief was Hugh Roe (Red Hugh) O'Donnell, who escaped his
treacherous imprisonment by the English at Dublin Castle (he was rescued,
after his bold escape, by The O'Hagan, and with the assistance of the Wicklow
clans) and later fought at Kinsale. Rory O'Donnell was with The O'Neill in the
Flight of the Earls at the beginning of the seventeenth century, while other
famous O'Donnells distinguish the pages of Irish and Continental history during the seventeenth and eighteenth centuries. A branch of the family (descended from Shane Luirg, son of Turlough O'Donnell of the Wine, Lord of
Tir-conaill in the early fifteenth century) became established in Limerick and
Tipperary.

The O'Friels (O Firghil) descend from Eoghan, nephew of Sedna, ancestor
of the Clann Dalaigh, and brother of the illustrious and sanctified prince of
the Cineal Conaill who established Iona in the sixth century: St. Columba
(also known as St. Columcille – see Chapter IV). The O'Friels were hereditary
abbots (erenaghs) of Kilmacrenan in the old Clann Dalaigh country in
Donegal. The O'Freil had the privilege of inaugurating The O'Donnell as chief
of the Cineal Conaill and lord of Tirconnell (Tir-Conaill).

Also closely related to the Clann Dalaigh, being of the same stock within
the Cineal Conaill, are the O'Boyles (O Baoighill), O'Cullinans (O Cuileannain)
and the Cineal Edna. The O'Boyles were one of the principal families of the
Cineal Connail. Originally chiefs of the Three Tuaths in the northwest of
County Donegal, when these lands passed into the hands of the MacSweeneys,
The O'Boyle became chief of Tir-Ainmhireach in the west of the same county.
This territory was afterwards known as Crioch Bhaoigheallach, or O'Boyle's
country, now the barony of Boylagh. During the wars attendant to the reign
of Elizabeth they spread into different parts of Ireland. The O'Cullinans (the
name was changed after about 1700 to the form Cullen) were chiefs around

Mullinashee in what is now the Barony of Raphoe, County Donegal. Several of the family, sons of the Chief, were important ecclesiastics at the end of the sixteenth and first half of the seventeenth centuries. Of these, Glaisne O'Cullinan (1558-1584), Cistercian Abbot of Boyle, was martyred (that is, murdered by the English) and Dr. John Cullinan (1585-1653) was Bishop of Raphoe and suffered much persecution, ending his career as a prominent supporter of Rinnuccini at the Confederation of Kilkenny.

The Cineal Enda or O'Dohertys (O Dochartaigh) were originally settled in Ardmire (Ard Miodhair) in the barony of Raphoe, but about the beginning of the fifteenth century they became lords of Inishowen in the northeastern corner of County Donegal. Afterwards they were one of the most influential families in Tirconnell (Tir-Conaill), retaining their position as lords of Inishowen down to the reign of James the First in the early seventeenth century, at which time their lands were confiscated as a result of the rebellion of Sir Cahir O'Dogherty. The O'Gallaghers (O Gallchobhair) descend from Maolchobha, High-King of Tara in 615. They were powerful in Tir-Conaill, and as marshalls of O'Donnell's forces, they took a prominent part in all the military actions of the Cineal Conaill during the fourteenth and subsequent centuries. Many of them were distinguished bishops of Raphoe and Derry.

The Cineal Conaill in Scotland were known as the Kindred of St. Columba, the great saint who founded Iona. This epithet was applied to all the descendants of St. Columba's great-grandfather, Conall Gulban, but was especially applied to branches within the clan devoted to ecclesiastical pursuits, especially in Scotland. Thus the Kindred was comprised of several early saints, and also of the hereditary abbots of Iona, Kells, Derry and Dunkeld, some of whom were descended from the Saint Columba's brother. The Kindred of St. Columba remained closely connected to the Abbey at Iona despite changes in political control and the distance from the Cineal Conall homeland in Donegal. In 1164 King Somerled of the Isles (see under MacDonald) invited the chief co-arb (see Chapter IV) of St. Columba to accept the Abbacy of Iona; but the Cineal Connaill would not allow the Columban primacy (which first went from Iona to Kells, and then to Derry in Donegal, the homeland of the Kindred) to pass from Derry back to the Hebrides.

The Abbacy was then offered to members of the O'Brollaghan branch of the Cineal Eoghan, a Derry-based ecclesiastical family with splendid masonic skills, but their talented representative at Iona died in 1203. This left a void at Iona, an absence of the Columban Kindred, and so Ranald, next King of the Isles had no choice but to follow the Scottish example at Scone and install a foreign order, in this case the Benedictine Order, at Iona. This inevitably led to high-strung local dissension by those who preferred the native way of the (Celtic) Columban church, which had had hereditary, non-celibate abbots of the Kindred administering the abbey estates. Finally, in 1204, the Cineal Conaill, led by two bishops and two abbots all of the Kindred of St. Columba,

raided Iona and demolished a monastery erected on Columban land by the
new Benedictine abbot, and proclaimed the then Abbot of Derry, who was a
descendant of St. Columba's brother, to be Abbot of Iona as well.

The Kindred of St. Columba had come into the Crown of Scotland in
earlier times, when Bethoc, daughter of Malcolm II, King of Albany married
Crinan (ca. 975–1045), Thane (temporal lord) and (hereditary) Abbot of
Dunkeld, and Seneschal (household officer or administrator) of the Isles.
Crinan's line was probably a branch of the Cineal Luighdheach, mentioned
above (Moncreiffe 211). The Cineal Luigheheach were heads of the Columban
church in Scotland since the removal of that primacy from Iona to Dunkeld
several generations before (see Chapter IV). The sons of Bethoc and Crinan
were King Duncan I of Albany (killed in 1040), whose descendants bore arms
of the colors red on gold; and Maldred, Ruler of Cumbria, who married the
daughter of the Earl of Beornicia, and whose descendants bore arms of the colors red on silver (white). From Maldred's son Gospatric, Earl of Beornicia
(which passed from English to Scottish control during his tenture, and whose
original Saxon House is represented in the male line by the Swintons of that
Ilk), are descended the families of *Dunbar, Dundas* and *Moncreiff.*

The *Dunbars* descend from the above mentioned Gospatrick, who was also
known as Earl of Northumbria and who was forced to flee that earldom, but
was later given the barony of Dunbar in East Lothian by his cousin Malcolm
III, Ceann-Mor ("great-head"), who was killed in 1093. Later his line acquired
additional lands in what is now southwest Scotland. His descendants, the earls
of Dunbar, thus became the head of an important Lowland family. In the fourteenth century their then chief married the heiress of the Randolf earl of
Moray, and by 1579 the Privy Council describes the Dunbars of northwest
Moray as a clan. The *Dundases* descend from a son of Gospatrick of Northumbria who was given a charter of the lands of Dundas in West Lothian about
the mid-twelfth century. They became an important landed family around
Edinburgh. John de Dundas acquired a charter of the barony of Fingask in
Perthshire in 1364–65.

The *Moncreiffes* take their name from the lands of Moncreiff in the parish
of Dunbarny in southeast Perthshire (Strathearn) on the north side of the
River Earn near its mouth. From their arms (coat of arms) and early history
they appear to be a branch of the House of Dundas. Sir Mathew of Moncreiff
obtained a charter from Sir Roger de Mowbray, Sheriff of Edinburgh,
Linlithgow and Haddington of the lands of Moncreiff and Balconachin, which
in 1248 were confirmed to him and erected into a free barony by a subsequent
charter from Alexander II. He also held the lands of Culdares and Duneaves
on the northeast side of Loch Tay in Atholl, which appear to have been his
family's earliest possessions. John de Moncreiff was granted a charter of Moncreiff by Alexander III between 1250 and 1286, and all these lands, including
those in Atholl and Strathearn, were formally incorporated into the barony

of Moncreiffe in 1455. William Moncreiff of that ilk rode with the earl of Atholl on a raid into Northumberland in 1296.

The Clann Donnachaidh or Robertsons (Mac Raibeirt) descend from Conan, bastard only son of Henry, Earl of Atholl (died in 1210), who granted Conan wide lands in the Rannoch district of western Atholl. Henry was a descendant of King Duncan I, mentioned above. The Robertsons take their clan-name, which means "children (descendants) of Duncan," from their early fourteenth-century chief Duncan of Atholl. They take the family name of Robertson from their fourth chief, Raibeirt Riabhach, "Grizzled Robert" Duncanson, whose lands were erected into the barony of Struan in 1451 by King James II as a reward for the previous capture of Sir Robert Graham, slayer of James I (see under Graham). The Robertsons were a vast and powerful clan in Rannoch, and very important in the history of the district. The Serpent and Dove supporters on the arms of their chief, Straun Robertson, allude to their belonging to the Kindred of St. Columba, whose name means "dove" of the church (there is an old proverb found on the privy seal of King Alexander III, a cousin of the line of Conan, which translates "be as wise as the serpent and gentle as the dove").

The Clan MacDuff descends from Gillemichael mac Duff, Earl of Fife in about 1133. But the significance of the name Duff (Dubh) goes back to the line of Duff, King of Albany in 967, whose descendants' patrimony was in Fife (the "kingdom" of Fife). His line, the Clan Duff, was collateral with the line of King Duff's brother, King Kenneth II, and the two lines alternated the High-Kingship of Albany until 1034, as both lines had their ultimate origin in sons of King Malcolm I of the line of the Cineal Gabhran who had inherited the Picto-Gaelic crown (hence their traditional descent, in the female line, from Conall Cearnach, traditional ancestor of the Cruithne).

Both of these lines ended in heiresses about the year 1034: The Line of Kenneth II ending in Bethoc, who married Crinan, hereditary Abbot of Dunkeld, of the Kindred of St. Columba, mentioned above; and the Line of Duff ending in Gruoch, who married Gillacomgan, Mormaer (King) of Moray, of the line of the Cineal Loarn. Their son, Lulach, was thus Chief of Clan Duff (in those presurname times of Picto-Gaelic succession) and King of Moray, and was as well a rival King of Albany. His daughter and heiress, the Princess of Moray and heiress of Clann Duff appears to have "married" Eth (Aedh, later Aodh, Gaelic form of Aethelred), Last Abbot of Dunkeld, who himself was the eldest of the four royal sons of Malcolm III (whose father was Duncan I, mentioned above, heir of the Royal line collateral to the Clan Duff) by his second wife, St. Margaret, a daughter of the Saxon King of England (Duncan II, son of Malcolm III by an earlier marriage, was the ancestor of the famous "Mac-William" claimants).

Eth seems to have been debarred from the throne, which could have been because of a blemish (a taboo) or perhaps because he was already an Abbot.

He was nonetheless the first earl of Fife, probably in right of his wife. His sons included Angus, King of Moray (killed 1130), and also Duff, Malcolm and Gillecoimded. These sons had a number of important inheritances to consider. There was the Kingship of Moray, and also the chiefship of the Clann Duff, and in the male-line, also the senior descent of, or position of precedence within, the royal Kindred of St. Columba in Scotland. The descendants of Duff (who predeceased his father Eth) took the latter two, as the senior line, while the descendants of Malcolm and Gillecoimded "MacEth" threw in their lot with the Moray-men, whose Gaelic laws would prefer the succession of the living brothers of their king, Angus, over his living nephews, the descendents of Duff. On the death of Eth (Aedh), the Moray-men rose under King Angus and his brother Malcolm MacEth (Mac Aedh) in an attempt to put Angus on the throne of the Scots (as a son of the Abbot-Earl Eth, and as representative of the dispossessed Clan Duff). This was a reaction in part to the Normanizing influence at the Scottish court of David I, and in fact they were defeated and Angus killed by David's Norman mercenaries. Malcolm (called "Jarl" or ruler of Moray by the Norwegians) married a daughter of Somerled of the Isles, and carried on the struggle until one of his sons, *Donald MacAedh*, was captured by the forces of King Malcolm IV in 1156.

At this point Malcolm became nominally reconciled with the King of Scots, and was made Earl of Ross, a post he held till his death in 1168. His grandson, Kenneth MacAedh, made a final attempt at the crown of the Scots in 1215, but was defeated and beheaded by the ancestor of the Ross clan, who subsequently became Earl of Ross (see Chapter IV). During these struggles, in about 1163, King Malcolm IV attempted to deprive Malcolm MacAedh of the earldom of Ross in order to give it to his own foreign brother-in-law, the Count of Holland (many knightly Flemings had already settled in Moray). Accordingly, the King transported many of the Moraymen *extramontanas Scociae*, that is, beyond the mountains of Scotland into Caithness, which was still under Norse control (Moncreiffe 145). The Jarl of Orkney and Caithness at the time was Harold, son-in-law of Earl Malcolm MacAedh.

It is in the extreme northwest of Scotland, in the district known as Strathnaver in western Caithness, that the later MacAedh chiefs appear in the early thirteenth century, and here the MacAedh chiefs gave rise to a very important clan, later known as the *Clann Aodha* or *MacKays (Mac Aodha*, earlier *MacAedh)*, whose chiefs held Strathnaver for many centuries. They were also known as the *Clan Morgan*, Morgan having been a favorite name in the royal house of Moray. They adopted their current arms in the seventeenth century to reflect their traditional kinship with the Forbes clan, but their original arms were three blue stars on silver, with a hand in chief, that is, the Royal arms and colors of the Kingdom of Moray, surmounted by a hand symbolizing "true family." They also share the "butcher's broom" plant badge (a symbol of tribalism) with their successors in the Kingdom of Moray, the Murrays and

Sutherlands. A branch went early to Ireland as gallowglasses (see under O'Crowley), the name being Anglicized there as MacCoy.

Duff mac Eth himself had two sons, Constantine MacDuff, second Earl of Fife, and Gillemichael MacDuff, third Earl of Fife (ca. 1133). From Gillemichael are descended the later earls of Fife (which earldom they held "by the grace of God," allodially, and not by feudal charter from the King of Scots), allies of the kings of Scots of the line of David I. As the descendants of Eth, first Earl of Fife, they bear as a coat of arms the Royal Arms of the King of Scots undifferenced, that is, without the "Royal Tressure" (double flory counterflory) that marks the arms of the line of King David I, younger brother of Eth. This marks the heraldic seniority of their line to that of the kings of Scots themselves, as per Norman practice.

These earls were the chiefs of Clan MacDuff, a clan-name combining the sense of "Clan Duff" and "Clan (Gillemichael) MacDuff." As the "senior" kindred and also as the heirs of the Sacred Family of Dunkeld, these earls held the most honored position of precedence in Scotland, an almost sacred position born of their lineage. The County of Fife is still referred to as the Kingdom of Fife, and the Earl's Kindred were legally accountable under a special code of ancient Scots law known as "the Law of Clan MacDuff," which meant that they could literally "get away with murder" (for a fee, and if they could first make it to the sanctuary cross of MacDuff near Abernethy in Strathearn). The earls of Fife held rich lands in the Lowlands of Fife, Stirlingshire, East Lothian and Midlothian, and these Lowland tracts were the chief seat of their power, which was centered in Fife. Nonetheless they also held wide lands in the Highlands of Perthshire, Banffshire, Inverness-shire and Moray.

The MacKintoshes, who inherited the chiefship of the Clan Chattan, are a branch of the Clan MacDuff (see under MacKintosh), as are the MacDuffs (MacDuibh), barons of Fandowie in the Strathbran district of Perthshire (a position they held as late as 1602). Alexander McDuff (sic), brother of the laird of Balanloan in Atholl, appears in a list of gentlemen on the Atholl estates who took part in the Rising of 1745. The MacDuffs of Bonhard in Perthshire are nineteenth-century representatives of this family.

However, the most important branches of the House of Fife, including the main branch, the earls of Fife, never adopted the patronymic of MacDuff. Instead the various branches of the House of Fife adopted such names as Wemyss, Abernethy, Spens, and Scrymgeour. The Wemyss take their name from the lands of that name on the other Fife side of the Firth of Forth opposite the city of Edinburgh. The ancestor of the family was Sir John de Methkil, son of Michael de Methkil (a place in Fife), who in 1228 witnessed a charter by Malcolm, seventh Earl of Fife, being himself descended of that house. He held land in east Lothian, and as John de Methkil he granted the church of Wemys (Wemyss) in Fife to House of Soltre sometime before 1240. His father was also known as Michael de Wemys. Sir David Wemyss was chosen ambassador to Norway in 1286. The family adhered to The Bruce during the Scottish War of Independence, and in 1316 David de Wemys witnessed the homage of Duncan, Earl of Fife, to the Abbot of Dunfermline. On the failure of the male-line of the earls of Fife (the earldom was resigned to the House of Stewart by the last of the original line, a countess, in 1372), and the male-line of the House of Abernethy (by 1334), the head of the Wemyss family became the senior male-line representative of the House of Fife, and were later vested in the undifferenced arms as chiefs of Clan MacDuff.

The *Abernethys* descend from the hereditary abbots of the Culdee monastery at Abernethy, and were the senior cadet (branch) family of the House of Fife. Hugh, Abbot of Abernethy, died about 1150. He was succeeded by his son Orm de Abernethy, who appears as a charter witness for the Bishop of St. Andrews before 1162. He may have given his name to the lands of Ormiston in East Lothian, which are contiguous with those of Salton, which were in the possession of his descendants, under their title of Lord Abernethy (a title which passed through heiresses after 1334, and ultimately to the Hamiltons by the sixteenth century). The House of Abernethy possessed the right to inaugurate the King of Scots as ecclesiastical representatives of the House of Fife branch of the Kindred of St. Columba. Between 1189 and 1196 King William the Lion granted the church of Abernethy to the Abbey of Arbroath, which had been founded in the early thirteenth century by King William the Lion (of the line of David I and the Kindred of St. Columba) as the seat of a new order in conjunction with the gradual secularization of the old Celtic abbeys, a task completed by about 1300 under King Robert Bruce. About the same time Lawrence, son of Orm de Abirnythy (*sic*), conveyed to the church and monks of Arbroath his whole right "In the advowson of the church of Abernethy." This can only refer to the kind of secularization of the old Celtic abbey-lands referred to in Chapter IV, for Lawrence de Abernethy retained the land and position of *dominus* or lord of Abernethy. The seal of Sir Alexander de Abernethy in 1296 bears the Abernethy coat of arms, a differenced version of the arms of the House of Fife, born on the breast of an eagle displayed (see under Lindsay).

The *Scrymgeours* have long been an important family around Dundee and in the Kingdom of Fife, and in the late fourteenth century they inherited a vast territory in Glassary in Argyle from the MacGilchrist lords of Glassary. The Scrymgeours descend from Alexander Schyrmeschur, son of Colyn, son of Carin of Cupar, who obtained in 1293 a tack or lease of the land of Torr, or Torer, in the parish of Cupar, Fife from Thomas de Kylmaron (also in Cupar). He held the office of Royal Bannerman, and in 1298 was made Constable of the Royal castle of Dundee by charter from the great Lowland war leader and Guardian of Scotland, Sir William Wallace. He was later executed by the English for carrying the Royal Banner for Bruce at the Battle of Methven. His ancestors appear in Coupar at least as early as the first half of the thirteenth century, and held the hereditary office of standard-bearer, or bannerman, of Scotland since the days of Alexander III (1249–1286).

In earlier times the leadership of the van of battle, which the Bannerman represented, was held by the King's royal Cineal Conaill cousins, the earls of Fife, chiefs of Clan MacDuff (as descendants of the last abbot of Dunkeld, also first earl of Fife). Taking into account the fact that the Scrymgeours arose in Cupar, the original demesne of the House of Fife, and also that they long held land in the barony of Dunkeld, it seems likely that the Scrymgeours inherited the sacred office of bannerman as a younger branch of the House of Fife. This would be consistent with the common practice of delegating hereditary duties to younger branches of the parent clan. This is supported by the arms of the family, which has the Royal "Lyon" of the House of Fife with the colors reversed (a common early method of marking cadetship or "cadency" in heraldry) and with the addition of a bent or "used" sword, as per the name. The name Scrymgeour is from the Old French "eskermisor"–"sword fighter" –a descriptive name which indicates that the original bearer was a skirmisher, that is, one who fights in the preliminary encounters of two opposing forces.

The task of the Bannerman was to carry the *vexillum regium*–the Royal lion-banner of Scotland–in the van of battle. This was an ancient function, for before heraldry came into general use in the latter part of the twelfth century, the armies of the kings of Albany had been led into battle by an abbot carrying a sacred reliquary, or *vexillum*. The specific reliquaries concerned here were, naturally, those connected with St. Columba: St. Columba's crozier, which was used in this capacity at least as late as 918, but more especially the "Brecbennoch" or "Battle-Victory" (Gaelic "Cath-Buaidh") reliquary of St. Columba (St. Andrew was the patron saint of the kingdom, that of Albany and its later acquisitions, but the Royal House had by this time long since regained its position as the chief family of the Columban Kindred in Scotland, and so St. Columba was of course its patron saint).

The first-mentioned reliquary probably went back to Iona and then Ireland with the final exodus of the Columban clergy from Dunkeld, but the Brecbennoch stayed in the possession of the now unrivaled Royal representatives of the Cineal Connaill in Scotland, the House of Fife and the line of David I. In 1211 William the Lion gave custody of the Brecbennoch to the monks of his newly founded monastery at Arbroath, granting along with it the lands of Forglen "given to God and to St. Columba and to the Brecbennoch" in return for service to the Royal army with the Brecbennoch. After doing such service, presumably with the Brecbennoch, at the battle of Bannockburn in 1314 the Abbot of Arbroath granted hereditary custody of the Brecbennoch to Malcolm de Monymusk (an estate in Aberdeenshire) early in 1315 "to be held by the said Malcolm and his heirs on condition that he and they shall perform in our name the service in the king's army which pertains to the Brecbennoch, as often as occasion shall arise." His family came to an end before 1400, but in any case the Scrymgeours had long been in possession of the similar but more important office of Bannerman. It was the creation of this office for the Fife Kindred (later represented by the Scrymgeours) who already had charge of the Brechennoch, that probably led to the Brechennoch being given to the Arbroth monks in the first place, as per the King's wishes. Yet an at least partly apocryphal story is told by Boece regarding the acquisition by the Scrymgeours of the post of bannerman of the *vexillum regium* and their name. In an early historical work, the *Cronikls*, Boece asserts that in the days of King Alexander I (1107–1124) or, as an inconsistency, King Malcolm (Malcolm IV?–1153–c. 1175), the King traveled to Monymusk to fight his rivals for the Crown (the Moray-men) but saw his bannerman "trembling for fear of enemies and not passing so pertly forward as he desired." At this point the King took the banner from him and gave it to one "Sir Alexander Carron," who was given the significant name *Scrymgeour*.

Later in the same book Boece asserts that Sir Alexander Carron won his new surname by going forward in a skirmishing party of picked men, with the *vexillum regium*, and defeating and killing the opposition. First of all, the date is far too early, as the family of Scrymgeour only held the office from the reign of Alexander III (1249–1246), and the first of the name Scrymgeour does not appear until the career of Alexander, grandson of Carin, who fought bravely as Bannerman for both Wallace and Bruce in the Scottish wars of independence. It is clearly he that this romantic story is really about, the character Sir Alexander Carron being apparently a combination of his name with that of his earliest recorded ancestor, Carin of Cupar, with the added flavor of an older "Brechennoch" tradition connected with the struggles of David I against the "Moray-men." The story is probably meant to contrast the bravery of Sir Alexander with the relative ineffectiveness of those other vexillum-bearers, the monks of Arbroth, hence the mention of the relatively obscure estate of Monymusk.

The *Spens* too are descended from the House of Fife, and appear to have branched off the main stem sometime after the family of Wemyss. They take their name from the office of Spence or Spense, from dispensa, Latin despensario, that of custodian of the larder or provision room, in this case apparently originally connected with Inchaffray Abbey in Strathearn. The post apparently evolved into a royal government office, in the same way that the Stewart or Steward of the King's household (that is, the whole Kingdom) himself became a royal officer of realm-wide responsibility. Several persons named Spensa or Dispensa are mentioned as government officials from the thirteenth century onwards, including one in 1529 for whom there is entry in the royal accounts of livery for "John Spens at the cupboard." Roger Dispensator witnessed a charter by the bishop of Moray between 1202 and 1222. Thomas Dispensator witnessed excambion of the lands of Dolays Mychel

(Dallas) in 1232. John Spens was bailie of Irvine, 1260, and Thomas de (a contemporary conventional form of Norman-French "le," also evident in Gaelic) Spensa witnessed a charter in favor of the Hospital of Soltre, Midlothian, between 1296 and 1324. One of these early Spenses was a scion of the House of Fife, and the office was probably hereditary in the family for a time. Thomas de Spensa and Laurence de Spensa appear as witnesses in Perth in 1375, and Henry of Spens witnessed a charter by Robert, Earl of Fife, about 1390. Fergus de la Spens held a tenement in Edinburgh in 1392 and John de Spensa was a burgess of Perth in 1426 and had a grant of lands in the earldom of Mentieth. The family held considerable estates in mid and eastern Fife towards the end of the sixteenth century including that of Lathallan. Thomas Spens was an important bishop of Aberdeen in the latter half of the fifteenth century.

Southern Ui Neill

The Southern Ui Neill alternated the High-Kingship of Tara with their cousins of the Northern Ui Neill. They established themselves near Tara in the late fifth century, as several of the sons of Nial of the Nine Hostages settled in the east of the territory of Mide (Westmeath and North Offaly) just west of Tara. By the seventh century the Southern Ui Neill were masters of Brega (which included the sacred center at Tara in what is now County Meath) and were also firmly established as masters of the whole of the expansive territory of Mide (Westmeath and North Offaly). This territory stretched across the center of Ireland to the Shannon, and included Uisnech, the important traditional center of the Island, as meeting-place of the traditional "five fifths" of Ireland.

Here the Clann Cholmain, a collateral line to the Sil nAedo Slaine (the Seed of Aed of Slane) of Brega, established themselves as overlords of Mide under the title of Rig Uisneg ("king of Uisnech"). The center of their power was in the heart of what is now Westmeath, and their royal residences reflect this, they being either on or by Lough Ennell in the center of Westmeath. Thus there were, through the tenth century, two overkingdoms of the Southern Ui Neill, the Sil nAedo Slaine of Brega (Meath with parts of Dublin and Louth) and the Clann Cholmain of Mide. The former were more important during the seventh century, and possessed the site of Tara, though their princes resided some five miles to the southeast at Lagore. Eight of their kings were also High-Kings of Tara, and with this monopoly went the overkingship of the Southern Ui Neill. But after the death of their king, Cinaed, in 728, it was the Clann Cholmain who monopolized the overlordship of the Southern Ui Neill (which included the right to alternate the High-Kingship of Tara with the Northern Ui Neill), except for a brief period between 944 and 956.

The Clann Cholmain thus became the royal clan of the Southern Ui Neill. They became established as kings in Mide (Westmeath and North Offaly) from the sixth century onwards. Their chief family in later times was that of

O'Melaghlin, later *MacLoughlin (O Maoilsheachlainn)* of Meath (now counties Meath and Westmeath, with north Offaly). The O'Melaghlins were kings of Meath, and descended from Maelsheachlainn, or Malachy II, High King of Ireland (died 1022) at the time of the rise of Brian Boru (ancestor of the O'Briens of North Munster or Thomond). After the Anglo-Norman invasion, the territory of Meath fell under the control of the Norman Hugh de Lacy, and the territory of the MacLoughlins was restricted to the barony of Clonlonan in the southwest of what is now County Westmeath. They were, however, one of only five Gaelic families privileged to use English Laws, which meant protection under the law of the conqueror. Nonetheless the property of the family was yet further reduced by the confiscations of the seventeenth century, and they sank into relative obscurity.

The *Cineal Fiachach* descend from Fiacha, son of Nial of the Nine Hostages. They were a great clan among the Southern Ui Neill, under the overlordship of Mide, and their original patrimony extended from Birr to the Hill of Uisneach in what is now County Westmeath. Their chief representatives in later times were the *MacGeoghegans* and the *Feara Ceal* ("the men of churches") or *O'Molloys*. The MacGeoghegans (Mac Eochagain) were chiefs of the Barony of Moycashel in the south of County Westmeath, though their ancient patrimony was much greater. They lost their estates in the Cromwellian confiscations of the mid-sixteenth century, and a branch of the family was transplanted to County Galway.

The *O'Molloys (O Maolmhuaidh)* were of the same stock as the MacGeoghegans, being originally of the same clan. At some time during the period of about 950–1050 the Cineal Fiachach divided their territory between their two great branches, the MacGeoghegans retaining the norther portion under the original clan-name of Cineal Fiachach, and the O'Molloys becoming lords of the southern portion under the clan-name of Feara Ceall. This territory, called after them Fircall, comprised the modern baronies of Fircall, Ballycowan and Ballyboy in the north of County Offaly, and remained in the hands of the family down to the first part of the seventeenth century. Many of this distinguished family had friendly relations with the kings of England and the government of the Pale from the Anglo-Norman invasion onwards, and though several leaders of the clan were active in resisting English aggression in Ireland during the Tudor period during the mid-sixteenth century, the chief of the name was made Hereditary Standard Bearer of the English standard in Ireland.

The *Cineal Laoghaire* descend from Loeguire, son of Nial of the Nine Hostages. They were seated in what are now the baronies of Upper and Lower Navan near Trim, County Meath, and in ancient times fell under the overlordship of Brega. Their chief representatives in later times were the *O'Quinlans (O Caoindealbhain)*, who descend from Caoindealbhan (died 925), chief of the Cineal Laoghaire in the early tenth century. The O'Quinlans were

were dispersed as a result of the Anglo-Norman invasion, and some of them settled afterwards in Tipperary.

The Fir Teathbha ("men of Teffia," an ancient semi-independent district covering a wide territory along the River Shannon and the north of Lough Ree in what is now the south of County Longford) trace their descent back to Maine, son of Nial of the Nine Hostages. Their original clan-territory embraced a great portion of what is now County Westmeath and also what is now the barony of Kilcoursey in the present County Offaly. Their chief representatives in later times were the *O'Caharneys* or *Foxes of Muintear Tadhgain*; also the *Corca Adhaimh* or the *O'Dalys*; also the *MacAwleys*; *Muintear Mhaoilsionna* or the *MacCarons*, and finally the *O'Brennans*.

The Muintear Tadhgain (descendants of Tadhgain, ninth of the line of Maine), the *O'Caharneys* or *O'Kearneys* (O *Catharnaigh*) also known as the Foxes (*Sionnach*), were originally chiefs of all Teffia, but in later times (after the Anglo-Norman invasion) their territory was restricted to Muintear Tadhgain, now the barony of Kilcoursey in Offaly. They were known by the surname of *Sionnach*, or Fox, from the cognomen of their ancestor, Catharnach Sionnach (Caharney the Fox), who was slain in the year 1084. The head of the family was known by the title of "An Sionnach" or the fox. It was one of the men of An Sionnach that assassinated the Norman de Lacy for making unnegotiated encroachments into O'Caharney territory. In the sixteenth century the head of the family was knighted and fell in with the English under Queen Elizabeth I.

The MacAwleys (Mac Amhalghaidh) were, prior to the English conquest of the sixteenth century, lords of a wide territory known as Calry (*Calraighe*) which in its broadest extent comprised land in the west of County Westmeath and north of County Offaly, but which was centered on Ballyloughloe in Westmeath. This territory was known to the English as MacGawley's Country. *The MacCarons (Mac Carrghamhna, formerly Mac Giolla Ultain)* descend from Carrghamhain, grandson of Giolla Ultain, great-grandson of Maoilsionna (whose name means "chief of the Shannon"), from whom they get their clanname of *Muintear Mhaoilsionna*. They thus originally commanded a terrritory on the east side of the River Shannon in Westmeath, and it is there that the MacCarons, or *Growneys* (O *Gramhna*, a corruption of "Mac Carrghamhna") are found in later times. Their territory was known by the name of *Cuircne*, now the barony of Kilkenny West in northwest County Westmeath. These lands passed into the possession of the Dillons not long after the Anglo-Norman invasion of the twelfth century, though the MacCarons maintained some independence as a clan down to the seventeenth century. In 1578 the English government granted one of them the office of "chief sergeant of his nation" along with lands in the "ploughland of Kilmacaron, which of old belonged to the chief of the nation of M'Caron."

The O'Brennans (O Braonain) were once a powerful clan of the Fir Teathbha in County Westmeath, but were dispersed into Connacht as a result of the Anglo-Norman invasion. The *Corca Adhaimh* or *O'Dalys (O Dalaigh)*, alias *Corca Adain* (race of Adam) are a branch of the Southern Ui Neill descended from Maine, son of Nial of the Nine hostages. They were originally seated in the present barony of Magheradernon in central County Westmeath. In later times they became a literary family of highest honor, and sent learned bards of their name to serve kings all over Ireland. The first of the family to become famous for his learning was Cuchonnacht na Scoile ("of the school") who died at Clonard in 1139. He was the ancestor of all the bardic families of the name. Beginning with Cuchonnacht, poetry and learning became a profession in the family, and he presided over a bardic school in Meath not far from, but connected with, the original territory of Corca Adhaimh.

From Corca Adhaimh, then, the family sent forth poetic professors to various parts of Ireland, where they started new literary families. About 1250 a branch of the O'Dalys, descended from Donough More O'Daly, a famous bard, became hereditary poets to the O'Loughlins, and settled at Finavarra, in the Burren of County Clare. To this literary branch belong the Dallys of Galway, whose ancestor settled in Ui Maine (County Galway) in the latter part of the fifteenth century. Raghnall O Dalaigh settled in South Munster (Desmond) about 1150 and became chief ollav (professor) in poetry to the MacCarthy. Other branches served such great names as the O'Reillys of Cavan, the O'Neills of Ulster, and the O'Connors of Connacht.

Another professional branch of the Fir Teathbha were the *O'Shiels (O Siadhail)*, a famous medical family that established various branches in Ulster and Offaly, serving as hereditary physicians and surgeons in Oriel, Inishowen and Delvin-MacCoghlan. Owen O'Sheil, the "Eagle of Doctors," was physician to the armies of the Confederate Catholics of Ireland from 1642 to 1650.

The Four Tribes of Tara were four princely families of the Southern Ui Neill, settled in the area of Tara in what is now County Meath. They represent the lineal descendants of the *Sil nAedo Slaine* kings of South Brega. From the beginning of the ninth century the Kingdom of Brega had divided into North and South Brega, with the kings of North Brega residing at Knowth some twelve miles northeast of Tara on the River Boyne, and the kings of South Brega remaining in the vicinity of Tara itself. The chief representatives of the original Four Tribes in later times were the families of *O'Hart (O hAirt)* and *O'Regan (O Riagain)*.

The O'Harts were dispossessed soon after the Anglo-Norman invasion of the late twelfth century. Afterwards they migrated westward to Sligo, where they became chiefs in what is now the barony of Carbury in North Sligo, where they possessed considerable estates down to the seventeenth century. The O'Regans were, prior to the Anglo-Norman invasion, kings of South Brega, and had taken a leading part in the wars against the Danes. They apparently alternated the Kingship of Brega with their northern cousins, for in the year 1029 the annalists record the victory of Mathghamhain O Riagain, King of Brega, over Sitric, Viking King of Dublin. The O'Regans were dispossessed soon after the Anglo-Norman invasion, and dispersed into what is now County Leix. Branches of the family later spread into County Limerick.

The MacKennas or Kennys (Mac Cionaodha) were chiefs of Truagh, now the barony of Trough in North Monaghan, but they were traditionally "Meathmen" ("Meath" was an area primarily associated with what is now Meath, Westmeath and North Offaly) by origin, and are a branch of the Southern Ui Neill. Branches of this family settled in the seventeenth century in Down and in South Munster.

The family of O'Higgin or Higgins (O hUigin) were a distinguished literary family of the Southern Ui Neill, originally settled in what is now County Westmeath. No fewer than eleven of them are mentioned in the *Annals of the Four Masters* as poets or professors of poetry between 1300 and 1617. A branch of the family settled early in Sligo, where they acquired large tracts of land in the southwest of that county.

The South Gaels

Eoghanacht

The South Gaels were known by the dynastic name of *Eoghanacht* (descendants of Eoghan). They rose to preeminence at Cashel in central Tipperary during the fifth century and were instrumental in the establishment of Gaelic as the dominant dialect in the South, much as the North Gaels were responsible for its establishment and prestige in the North (without the prestige of the Eoghanacht as the dominant group during the critical early centuries surrounding the establishment in Ireland of the Church – and hence of *writing* – the other Munster tribes, being a geographically remote pre–Gaelic population, would not have adopted Gaelic as a written *lingua franca*). The Eoghanacht had close ties with the church, and a number of abbots of the Eoghanacht line were elected to kingship during the Viking period in the ninth and tenth centuries.

The true branches of the Eoghanacht descend from *Conall Corc*, their first great king, though some Munster tribes (such as the Ui Fidhgheinte of the Erainn) had themselves nominally tacked on to the traditional stem as descendants of *Mug Nudat* (alias *Eoghan*), mythic traditional ancestor of Conall Corc. This, together with the fact that Mug Nudat means "the slave of Nuadu" (a divine pre–Gaelic ancestor figure) suggests that the Eoghanacht early consolidated their traditions with that of their subject-tribes in Munster.

The MacCarthys (Mac Carthaigh) were the chief family of the Eoghanacht, being of the Chaisil (Cashel) branch, descended from Ceaillachan of Cashel,

King of Munster in 954. As a result of the Anglo-Norman invasion they were driven from the plains of Tipperary into Cork and Kerry where they remained very powerful down to the end of the seventeenth century. They were divided into three great branches, the heads of which were known respectively as Mac-Carthy More (the Great MacCarthy) centered in Kerry, MacCarthy Reagh, Lord of Carbery in southwest Cork, and MacCarthy of Muskerry in west Cork. The *MacAuliffes (MacAmhlaoibh)* of Castle MacAuliffe in Cork were an important branch of the MacCarthys. Their territory stretched northwest from Newmarket to the borders with Kerry and Limerick. The *O'Meehans (O Miadhachain)* were a branch of the MacCarthys, seated at Ballymeehan in Leitrim.

The *O'Keeffes (O Caoimh)* descend from Art Caomh, son of Finguine, King of Munster in 902, a cousin of Ceaillachan of Cashel. They were pushed by the Anglo-Norman invasion from the barony of Fermoy in north-central Cork westward into the northwest of the barony of Duhallow. They remained in possession of their new territory, called after them "Pobble O'Keeffe," to the end of the sixteenth century.

The *O'Sullivans (O Suileabhain)* are also a branch of the Eoghanacht Chaisil. Their original patrimony, prior to the Anglo-Norman invasion, was along the River Suir in the plains of Tipperary, their principal seat being at Knockgraffon, about two miles north of Cahir. In 1192 they were forced out of their territory and settled in the mountains of Cork and Kerry, where they divided into several branches under chiefs, the most important of which were O'Sullivan More, possessor of the barony and castle of Dunkerron, near Kenmare; and O'Sullivan Beare, who owned Beare, now the baronies of Beare and Bantry on the southwestern peninsula of Cork and Kerry.

The *MacGillycuddys (Mac Giolla Chuda)* are a sixteenth-century branch of the O'Sullivan More branch of the O'Sullivans. They gave their name to MacGillycuddy's Reeks, the mountain range in central Kerry, their chief being known as MacGillycuddy of the Reeks.

The Ui Eachach Mumhan

The *Ui Eachach Mumhan* (Munster) or *Eoghanacht Raithlinn* were an early branch of the Eoghanacht descended from Cas, son of Conall Corc. They inhabited the territory in Desmond between the upper reaches of the Lee and the Blackwater in the south of County Cork, and were thus somewhat isolated from the rest of the Eoghanacht, though they were nonetheless powerful. In the sixth century they divided into two great branches, the *Ui Loegairi* (later *Cineal Laoghaire*) of the western part, and the *Cineal nAeda* (of whom Feidlimid was king of Munster in the late sixth century) farther to the east between the mouth of the Lee and the River Bandon. The main line of the Cineal nAeda gave rise in the late seventh century to the further sub-clan of *Cineal mBecce* (later *Cineal mBeice)*, inhabiting the eastern part of the original territory (called after them "Kinelmeaky," now the barony of that name) between the Cineal Laoghaire in the west and the rest of the Cineal nAeda (later Cineal Aodha), under that name, in the east.

The *Cineal Aodha* or *O'Callaghans* (*O Ceallachain*) later claimed descent from an Aodh (older "Aed") in the pedigree of the Eoghanacht of Cashel, and claimed Ceaillachan of Cashel himself as their ancestor, though admitting that they took their name from a namesake of his some generations later. They gave their clan-name to their original territory, now the barony of Kinalea in the south of County Cork between Cork and Kinsale, from which they were driven soon after the Anglo-Norman invasion by Fitzstephen and de Cogan. Afterwards they settled on the banks of the Blackwater, west of Mallow, where they became chiefs of a territory called after them "Pobul Ui Cheallachain." They held this land down to the Cromwellian confiscations of the mid-seventeenth century, after which the head of the family was transplanted to Clare.

From the eighth century onwards the main representatives of the ruling Ui Eachac Mumhan were the Ui Loegairi and the Cineal mBecce. Their chief clan-families in later times were: Of the former, the *Cineal Laoghaire*, alias *Clann tSealbhaigh*, or *O'Donoghues* (*O Donnchadha*) of Desmond (South Munster), and of the latter, the *Cineal mBeice* or *O'Mahonys* (*O Mathghamhna*). The *O'Donoghues* take their name from their ancestor Donnchadha, son of Domhnall, son of Dubhdabhoireann, King of Munster. Domhnall commanded, conjointly with Cian, ancestor of the O'Mahonys the forces of Desmond at the battle of Clontarf in 1014, which culminated the Viking wars. The descendants of Domhnall assumed for a time the surname of O Domhnaill, but afterwards took their name from Donchadha. They take their clan-name of Cineal Laoghaire from Laoghaire, fourth in descent from their ancestor Corc. The original patrimony of the O'Donoghues lay in west Cork, but in the time of the Anglo-Norman invasion in the late twelfth century they were driven westward from their territory by the MacCarthys and O'Mahonys and settled in Kerry, where they became lords of all the country around the Lakes of Killarney, to which they gave the name of Eoghanacht Ui Dhonnchadha (Onacht O'Donoghue). The O'Donoghues divided early into two great branches: The O'Donoghues of Loch Lein, the head of which was known as O'Donoghue More (The great O'Donoghue) and resided at Ross Castle at the southern end of the Lakes (the castle was built by them in the fifteenth century), and the O'Donoghues of Glenflesk, the head of which was known as O'Donoghue of the Glen. The estates of O'Donoghue More were confiscated in the reign of Elizabeth, but O'Donoghue of the Glen retained considerable property into modern times, and is now known as "The O'Donoghue." The *O'Moriartys* (*O Muircheartaigh*) are an early branch of the O'Donoghues, and were originally chiefs of the territory lying at the end of Dingle Bay around Castlemaine in County Kerry. Although in 1210 their then chief, by way of alliance, married the daughter of a leading Fitzgerald, their influence was nonetheless reduced as a result of the encroachments of the Fitzgeralds.

The *Cineal mBeice* or O'Mahonys descend from Mathghamhain (slain at Clontarf in 1014) whose father Cian (son of Maolmuadh, King of Munster in 978) commanded the forces of Desmond at the battle of Clontarf in 1014 jointly with the ancestor of the O'Donoghues, and whose mother was a daughter of Brian Boru (see under O'Brien). They gave their clan-name to their territory, now known under the phonetically Anglicized form Kinelmeaky, an extensive district along the River Bandon in the south of County Cork. As a reaction to the pressure caused by the Anglo-Norman invasion of the late twelfth century, they expanded westward into the territory of their collateral kinsmen, the Cineal Laoghaire. Afterwards their power extended from Kinelmeaky southwards to the sea, where their fortified stronghold of Rosbrian lay off the coast of southwest Cork.

The *Eoghanacht Mag Geirginn* inhabited the district in northeast Scotland between the Tay and the Dee, and were especially associated with Angus and what is now known as Kincardineshire (formerly "The Mearns"). They traditionally descend from Conal Corc, grandfather of Oengus, King of Munster (490), who is said to have sojourned in Albany, or Scotland, where he married the daughter of Feradach, King of Cruthentuath (Pictland), thus establishing the Eoghanacht of the district of Mag Geirginn. His descendants by her included his son Cairbre (or Coirpre) Cruithnechan ("Cairbre Pictling"), ancestor of the Mag Geirginn branch, also known as Cairpre "mac na Cruithnige" (the son of the Pictish woman), and also his son or grandson Maine Lemna, ancestor of the Lemnaig, later the ruling family of the Levenax (later Lennox). Thus established, the Eoghanacht maintained their individuality at least until the reign of Oengus mac Forggusso, King of the Picts (died 761), who was one of them, and may have been the "Oengus" after whom "Angus" is named.

The district of Atholl (New Ireland) appears about the beginning of the eighth century, with a king of its own, and this may represent a later patrimony for the male-line representatives of the Eoghanacht in Scotland, in as much as they maintained their individual patrilineal traditions within still-matrilineal Pictland. That they did so is indicated by the traditional male-line descent of the medieval ruling family of the Lennox from Maine Lemna, son or grandson of Conall Corc. The nearby district of the Lennox apparently followed Atholl as this group's patrimony as they emerge as its ruling dynasty in the early twelfth century, having been for some time its Mormaers and afterwards its earls (it is interesting to note the continuation of distinctively South-Irish royal names, such as Corc among the House of Lennox even as late as the fourteenth century). The family, known simply as "de Lennox," held the earldom until it passed to the Stewarts of Darnley through an heiress in the early fifteenth century (after the unjustified beheading of Duncan, the last earl of the House of Lennox by James I in 1425 for his relationship to the House of Albany). Afterwards, a family of the name of *de Levenax* (later "Lennox"), a branch of the House of Lennox, settled in South Galloway where they appear as early as 1508 as followers of the Earl of Cassilis and acquired wide lands in Kirkcudbright (Lennox is also one of the name-titles of the Gordon-Lennox dukes of Richmond, Lennox and Gordon, descendants of a natural son of Charles II).

The MacFarlanes (*Mac Pharlain*) descend from Parlan, whose great-grandfather Gilchrist of Arrochar was a younger son of Alwyn, Earl of Lennox about 1200. On the death of Earl Duncan the chiefs of the MacFarlanes claimed to be chiefs of the whole kindred of the House of Lennox, as heirs-male to their kinsmen the earls. The earldom was granted to the Stewarts of Darnley, as mentioned, and the district was consolidated by the marriage of the MacFarlanes' then chief, Andrew MacFarlane of Arrochar, to a daughter of the new earl. Their son, Sir Iain MacFarlane, used the old-style chiefly title of Captain of Clann Pharlain, and led the warlike clan under the Earl of the Lennox at the battle of Flodden in 1513. The MacFarlanes were described by a contemporary as "men of the head of Lennox, that spake the Irish and the English-Scottish tongues, light footmen, well armed in shirts of mail, with bows and two-handed swords" (Moncrieffe 139). The MacFarlanes had island strongholds in upper Loch Lomond, while the chief's residence was the primitive house at Arrochar on the shore of Loch Long.

The Buchanans (*Canonach*) take their name from the barony of Buchanan on the eastern side of Loch Lomond. They were an ecclesiastical family devoted to St. Kettigern, their Gaelic patronymic being *MacAuslan* (*Mac Absalon*), from a local ecclesiastic of the early thirteenth century. Sir Absalon of Buchanan (*buth chanain*, "house of the canon") appears in the early thirteenth century as the temporal lord of what were probably recently secularized church-lands (see page 106). As Absalon son of Macbeth, he was granted the island of Clarinch opposite Buchanan by the Earl of Lennox in 1225. There is a family tradition connecting the Buchanans with Moray, or at least the Moray area. Both the name "Macbeth," and the original Buchanan arms of "three bears heads," could indicate a connection of their ecclesiastical line with the family known as "of the Aird" (see page 56). In any case, as the then laird of Buchanan appears as Steward of the Lennox in 1238, either he, or his father, probably married into the House of Lennox, for stewartrys were reserved for younger branches of the earl's family (see under "Drummond" and in Chapter IV). In the early fifteenth century the Buchanan chiefs married into the discouraged House of Albany (Stewarts), and thus became the nearest lawful heirs of this house; hence the black royal "lyon" in the Buchanan arms — a symbol of mourning.

Other branches of the House of Lennox include the *Leckies* or *Leckys* of

Croy-Leckie, who descend from Corc, younger brother of Gilchrist of Arrochar, ancestor of the MacFarlanes (John Leckie of Croy-Leckie, the then head of the family, married a daughter of MacGregor of Glengyle by his wife, a Campbell of Glenfalloch, and thus became brother-in-law to Rob Roy, whom he joined at Sheriffmuir); and finally also the *MacAulays (Mac Amhalghaidh)* of Ardencaple in Dumbartanshire.

The MacAulays were chiefs of the district along the east shore of Gare Loch, between Loch Long and Loch Lomond. They descend from Aulay Arngapill, or Ardincapill, of that Ilk who is mentioned in 1513. He himself descended from a long line of barons of Ardencaple (Morice de Arncappel rendered homage in 1296, Johannes de Ardenagappill was a charter witness about 1364, and Arthur de Ardincapel witnessed a charter by Duncan, eighth Earl of the Lennox about 1390). Though not originally descended from the House of Lennox, they seem to have inherited the leadership of some of the earls' kindred of the name of MacAulay, for the Aulay is distinctive to that family (the House of Lennox); that is, Amalghaidh mac Amhalghaidh (Aulay mac Aulay), son of Aulay, was a younger son of Alwin, second Earl of the Lennox about 1200. Furthermore, Alexander Ardincapple, Aulay Ardincapill's representative in the reign of James V (1513–1542), adopted the surname of MacAulay in order to better represent the clan at the head of which he found himself, that of MacAuley: Alexander Ardincapple, "then the head of the family, took a fancy to call himself Alexander MacAulay of Ardincapple, from a predecessor of his of the name of Aulay, to humour a patronymical designation as being more agreeable to the *head of a clan* than the designation of Ardincaple of that Ilk" (Black 29). Alexander's taking the name of MacAulay seems tantamount to acknowledging the name and line of the clan he represented, hence the inclusion of his family in the discussion of the Lennox kindred. Awla McAwla of Ardencapill appears in 1536, while another Awla McAwla was clerk of the watch of Queen Mary's guard 1566. Getting back to the pre–Ardincapple MacAulay kindred, Sir Duncan MacAulay, son of Aulay mac Aulay, joined Robert the Bruce in the time before Bannockburn, and his son Aulay "de Faslane" was given the office of Tosheagor, or heritable bailie, by Malcolm, Earl of the Lennox. His son Walter was the Walter de Faslane who married the heiress of his kinsmen Donald, Earl of the Lennox, thus keeping the earldom within the House of Lennox for the time (this situation was analogous to the marriage, some 200 years later, of Mary Queen of Scots, heiress of the Royal House, with Lord Darnley, the Stewart heir-male). It is probably a cousin of the above family that appears as "Iwar McAulay in Lennox" in 1326. The stronghold of the MacAulays was Ardencaple Castle, sold in 1767 and now in ruins.

X. The Vikings and Normans

The Vikings and Normans are ethnically linked because of their common descent from the Norwegian group of Viking raiders and settlers of the ninth to eleventh centuries. The Vikings *per se* came directly to Ireland and Scotland during this period, and in Ireland they established the first towns as coastal trading centers, as merchant activity was a natural second stage to their original ferocious naval raiding. They became completely Gaelicized. The twelfth century brought Anglo-Norman settlers to Scotland, and Anglo-Norman invaders to Ireland. The Normans first appear as mixed Danish and Norwegian settlers in tenth-century Normandy, a province of France which these Vikings wrested from the French and made a dukedom, and from which province they subsequently invaded England in 1066. Their original introduction into the Frankish and Gallo-Roman world in Normandy changed military technology forever, for these acculturated Vikings, afterwards known as Normans, swept forward from Normandy into England and later Gaeldom with "Mote and Bailey" castles (where the Gaels had raided, exacted tribute and then gone back to their own territory, the Normans confounded the Irish by actually squatting on the invaded land with castles, thus physically denying it to its erstwhile owners). The Normans also utilized disciplined and armored Frankish-style cavalry, thus introducing the mounted knight. They invaded both England and Ireland with similar success, though in the Gaelic area they were influenced as much as they influenced. They eventually became to a very large degree, "more Irish than the Irish," adopting Gaelic lifestyles, language and kinship patterns.

The Viking Clans

The Viking clans descended from the Norse who settled in Gaeldom before the Normans include the *Clann Fearghaille*, the *Clann Guinne*, the *Siol Tormod* and *Siol Torquil*, the *MacCotters*, the *O'Doyles* and the *MacCorquodales*.

THE VIKINGS
AND NORMANS

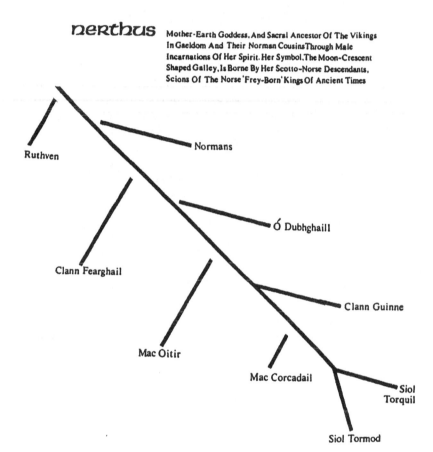

ᚾᴇʀᴛʜᴜs   Mother-Earth Goddess, And Sacral Ancestor Of The Vikings
In Gaeldom And Their Norman Cousins Through Male
Incarnations Of Her Spirit. Her Symbol, The Moon-Crescent
Shaped Galley, Is Borne By Her Scotto-Norse Descendants,
Scions Of The Norse 'Frey-Born' Kings Of Ancient Times

Ruthven

Normans

Ó Dubhghaill

Clann Fearghail

Clann Guinne

Mac Oitir

Mac Corcadail

Siol
Torquil

Siol Tormod

*Unconnected Lines Indicate That Descent Is Implied By Ethnicity

The Clann Fearghaill

The Clann Fearghaill or O'Hallorans (*O hAllmhurain*) were chiefs of Clann Fearghaile, an extensive district named after them which lay just west of Galway City. They maintained their leading position in Iar-Connacht (the largely barren territory west of the province of Connacht proper) up to the end of the sixteenth century. Being originally Norse in extraction, they probably were connected with the origin of Galway City itself, before the Normans came to Galway and monopolized its merchant enterprises after the twelfth century.

The Clann Guinne

The Clann Guinne or Gunns (*Guinne*) descend from Gunni, grandson of Sweyn Asleif's son, famed in the sagas as a wily and daring Viking in the twelfth century. Gunni's wife, Ragnhild, was the daughter of the Norse Earl of Caithness and Orkney. She carried to the Gunns large estates in Caithness and Sutherland. The territory of the Gunns was in the Highland part of Caithness, where they formed a buffer state between the earls of Caithness in the northeast, the MacKays to the west and the MacKays' rivals, the earls of Sutherland, to the south. The chiefs of the Gunns held the hereditary office of Crowner of Caithness in the fifteenth century, an important position in the north, and from early in that century they carried on a vicious blood-feud with the Keiths of Ackergill, a northern branch of that family. The *MacKeamishes*, or *Jamesons* descend from James, the chief of the clan, who was the son of George, Crowner of Caithness in 1464. The Gunn chiefs' patronymic title in Gaelic, Mac Sheumais Chataich (The MacJames, or Jameson, of Caithness), is derived from the same famous James.

The MacCotters

The MacCotters (Mac Oiter) were seated at Carrigtwohil, near the city of Cork. The townland of Ballymacotter indicates their early presence in the area. It is interesting to note that the MacCotters, like the other Norse families in Ireland, the O'Hallorans and the O'Doyles, were settled in areas adjacent to coastal settlements which were originally Norse.

The O'Doyles

The O'Doyles (O Dubhghaill) originated in the coastal regions of southeast Leinster (Counties Wicklow and Wexford). "O Dubhghaill" means "dark foreigner," an epithet applied to the Norse settlers of the area by the native Gaelic inhabitants, and hence there may be more than one Norse ancestor for families so named. In any case, the main sept of the name was located in the area of the Wexford-Wicklow border, from which area branches spread throughout the southeastern region, and beyond. In keeping with their Norse origin, families of the name have always been more numerous in the maritime

areas originally settled by their Viking ancestors. Owen Doyle appears as a
gentleman of Arklow, County Wicklow about 1600.

The MacLeods (Mac Leoid)

The *Siol Tormod* and *Siol Torquil* are the two great independent branches
of the Clan MacLeod (Mac Leoid). The MacLeods descend from Olaf the
Black, King of Man and the North Isles in the thirteenth century. King Olaf
was of the Norse House of Godred Crovan, King of Man, Dublin and all the
Hebrides, who fought for King Harald Haardrade of Norway in his abortive
attempt to conquer England in 1066. The MacLeods originally quartered the
Black Galley in their arms, which was the symbol of the old Norse Kings of
Man. In the seventeenth century they adopted instead a quartering of the
"Three Legs of Man." Their eponymous ancestor was Leod, son of Olaf the
Black. His two sons were the founders of the Siol Tormod and Siol Torquil
branches of the clan, the former of which is generally considered the senior
of the two (this has been disputed by the Torquil branch).

The *Siol Tormod* held the peninsula of Harris in the Outer Hebrides, the
district around Glenelg on the mainland, and the large district around
Dunvegan in western Skye. Dunvegan Castle is still the seat of the chief of all
the MacLeods, as it has been for over 700 years. The *Siol Torquil* held the Island
of Lewis, part of Skye, and also the mainland district between Loch Ewe and
Loch Torridon until they were overthrown by the MacKenzies early in the
seventeenth century. A younger branch, the *MacCallums* or *Malcolmsons (Mac
Giolla Chaluim)*, or MacLeods of Raasay, held the Island of Raasay until the
mid-nineteenth century (their chief's designation was "Mac-Gille-Chaluim").
The Clan Malcolm, the MacCallums or Malcolms of Poltalloch in Argyle, are
a branch of the Raasay clan. They were taken in under the protection of the
Campbells of Lochow, for whom they appear as hereditary constables of the
castles of Craignish and Lochaffy as early as 1414. The *MacCabes (Mac Caba)*
are a branch of the MacLeods from the Hebrides who settled in Breffny (Cavan
and West Leitrim), Ireland, as captains of gallowglasses (heavily-armed
soldiers) to the O'Rourkes and O'Reillys beginning the mid-fourteenth
century.

The *Morrisons*, or *Clann Mac Giolla Mhoire*, descend from Gillemoire, illegitimate brother of Leod, thirteenth century ancestor of the MacLeods.
Their territory lay in the extreme north of Lewis, the Morrrisons being
hereditary brieves, or brehon judges, for the whole island. In the mid-
fourteenth century their chiefly line passed through an heiress, who married
a MacIan MacDonald of Ardnamurchan. The haughty heiress persuaded her
MacDonald husband to change his name to Morrison, and he afterwards
became "one of the best brieves of Lewis." They had a falling out with their
kinsmen, the Siol Torquil, about the year 1600, which led directly to the
MacKenzie takeover of Lewis.

The MacCorquodales

The MacCorquodales (Mac Corcadail), whose name means "son of Torquil" (Thor's kettle), appear since earliest memory as the barons of Phantelane, an extensive mountainous district on the northeastern shore of Loch Awe, bordered on the north by Loch Etive and on the northeast by the Pass of Brander. As such their chiefs were known as Baron MacCorquodale, or as "MacCorquodale of that Ilk" (here "Ilk" indicates chiefship of the "Name"— the MacCorquodales were the earliest family to be officially so designated). Their chief's Gaelic designation was "Mac-a-Bharain," or "son of the Baron" (barons had life-and-death judicial authority in their territories). Tradition relates how their Norse ancestor was for his services awarded with territory on the north shore of Loch Awe by an early Lord of Argyle.

The Ruthvens

The Ruthvens take their name from an old barony of the name in Angus. Thor, son of Swein, was a witness to royal charters between 1127 and 1150. Besides Ruthven, he held the lands of Trauernent (Tranent), the church of which he granted to the monks of Hollyrood. Swan, son of Thor, held land in Perthshire, and assumed the designation "de Ruthven." He also held the lands of Crawford in Clydesdale with William de Lindsay as his vassal. William Ruthven of that Ilk was created Lord Ruthven in 1488. William, fourth Lord Ruthven, was in 1581 created Earl of Gowrie. He was an ultra-Protestant, and led the famous Ruthven Raid. He also detained James VI at Ruthven Castle for ten months. In the famous Gowrie conspiracy of 1600, John, the third Earl of Gowrie, and his brother, the Master of Ruthven, were killed by supporters of James VI after they had allegedly attempted to assassinate the King. Afterwards the name of Ruthven was banned by an act of Parliament, but in 1641 another act allowed the Ruthvens of Ballindean, Perthshire, to retain their name.

Sir Patrick Ruthven (1575-1651) was in the service of the King of Sweden from 1612, and was knighted by Gustavus Adolphus. He returned to Scotland in 1638 to join Charles I, and was created Lord Ruthven of Ettrick in 1639. He held Edinburgh Castle for the King from February to July of 1640, and fought at Edgehill. Later he was created Earl of Forth and Earl of Brentford.

The Norman Families

The Normans came to Ireland mostly from the Welsh Borders, in the wake of the Anglo-Norman invasion of 1169. They came to Scotland as guest-settlers and allies to the Kings of Scots (who prized them for their chivalry and for their military and administrative skills) beginning with the reign of David I in the first half of the twelfth century (see Chapter IV). They included families of

Norman, Flemish, Welsh and Breton descent, the military aristocracy of England at the time. When these invaders met the disarrayed charge of the native Gaelic warriors on the open plains of Ireland, they usually swept the Irish from the field with their awesome three-pronged attack: First the deadly flight of arrows from the distant and invulnerable Welsh crossbowmen, then the organized charge of that "new animal," the charger-mounted armored knights with their long swords, and finally the follow-through onslaught by unrelenting lines of disciplined Flemish infantry. Combine these demonstrations of bold, courageous and creative military innovation with the savvy, pragmatic yet treacherous political machinations of the Normans and their Royal English masters and you have the result: Within 80 years nearly three-quarters of Ireland was under Norman control.

The Barrys (de Barra) descend from Philip de Barry, one of the earliest Anglo-Norman invaders. He was a nephew of Robert FitzStephen, who granted Philip the lands now represented by the baronies of Barrymore, Orrery and Kinelea in County Cork, originally the clan territories of Ui Liathain, Muscraighe-tri-maighe and Cineal Aodha, respectively. The Barrys became one of the most numerous and powerful families in Munster. They divided into several branches, the heads of which were known respectively as "An Barrach Mor" (the Great Barry), "An Barrach Ruadh" (the Red Barry), "An Barrach Og" (the Young Barry), "An Barrach Maol" (the Bald Barry) and "An Barrach Laidir" (the Strong Barry). The Barrys of Rathcormac and Bally-nagloch, County Cork, adopted the Irish patronymic surname MacAdam (Mac Adaim). There was also a branch of the family in County Wexford. The Barrys suffered considerably as a result of the wars of the seventeenth century, but are still numerous and respectable throughout Munster.

The Brownes (de Brun) were one of the Tribes of Galway, the mostly Norman merchant families of that city from the Middle Ages that included the Athys, Blakes, Bodkins, Brownes, Darcys (O Dorchaidhe), Deanes, Fants, Frenches, Joyces, Kirwans, Lynches, Martins, Morrises and Skerrets. The Brownes first came to Ireland at the time of the Anglo-Norman invasion in the twelfth century. They first appear in northeast Mayo as one of the families of Norman introduction that wrested the territory of Tirawley away from the Ui Fiachrach tribe. From there they intermarried with the Lynches of Galway City, where they afterwards became one of the tribes. Subsequently they intermarried with the O'Flahertys and O'Malleys, the leading native families of the Iar-Connacht, or extreme western region, thus securing their position in that quarter.

The Burkes (de Burc) rank with the Fitzgeralds and Butlers as among the most powerful and influential of the Anglo-Norman settlers in Ireland. They descend from William Fitz Adelm de Burgo, who came to Ireland in 1171 in the company of Henry II, who first made him governor of Wexford, and later, in 1178, made him Chief Governor of all Ireland (that is, all Ireland that was actually under Anglo-Norman control). In 1179, Fitz Adelm obtained a grant of a great portion of Connacht, although settlement there was not effected for some time. By marriage with the heiress of the de Lacys, Walter de Burgo, descendant of the Fitz Adelm, acquired the Earldom of Ulster, etc., and the Burkes became the greatest Anglo-Norman family in Ireland. On the murder in 1333 of William, the Brown Earl of Ulster, leaving only an infant daughter, the leading male representatives of the Burkes adopted the Brehon Law (the law of the Gael), which provided for a male succession. They divided the lordship of Connacht between them, and proclaimed themselves Irish chiefs under the style of MacWilliam Uachtar (the Upper MacWilliam) and MacWilliam Iochtar (the Lower MacWilliam), the former holding Galway and the other County Mayo. They did so in full defiant view of a castle of English garrison, standing without the walls some distance back, while symbolically changing their English clothing for Gaelic garb. There were several branches of the family, and these adopted from their respective ancestors the patronymics of Mac-Davie (Mac Daibhidh), MacGibbon (Mac Giobuin), Jennings (Mac Sheoinin), MacRedmond (Mac Reamoinn) and MacPhilbin (Mac Philbin).

The MacDavies were settled in the north of County Galway along the Roscommon border. The MacGibbons were seated on the west side of Croagh Patrick in County Mayo. The Burkes also possessed the Barony of Clanwilliam in County Limerick. There is a late medieval knight's effigy of the Burkes at Glinsk in County Galway. Thoor Ballylee, the home of William Butler Yeats in the Kiltartan country of County Galway, was originally a Norman keep built there by the Burkes.

The Butlers (de Buitileir) descend from the Norman Theobald Fitzwalter, whom Henry II appointed to the post of Chief Butler of Ireland in the late twelfth century. Theobald was besides granted the baronies of Upper and Lower Ormond, and other lands in Kilkenny and Tipperary. In 1328 the then head of the family was created Earl of Ormond. Their chief seat was long at Kilkenny castle, from which they exercised great influence and power.

The Chisholms (Siosal), who came to form a clan in the Highland territory of Strathglass and Glen Affric in Inverness-shire, descend from the Saxon-Norman family of the name, settled in the border region of Roxburghshire and Berwickshire (this Lowland family is still extant). The Chisholms seem from their arms to have been closely related to the Swintons of that Ilk, a great Lowland family, the male-line representatives of the old Anglo-Saxon Beornician Royal House.

Robert Chisholm of that Ilk in Roxburgshire became Royal Constable of Castle Urquhart on Loch Ness in 1359, by succession from his maternal grandfather, Sir Robert Lauder of the Bass, the previous constable. He also inherited from Lauder lands near Elgin and Nairn, and he soon became Sheriff of Inverness and Justiciar of the North as well. His son, Alexander, acquired wide possessions in the north by virtue of his marriage to Margaret, daughter of

Wiland of the Aird (though ultimately through heiresses from the Bissets). The mother of Margaret was Maud, daughter and co-heiress of Malise, Earl of Strathearn, Caithness and Orkney, by his wife Marjory, daughter of the fifth Earl of Ross. The Chisholms may have acquired their possessions in Glen Affric from that side. The Chisholms were ardent Jacobites, were out under the Earl of Mar in 1715, and fought for Prince Charles in the 1745 rising.

The Gordons (Gordon) of the Highlands descend from a Lowland family, a cadet house of the Swintons of that Ilk, who were themselves the male-line representatives of the old Anglo-Saxon royal house of Beornicia, the old kingdom from the Tyne to the Forth along the eastern coast. These Lowland Gordons took their name from their lands: The lands of Gordon in Berwickshire. They also held the lands of Huntly nearby, and later cadet branches held other territories in the Lowlands. Adam of Gordon witnessed a charter about 1195.

A later Sir Adam of Gordon was a close supporter of the Red Cummin, the Lord of Badenoch murdered by Bruce in 1306. After mistreatment by the English allies of the Cummin-Balliol faction, this Adam joined the Bruce in time for the Battle of Bannockburn in 1314, and became an important ally. He was awarded with huge tracts of Highland territory in what had been Clan MacDuff territory, especially the lordship of Strathbogie, the capital of which they renamed Huntly. Thus did the Gordons come to the Highlands. The family rose to great power in the northeast, becoming by the seventeenth century one of the three most powerful families in northern Scotland, together with the Murrays in Atholl and the Campbells in Argyle. The power of the Huntly Gordons was raised in stages, all the way to a dukedom by 1684.

Branches of the Gordons settled in Aberdeenshire, where they founded clans under Gordon Chieftains. In 1408 the heiress of the main Huntly (Aberdeenshire) line married Sir Alexander Seton, who assumed the name of Gordon, and spent much of his time increasing the clan following by encouraging his vassals to take the name of Gordon (notice the mixture of feudalism and clanship). Their son was created Earl of Huntly in 1449, and thus this family remained the senior line of the Gordons.

The Colquhouns (Colchun) descend from Humphrey of Kilpatrick, who was granted the lands of Colquhoun in Dunbartonshire by Malcolm, Earl of Lennox about 1241, from which lands his descendants took their name. About 1368 Sir Robert Colquhoun married the "Fair maid of Luss," heiress of an ancient, ecclesiastical family who were hereditary guardians of the Bachuil, or crozier, of St. Kessog, the martyr who is associated with the church of Luss (which saint the Luss family was probably related to). Their descendants, the Colquhouns of Luss, while still holding the old Colquhoun castle of Dunglass, became leaders of an important clan in the area of Loch Lomond. In 1457 the lands of Luss were erected into a free barony by King James II, after which the then chief built the now ruinous castle of Rossdhu on Loch Lomond.

The Condons (de Canntun) were a Norman family well known in Cork, who early formed a Gaelic-style sept, and who formerly held extensive possessions in the northeast of that county, in the area of what is now the Barony of Condons, which is named for them. Their principal stronghold was the Castle of Cloghleagh near Kilworth. Mitchelstown, County Cork, is named after one of them.

The Cummins (Cuimean) descend from Richard Cummin, or Comyn, Lord of Northallerton, nephew of an important Norman noble under David I. Richard married the granddaughter and eventual heiress of King Donald III, whose family held land in Lochaber and Badenoch in the central Highlands below the Great Glen. The descendants of Richard Cummin became lords of Badenoch, holding much of Lochaber and the Great Glen as well. During the thirteenth century the family became the most powerful family in Scotland, holding nearly a quarter of the Scottish earldoms by right of marriage. In 1291 their then chief, the Black Cummin, was one of the competitors for the Crown of the Scots. His son, the Red Cummin, was murdered by his rival, Robert the Bruce, in 1306, and in the ensuing wars the Cummins were ruined. A few Cummins survived in Buchan, while the descendants of Sir Robert Cummin, uncle of the Red Cummin, settled in the territory between the Spey and the Findhorn, on the borders of Badenoch, receiving grants of land from David II and Robert II. They became chiefs of the clan branch of the family, the head of which is known as Cumming of Altyre.

The Cusacks (de Ciomhsog) were a distinguished Norman family of the Pale, the English territory around Dublin, branches of which spread into neighboring Meath and Leinster. Members of the family were active on both sides, Irish and English, during the wars of the sixteenth and seventeenth centuries.

The Daltons (Dalatun) came to Ireland with the Anglo-Norman invasion, and were active in the Pale in early times, two of the family being members of the Dublin Guild-Merchant in 1226. Later the Daltons appear as lords of Rothconrath in County Westmeath, but they lost their estates in the Cromwellian and Williamite confiscations of the seventeenth century.

The Darcys (Dairsigh) The Darcys or D'Arcys were a distinguished Norman family in England. The founder of the Irish branch was Sir John D'Arcy, chief justiciary of Ireland, in about 1325. He received large grants of land in Meath which remained in the hands of his descendants down to the confiscations of the seventeenth century. Platten, County Meath, was the first Irish home of the family, and from this place came all other branches of the family in Ireland.

The de Courcys (de Cursa) are a distinguished Norman family whose ancestors came to England with William the Conquerer. In 1177, Sir John de Courcy came to Ireland with a grant from Henry II of the whole of Ulster, which he invaded, causing great slaughter. His son, Milo de Courcy, was created Baron of Kinsale by Henry III, and since that time the family has been mainly associated with the area south of Cork City.

The Dillons (Diolun) came to Ireland with the Anglo-Norman invasion. Sir Henry Dillon received from King John large grants of land covering much of Westmeath, known in later times as Dillon's Country. His descendants became barons of Kilkenny West, a barony on the western side of County Westmeath. A branch settled in Mayo. The Dillons were high in the service of the Stewarts, and after the fall of the Stewarts, they became famous as colonel-proprietors of Dillon's Regiment in the French service. One of them was made a French count in 1711.

The Fagans (Fagan) appear as early as 1200 as extensive property holders in the city of Dublin. Soon afterwards they are found seated at Feltrim, County Dublin. Branches settled in Cork and Kerry: The Cork branch descends from Christopher Fagan, who took refuge there for political reasons in 1497, while the Kerry branch became famous in the service of France in the eighteenth century.

The Fitzgeralds (Mac Gearailt) called collectively the "Geraldines," descend from Gerald, Constable of Pembroke in Wales, whose wife was Nest, daughter of Rhys Ap Tewdwyr, King of South Wales. Gerald flourished in the early part of the twelfth century. His son, Maurice Fitzgerald, ancestor of the Irish Fitz-Geralds, was one of the allies of Strongbow, the leader and organizer of the Anglo-Norman invasion. Maurice received grants of land in several parts of Ireland, and his descendants were, with the Burkes and Butlers, among the most powerful of Norman families in Ireland, and members of the family often filled high offices in Ireland under the English Crown. The Leinster branch of the family held for many centuries the Earldom of Kilare, while the Munster branch held the Earldom of Desmond. A branch of the Fitzgeralds, the *Barrons (Barun)* of Burnchurch, County Kilkenny, assumed the surname of Barron from their title in those parts, and remain a highly respectable family in that area and Waterford. The *MacMorises (Mac Muiris)* or *Fitzmaurices* were a branch of the Geraldines who became lords of Lixnaw in County Kerry, and became famous for their resistance to the English invaders of the sixteenth century. In 1333 the then Earl Palatine of Desmond created three hereditary knights, two of whom were sons of a John Fitzgerald. The two lineal male descendants and heirs of these two brothers are still known respectively as the Knight of Glin and the Knight of Kerry.

The MacGibbons (Mac Giobuin) or *Fitzgibbons* descend from Gilbert de Clare, who about 1300 possessed the manor or Mahoonagh and other valuable estates in southeastern County Limerick. The head of this family is the White Knight, one of three hereditary knights so named in 1333 by the Earl of Desmond. A branch of the family settled in County Cork, where they were chiefs of a territory known as Clangibbon.

The Frasers (Friseal) descend from a Norman family named de Frisselle (Norman-French "the Friesian") or de Freseliere that settled in Tweeddale and Lothian, where the name is still extant. Some of them, including the main line of the family, adopted the alternate name of Fraissier, which means strawberry bearer, as a pun on their name because they adopted fraisses, or strawberry flowers, as armorial bearings in the twelfth century. The first of the family recorded in Scotland was Sir Simon Fraser, who in 1160 held part of the lands of Keith in East Lothian, called after him Keith Simon. These lands later passed through Simon's granddaughter to the Keiths, Great Marischals of Scotland. The Frasers were important in the conflicts surrounding the Scottish war of independence in the late thirteenth and early fourteenth centuries. Sir Alexander Fraser, Chamberlain of Scotland, was one of the heroes of Bannockburn in 1314, and married a sister of Robert the Bruce. His line became established in Stirlingshire, and later inherited wide lands around Philorth in northeast Aberdeenshire from the Rosses in 1375. They are now represented by Lord Saltoun. A younger branch of the family, descended from Sir Alexander Fraser's younger brother Simon Fraser, acquired the lands of Lovat at the mouth of the Beauley Firth by marriage to the last of a series of heiresses of the Bissets. It is from this Simon that the Highland Frasers of the Loch Ness and Strathglass area descend, their chiefs being known by the Gaelic title Mac Shimidh (MacKimmie), which means "the son of Simon." Sir Hugh Fraser of Lovat, Sheriff of Inverness, was made Lord Lovat about 1431. The Highland Frasers were important supporters of Prince Charles in 1745.

The Frenchs (de Freins). The ancestors of the Irish Frenchs were one of the original Norman families in England, a branch of which settled in County Wexford about 1300. A branch of the Wexford family settled in Galway in the early fifteenth century, where they became one of the more prominent of the tribes of that city. Walter French became Sovereign (Mayor) of Galway in 1444.

The Grahams (Greumach) are an Anglo-Norman family, and take their name from the manor called Grey Home (OE. "Graeg-ham") in the Domesday Book of William the Conquerer. The first of the family in Scotland was William de Graham, a companion of David I (David I was also an English earl) who received from David I the lands of Abercorn and Dalkeith about 1128. The Grahams have been very prominent in Scottish affairs since the thirteenth-century wars of independence, when they were important allies of Wallace and Bruce. The first to come to the Highlands was Sir Patrick de Graham, who married into the native House of Strathearn, receiving land on Loch Lomond and other estates which he later exchanged for lands at Montrose in Angus.

In 1445 Sir Patrick Graham "of that Ilk" was made Lord Graham (lords were just beginning to be distinguished from lairds, or landholders, in the new peerage that was developing), and the third Lord Graham was made Earl of Montrose by James IV in 1504. James, the fifth Earl of Montrose, was one of the greatest military commanders in European history. Another famous Graham royalist appeared in the next generation. This was John Graham of Claverhouse, Viscount Dundee (a cadet of the House of Montrose) known to history as Bonnie Dundee (or as "Bloody Claver's" by the Covenanters he campaigned against).

In the early fifteenth century the then Graham chief's half-brother Patrick Graham married Robert II's granddaughter, who was the heiress of the new Stewart Earldom of Strathearn, and their son, Malise Graham, was thus heir of Strathearn. Patrick Graham was killed by the Drummonds in 1413, leaving the infant Malise in the guardianship of Patrick's younger brother Sir Robert Graham of Kinpoint. In 1427 James I seized the rich Earldom of Strathearn, giving Malise instead the almost empty title of Earl of Mentieth, and packing him off to England as a hostage-prisoner for almost 26 years. Sir Robert Graham, the boy's uncle and guardian protested in vain, and finally raided the King at Perth and killed the King himself, for which act he was later tortured to death. This line continued, however, and in 1631 the then Earl of Mentieth renewed his claim on Strathearn, but was in 1633 forced to accept the Earldom of Airth instead.

The *MacGilvernocks* (*Mac Giolla Mhearnaigh* – "Son of the servant of St. Ernan"), a sept of the Graham's Highland Border regions, Anglicized their name as Graham. This was the family of the Reverend Archibald Graham, last Bishop of the Isles, 1680–1688.

The *Grants* (*Grannd*, from the Norman-French "le Grand," meaning "the big") are a Norman family introduced into the north of Scotland by the Bissets on the return of some of them from their exile of 1242. In England the Bissets and the Grants possessed adjoining lands in Nottinghamshire and were intermarried. In 1246 King Henry III of England granted Lowdham to Walter Byset till he should recover his lands in Scotland. The adjacent manor of East Bridgeford was then held by William le Grant, who had married Alfreda Byset, a Bisset heiress. They are first recorded in Scotland when Laurence and Robert le Grant appear as witnesses to a grant by the Bissets to Beauly Priory near Inverness in 1258. Later, as Sir Laurence le Grant, the former appears as Sheriff of Inverness, while Robert is recorded as holding land in nearby Nairnshire. As sheriffs of Inverness, the chiefs of the Grants became established in the Glenmoriston area around their center at Castle Urquhart on the northeastern shore of Loch Ness, and acquired blood-ties to the native-men of the district, who held themselves connected to the MacGregors, which may simply indicate their traditional connection to Argyle. In this connection it should be mentioned that the arms of the MacArthurs, formerly princes in Argyle till 1427, could be taken as a differenced version of the arms of the Grants as both color and the "Cross Moline" are standard marks of difference to show blood-relationship. There did exist a famous Norman family of Grants in the early thirteenth century with the same armorial motto as the Scottish Grants: "Stand Fast,"–Latin, *Tenons Ferme*. Nevertheless, the arms of the Grants, three golden antique crowns on red, may have been inherited at the time that the Grants settled in Scotland around 1258, hence the possible MacArthur connection (a similar inheritance of arms happened in the case of the Haldanes of Gleneagles).

In any case, since the Frasers quarter the Grant arms for their Highland inheritance (see above), they probably inherited Lovat ultimately from a Bisset heiress, but more immediately through a Grant heiress. Notwithstanding their growing clan following, the Grants did not gain a real foothold in the Highlands until 1434, when their then chief, Sir Iain Grant, Sheriff of Inverness, acquired a vast district in Strathspey by marriage to the daughter and heiress of Gilbert of Glencairnie, the descendant of a younger son of the House of Strathearn (see Chapter VI). Afterwards they came to dominate Strathspey from Aviemore to Rothes.

The Hacketts (Hacaed, Haiceid) came to Ireland with the Anglo-Norman invasion in the twelfth century, settling in what is now Counties Kildare, Carlow and Kilkenny. They are well known in Anglo-Irish records, and one of them, Peter Hackett, was Archbishop of Cashel in 1385. Townlands of the name appear as Ballyhackett or Hackettstown in Counties Dublin and Kildare, and Hackettstown, County Carlow is still extant. A branch settled in Connacht and became Gaelicized, forming a small sept known as *MacHackett*. They were seated at Castle Hackett, six miles southeast of Tuam. Some of these were known as Guckian.

The Hamiltons (Hamultun) were an important Anglo-Norman family of the Lowlands. In 1474 James, the first Lord Hamilton, married the Princess Mary, sister of James III. Their son, James, second Lord Hamilton, Heir Presumptive to the Scottish Throne, was in 1503 created Earl of Arran, and given the Island of Arran with the earldom. Arran had come to the Stewarts, his mother's family, through an heiress of Angus, Son of Somerled, Lord of Bute and Aran, ca. 1200.

The Hays (Mac Garaidh) are an Anglo-Norman family descended from William de la Haye, Butler of Scotland, who came to Scotland about 1160. He married the Celtic heiress of Pitmilly near the Tay estuary, and was also made first Baron of Erroll. Their son David, second Baron of Erroll, married Ethna, daughter of Gilbert Mac Ferteth, Earl of Strathearn, thus establishing the main Hay line (David's younger brother Robert and younger son William founded Lowland houses of the name). Gilbert de la Haye, third Baron of Erroll and Sheriff of Perth was one of the co–Regents of Scotland in 1255 and 1258. He married a Cummin, but nevertheless his grandson, Sir Gilbert, the fifth Baron of Erroll, was an important follower of The Bruce, who made him hereditary Constable of Scotland after the battle of Bannockburn in 1314. In 1452 the then chief, William, Lord Hay was created Earl of Erroll. The seventh Earl of Erroll's mother was the daughter and heiress of Lyon Logie of that Ilk, Baron of Logiealmond, which inheritance, together with the Barony of Caputh on the border of Atholl and Gowrie gave the Hays land and influence in the Perthshire Highlands. The ninth earl was an important leader of the

Counter-Reformation at the end of the sixteenth century together with the Huntly Gordons under their chief, the "Cock of the North." Another branch of the Hays settled early on the Moray Firth as barons of Lochloy, and intermarried with the local clans. Sir William de la Haye, Baron of Lochloy, was sheriff of Inverness in 1296.

The Jordans (Mac Shiurtain) descend from Jordan (Shiurtain) D'Exeter, an Anglo-Norman knight, whose descendants acquired extensive holdings in northeast Mayo after the Anglo-Norman invasion. The present Barony of Gallen in northeast Mayo was formerly known as "MacJordan's Country." Though they remembered their descent from the D'Exeter family, they nonetheless formed a sept on the Gaelic model. In 1571 they are called "very wild Irish" by an Elizabethan official. A branch was also settled in County Clare.

The Keatings (Ceitinn) were among the first Anglo-Norman invaders, settling first in County Wexford, where they obtained large grants of land. They later spread into Counties Leix, Carlow, Kildare, Tipperary, and Waterford. The Leix and Carlow branches became Gaelic-style septs. The name is also prominent in Anglo-Irish records, in which Keatings are found filling important positions, mainly as sheriffs and later as members of parliament. Dr. Geoffrey Keating, the Gaelic-speaking priest, was an important historian in the late sixteenth and early seventeenth centuries.

The Keiths (Ceiteach) take their name from the lands of Keith in East Lothian, which passed through the granddaughter of Simon Fraser, ancestor of the Frasers, to Sir Robert Keith, who got a grant of Keith from King John Balliol in 1294. Sir Robert joined Robert Bruce in 1308, and became Justiciar and Great Marischal (commander of the royal army) of Scotland. He commanded the cavalry at Bannockburn in 1314, and was killed at Neville's Cross in 1346. The office of Great Marischal remained hereditary in his family, and in 1458 Sir William Keith, the then Great Marischal, was created Earl Marischal by King James II. A cadet of his family married one of the heiresses of the Cheynes of Akergill, and settled in Caithness, where his family long had a sanguinary feud with the Clann Gunn. The Earls Marischal exerted great influence on Scottish affairs through many generations, and the family acquired broad lands in the lowlands of Aberdeenshire, Kincardineshire and West Lothian. James Keith, younger brother of the tenth Earl Marischal, was out in the Jacobite rising of 1715, and later became a Field-Marshal under Frederick the Great.

The Kinnairds take their name from the Barony of Kinnaird in the Gowrie district of East Perthshire (not the Atholl Kinnaird). The first person of the name was Radulphus Ruffus, who received a charter of the lands of Kinnaird from King William the Lion about 1180. Richard of Kinnaird, grandson of Radulf Ruffus, appears in the early thirteenth century, and Rauf de Kynnard in 1296. William Kynnard of that Ilk appears in 1546. George Patrick Kinnaird of that Ilk, a member of Parliament and Privy Councilor, was made Lord Kinnaird in 1682 and died in 1689. The castle of Kinnaird was built in the fourteenth or fifteenth century.

The Lacys (de Leis) originally came over to England from Normandy with William the Conqueror in 1066. The first of the family in Ireland was the famous Hugh de Lacy, who was granted the whole of the kingdom of Meath, which included what is now Meath, Westemeath, Dublin, etc., and which was, before the invasion, in the hands of the Southern Ui Neill, under the O'Melaghlins (O'Melaghlin had Hugh de Lacy assassinated by an axman in 1186, for reneging on an agreement). Hugh de Lacy married as his second wife the daughter of the Irish High-King Roderick O'Connor. Owing to the failure of the male line, this territory passed out of the family, although cadets of the house remained in the area. A distinguished branch of the de Lacys, claiming descent from the O'Connor marriage, settled in Limerick, where they had castles at Ballingarry, Bruree, Bruff, and elsewhere. Pierce Lacy of Bruff was a famous captain in the wars against Elizabeth I in the late sixteenth century. Hugh Lacy, Bishop of Limerick from 1557–1581, was removed from his post by Queen Elizabeth and died in prison ten years later. Col. John Lacy was a member of the Supreme Council of the Confederate Catholics in 1647, and was specifically excluded from amnesty after the fall of Limerick in 1651. Count de Lacy, of the Ballingarry family, left Ireland with Patrick Sarsfield after the second siege of Limerick (in which he took a prominent part though only thirteen years of age at the time), and distinguished himself in the service of Peter the Great of Russia. His son became an Austrian field-marshal, while others of the family rose to fame in the service of Russia and Spain.

The Lindsays take their name from the district of that name south of the Humber in England, which they held as Anglo-Norman knights as early as 1086. Sir Walter de Lindsay, who appears in Scotland before 1120, was a friend and supporter of David I, who had been Earl of Huntingdon in England before his accession to the throne of the Scots.

The Lindsays acquired land in the hill district of Clydesdale, the estate called Crawford, which they held under the Ruthvens. William de Lindsay of Crawford was also Baron of Luffness, and his son by his first wife founded a Lowland baronial house of the name. William de Lindsay, his son by his second marriage, was Steward to the Steward (or Stewart) of Scotland, and adopted as his arms a differenced version of the arms of the Stewarts, significant to that office. Sir Alexander de Lindsay, though knighted by Edward I of England, nonetheless fought for Wallace and Bruce in the Scottish wars of independence, forfeiting his vast English estates for the Scottish cause. His wife was a sister of the Stewart of Scotland (House of Stewart), and their son, Sir David de Lindsay, Lord of Crawford, married in 1324 the co-heiress of the great Abernethy family of the Clan MacDuff. These great marriages are aptly reflected in the Lindsay arms. The family acquired the Highland district of Glenesk in Angus by marriage to the heiress of the Stirlings of Edzell. This together with their Abernethy lands in Angus amounted to about two-thirds of the county. Sir David Lindsay was created Earl of Crawford in 1398, and was overlord of the Highland district of Straithnairn. The Lindsays had a fourteenth century feud with the Lyons of Glamis, and a fifteenth century feud with the Ogilvys. Later Lindsay earls of Crawford were intimately concerned with rebellion at home and military service abroad. The Lindsays were famous for their chivalry and their knightly skill, and also for their patronage of distinctively Anglo-Scottish literature and art.

In 1390 Sir David Lindsay of Glenesk, afterwards first Earl of Crawford, as Champion of Scotland, fought a duel on London Bridge against the English Champion, Lord Welles, having accepted a challenge issued by the latter to all Scotsmen. This was fought before the King and Queen of England on the day of the Feast of St. George. Lindsay defeated Lord Welles handily, yet what is more remarkable is that he dismounted and remounted in full armor without assistance, in order to refute an allegation that he was fastened in the saddle. In the following foot-combat, Lindsay manfully lifted his opponent on the point of his dagger, and hurled him to the ground, again while both knights were in full armor. Afterwords Lindsay assisted Lord Welles by leading him gently by the hand into the presence of the King and Queen. Two years later, as a member of a posse led by Sir Walter Ogilvy, hereditary Sheriff of Angus (ancestor of the earls of Airlie) in pursuit of a *Clann Donnachaidh* (Robertson) raiding party from Atholl, Lindsay was himself severely wounded, and the Sheriff of Angus killed, as the result of being ambushed by the very Athollmen they were chasing. A Highlander, though pinned to the ground at the time by Lindsay's lance, nonetheless managed to cut him to the bone, through his steel leg-armor, by means of a two-handed claymore.

The Livingstons descend from a Saxon named Leving (Latin: Leuing) who settled in Scotland under David I in the early twelfth century. He was granted the lands in Edinburgh which from him were called Levingestun. These lands were called in early Latin Charters *villa Leuing*. Turstanus filius Leuig (Latin for Leuing) granted to the monks of Hollyrood in Edinburgh the church of Leuiggestun (Livingston) with other holdings in the reign of Malcolm IV (ca. 1155).

Sir Archibald de Levingestoune appears in 1296, while James of Leyffingstoun was Great Chamberlain of Scotland in 1456. His family became earls of Linlithgow and Callendar, and held the ancient Thanage or Barony of Callendar in Stirlingshire by inheritance with the native line, (one of whom, Richard Callendar, a descendant of Eva of Lennox and Duncan de Callendar, was constable of Stirling Castle in 1282). James Livingston of Skirling was Baron of Biel and Keeper of the Privy Purse to King Charles I. In 1641 the King granted him a 19-year lease of the "lands and teinds" of the bishoprics of Argyll and the Isles, followed in 1642 by a grant of the spiritualities and temporalities of the same bishoprics for life, with other provisions. The representative of this line, Sir James Livingston of Kinnaird, was created Earl of Newburg (Fife) by Charles II shortly after Charles' restoration and return from France (he had been granted a viscountcy in 1647 by Charles I). James raised the King's Life Guard of Horse, "the private gentlemen of the Kings Life Guard," composed largely of Perthshire gentry, on Leith Links, Edinburgh, in 1661. This regiment was later commanded by the Marquis of Tullibardine (of the Perthshire Murrays). It should be noted that some Pennsylvania Germans Englished their name of Loewenstein as Livingston.

The Lynches (de Linse) came to Ireland with the Anglo-Norman invasion, and settled at Knock in what is now County Meath. At the start of the fourteenth century a branch of the family settled in Galway City, where they became the most important of the mostly Norman tribes of that city, often serving as mayors. Several of the name were attainted, their property confiscated, at the end of the Jacobite wars of the late seventeenth century.

The MacCostellos (Mac Oisdealbhaigh) were one of the first Anglo-Norman families in Connacht, settling in Mayo, in what became the Barony of Costello, which originally included part of neighboring County Roscommon (their sixteenth-century seat was near Ballaghadereen, now in Roscommon). They were the first of the Norman invaders to adopt a Gaelic name, which marks their descent from Oistealb, son of the famous Gilbert de Nangle (Latin: de Angulo), who was one of the first Anglo-Norman invaders. His family, the de Angulos, obtained vast estates in Meath, where they were Barons of Navan. The family thence spread into Leinster and Connacht, where the leading family adopted the Gaelic patronymic Mac Oisdealbhaigh, as we have seen. Those in Leinster, and those in Connacht that did not adopt this form, became Nangles (de Nogla); while those in Cork became Nagles. The Waldrons (Mac Bhaildrin) are a branch of the MacCostellos in Mayo.

The Bissets' (Biseid) ancestor came to Scotland in the train of William the Lion on his return from captivity in England. The first recorded in Scotland was Henricus Byset, who witnessed a charter by William the Lion granted before 1198. His son John Byset witnessed a charter by Henry de Graham in 1204, and was granted wide lands in northern Scotland by the king. The descendants of this John Byset became very powerful barons in the North, but their power was broken as a result of the murder of the young Earl of Atholl by Walter Byset, Lord of Aboyne. He and his nephew, John Byset (founder of the Priory of Beauly in 1231) were exiled from Scotland (another Bisset, Sir William, was freed from guilt), and took refuge in the Glens of Antrim, where they carved out a territory under de Burgo, Earl of Ulster. From this John descends the family of MacKeown (Mac Eoin—son of John) of the Glens of Antrim. It was through an heiress of this family that the Glens came to the Mac-Donnells. In Scotland the Bissets continued to be a family of importance, although most of the old estates passed through heiresses to the Frasers and

Chisholms. The Bissets of Lessendrum are among the oldest families in Aberdeenshire.

The Martins (Mairtin) came to Ireland with Strongbow in the twelfth-century Anglo-Norman invasion. They became one of the famous, mostly Norman merchant families of Galway City, known collectively as the Tribes of Galway. The Martyns of Tullyra, County Galway, were one of the few Catholic families ever to be excluded from the harsh penal code, owing to their assistance of Protestants during the Catholic ascendancy of the seventeenth century.

The Menzies (Meinnearach) are a branch of the Anglo-Norman family of de Meyners of England, where the name has taken the form of "Manners" (of Etal and Rutland). The first of the name in Scotland was Sir Robert de Meyners, who was at the Court of Alexander II by 1224, and was created Great Chamberlain of Scotland by 1249. Alexander de Meyneris or Meinzeis had a charter of the lands of Durisdeer in Nithsdale from Robert I, and also held Weem and Aberfeldy, and Fortingal in Rannoch, or West Atholl (Fortingal later passed through an heiress to the Stewarts), and Glendochart, in Breadalbane. The Menzies fought for The Bruce at the Battle of Bannockburn in 1314. Sir Robert de Mengues, Knight, had his lands erected into the Barony of Menzies in 1487. The last chieftain of a distinguished fourteenth-century cadet branch, the Menzies of Pitfoddels (their young chieftain had carried the Royal Standard at the battle of Invercarron in 1650) settled his estate of Blairs on the Catholic church, which is now Blairs' College near Aberdeen, and which holds the surviving muniments of the old Scots College of Paris. The Menzies appear in the Roll of the Clans, 1597. Though after the Stewarts were driven from the throne in 1688 the chief of the Menzies favored the new government, the Menzies nonetheless were out in support of the Stewarts in the 1715 and 1745 Risings (though the chief sat out the 1745 Rising, the clan was out under Menzies of Shian). Menzies of Culdares introduced the first Larch trees to the Highlands in 1738, which was important to the reforestation of the Highlands. The Menzies of Culdares and Arndilly (Speyside) have inherited the chiefship. The name is pronounced "Meeng-us."

The Morrises (de Moireis: Latin "de Marisco"; Norman-French "de Marreis") are of Norman origin, and were a very powerful family in the south of Ireland attached to the Butlers of Ormond. They became Gaelicized, and adopted the patronymic name of Mac Muiris, now usually Morrissey. In 1485 a branch of these Ormond Morrises settled in Galway City, where they became one of the famous and mostly Norman tribes, or merchant families, of that city. They were prominent in the affairs of Galway City down to the time of Cromwell and the submergence of the Catholic aristocracy.

The Nugents (de Nuinnseann) settled to Ireland at the time of the Anglo-Norman invasion in the twelfth century, having come to England with William the Conqueror in 1066. In Ireland the family settled in what is now

Meath and Westmeath. Gilbert de Nugent was made Baron of Delvin by Hugh de Lacy, and that title continued in the family down to the year 1621, when Richard Nugent, Baron of Delvin, was created Earl of Westmeath. The *Nugents* of County Cork are known in Irish as Uinnseadun, which is a Gaelic rendering of the Norman French "de Wynchester," or of Winchester, Winchester being an ancient city in Hampshire, England, from which this branch of the Nugents came to Cork. The Nugents of Cork formed a clan after the Gaelic fashion, their chief residing at Aghavarten Castle near Carrigaline.

The *Powers' (de Paor: Norman-French "le Paor")* ancestor came to Ireland with Strongbow in the twelfth-century Anglo-Norman invasion. Strongbow granted him the territory of Waterford, where the family flourished and became Gaelicized, spreading into the adjoining counties of Kilkenny, Wexford, Cork and Tipperary. Baron le Paor was one of the great Norman lords who took part in the thirteenth century occupation of Connacht, where Powers settled for a while under the Burkes. Many of the family have held high position in the Roman Catholic church, especially as Bishops of Waterford. In 1535, Sir Richard le Poer was created Baron of Curraghmore (an English title), yet a number of Powers were prominent on the Irish side in the wars of the seventeenth century, some serving in King James' Irish Army. In spite of their Jacobite sympathies, the leading landholders of the name succeeded in retaining much of their estates.

The *Purcells (Puirseil)* came to Ireland from England (where the family is still extant) about 1250, and became one of the most influential Anglo-Norman families of Ormond (Kilkenny and Tipperary), as adherents of Butler earls of Ormond. The Purcells had many castles and manors in that district. The head of the family was known as the Baron of Loughmore (near Thurles), and the ruins of his stronghold, Lochmoe Castle, are still to be seen. The title of Baron of Loughmoe was conferred upon the head of the Purcells by the first Earl Palatine of Ormond (the English government, jealous of the power of the Norman barons, refused to recognize this Loughmoe title – to no effect). Important branches of the family settled at Ballyculhane in County Limerick, and at Crumlin in County Dublin. The Purcells were prominent on the Irish side in the wars of the seventeenth century, one being one of Patrick Sarsfield's right-hand men.

The *Rothes (Rut)* are descended from John Fitz William Rothe of northern Rothe, County Lancaster, who came to Ireland with the Anglo-Norman invasion. The Rothes came to Kilkenny about 1390, and became important in that county. They had their chief seats at Ballyraughtan and Tulloghmaine in County Kilkenny, and a branch of the family became one of the tribes, or merchant families of the city of Kilkenny. The branch settled at New Ross, County Wexford, is descended from John Rothe, Esquire, of Ballyevan, who died about 1585. He was a younger son of Robert Fitz David Rothe, Esquire, of Ballyraughtan. General Michael Rothe served with distinction in the Irish army of James II in the late seventeenth century, and was later commander of Rothe's Regiment of Cavalry in the Irish Brigade in the service of France.

The Sarsfields (de Sairseil) call themselves after a manor in Herefordshire, and came to Ireland with the Anglo-Norman invasion. The first of the family in Ireland was Thomas de Sarsfield, chief standard bearer to King Henry II of England, who was in Ireland in 1172. Branches of the family settled in Counties Cork and Limerick in the twelfth century, and later a branch of the Cork family settled in County Dublin. In the seventeenth and eighteenth century several members of the family, representing all the branches, had successful military careers in the French service. Patrick Sarsfield, hero of the Jacobite wars, was of the Dublin branch, and was a great-great grandson of Sir William Sarsfield, Mayor of Dublin in 1566.

The Sinclairs (de Sincleir) derive their name from St. Clair in the arrondissement of Pont d'Eveque, Normandy. In 1162 Henry de St. Clair, Normandy, received a charter of the lands of Herdmanston in Haddingtonshire from the de Morville Constable of Scotland, whose sheriff he was. The lands of Haddingtonshire continued in this branch of the family into modern times, and one of this branch was with Bruce at the battle of Bannockburn in 1314 (their arms difference as blue the Black Cross of the main line of the Sinclairs). Sir William Sinclair, son of Robert de St. Clair in Normandy by his wife, the daughter of the second Comte de Dreux, in France, was in 1280 granted the Barony of Rosslyn and other lands by Alexander III, whose favorite he was. Sir William was Sheriff of Edinburgh, Haddington, Linlithgow and Dumfries, and also Justiciar of Galloway, and was guardian, or foster-father, to Alexander, heir to the Kingdom of Scots, who died in 1283 or 1284. In 1285 he went to France to escort Alexander III's queen-elect, the daughter of his kinsman, the fourth Comte de Dreux. Younger sons of his line were established in Berwick and Invernesshire before the marriage of his great-grandson to Isabel, daughter of Malise, Earl of Strathearn, Caithness, and Orkney.

Isabel was designated primary heiress for Caithness by her father, and Henry Sinclair, their son was made Jarl (Norse equivalent of Scottish earl or Latin comes) of Orkney by the King of Norway, under whose control Orkney at the time was. Younger sons of this line were granted lands in Aberdeenshire, and Henry's grandson, William Sinclair, the last Jarl of Orkney, was granted the old family earldom of Caithness in 1455. Orkney was resigned by him in 1470, to the King of Norway, under pressure by the King of Scotland (sovereignty over Orkney had fallen peacefully into the possession of the King of Denmark, who in 1469 had given it over to James III of Scotland, when the latter married his daughter). Afterwards Orkney became Crown property.

The Sinclairs of Caithness were a powerful territorial family, and though many of their tenants assumed their name, the relationship of the Sinclair earls to those vassals remained feudal, though the two were often linked together through younger branches of the earls' family, whose chieftans held the usual clan-relationship with both parties. The Sinclairs of Rosslyn descend from the second son of William, last Earl of Orkney, and held the castle of Rosslyn in County Edinburgh. The strongholds of the earls of Caithness were the castles of Girnigoe and Mey (or Barrogill) in Caithness. The *Linklaters* (Old Norse "Lyngklettr") derive their name from a place in Orkney, and being regarded as kin to the original line of earls, or jarls, of Orkney, are regarded as a sept of the Clan Sinclair.

The *Spaldings* take their name from the town of Spalding in Lincolnshire, England. They appear in Scotland from about 1225, when Radulphus de Spalding witnessed a charter of a mill in Kincardineshire. Magister (a church office) John de Spaldyn witnessed a grant of lands in Aberdeen about 1294, and appears as canon of Elgin in 1300 and 1304. A Symon de Spalding was a parson (parish priest) in Ayrshire, and Peter de Spalding held lands and tenements at Berwick, and was a burgess of that town, in 1318. All of these de Spaldings may well be related, given their chronological progression, and as two of the three living around 1300 are non–Celtic and thus by rule were celibate Catholic churchmen, the Spaldings probably descend from the above-mentioned Peter, who helped Robert the Bruce overcome the governor of Berwick (whom Peter considered too severe) in The Bruce's siege of that town in 1318. In May of the following year he received as a reward for his services and in exchange for his Berwick lands (it may have been too hot for him to stay around Berwick) the lands of Ballourthy (Balzeordie) and Petmethey (Pitmachie) in Angus, together with the keepership of the royal forest of Kylgerry. The Spaldings became an important family in the Dundee area, and in 1587 were included in the roll of "Clans that have captains, chiefs and chieftains on whom they depend."

The *Walls* (*de Bhal*, Norman-French *"de Valle"*) descend from the Norman William de Valle, who came to Ireland with Richard de Clare, Earl of Pembroke, alias Strongbow, in 1172. William had four grandsons, each of whom founded families in various parts of the country between Waterford and Tipperary. In 1335 two of them, John de Vale and Walter de Vale, accompanied Sir John D'Arcy, the Chief Justiciary, on an expedition to Scotland. By the sixteenth century branches of the family were settled throughout the counties of Kildare, Carlow, Kilkenny, Tipperary, Cork, Limerick and Galway. In Galway they formed a distinct clan or sept in the Gaelic way, with a "chief of the name." Some of these were known as *Faltagh* (Faltach), a case-form of de Bhal in Gaelic. The Limerick branch held the manor of Dunmoylan from the thirteenth century down to 1580, when Ulick de Wale, though blind from birth, was put to death by the Englishman Pelham, who confiscated his lands. The head of the Limerick branch was known as An Faltach, which means "The chief of the Walls."

The *Stewarts* (*Stiubhard*) take their name from the office of Steward or Stewart of Scotland, the Anglo-Saxon title equivalent to the Norman Seneschal, or household officer. The distinctive arms of the Stewarts, the

"Fesse Chequy," alludes to the counting board used in their hereditary duties during the High Middle Ages. The ancestors of the Stewarts were Seneschals of the counts of Doll and Dinan in Brittany, to whom they were related, as per Medieval custom. Alan Fitz Flaald was in England before 1101, and his two sons, William and Walter, were the progenitors of the FitzAlan earls of Arundel in England, and of the House of Stewart in Scotland, respectively. Walter was in Scotland before 1164 and was created Stewart of Scotland by King David I. He was granted wide territories in Renfrewshire and East Lothian, and commanded the King's army which defeated Somerled of the Isles in 1164. He founded the Abbey of Paisley, near Glasgow, and passed the office of Stewart to his descendants, the second of which (the grandson of Walter) adopted the title as his surname. He himself had several sons, including Alexander, fourth High Stewart, and Walter, ancestor of the *Menteiths*, a branch of the Stewarts who took their name from their earldom. Alexander's son James, fifth High Stewart, inherited the Islands of Bute and Arran, as well as the royal name James from his mother, who was the heiress of Seumas (James) mac Angus mac Somerled, of the Royal House of the Isles. Walter, sixth High Stewart, was prominent at Bannockburn on the Scottish side, and Robert the Bruce later gave Walter his daughter Marjory's hand in marriage. She became heiress of the House of Bruce when her brother David II failed to have children, and so Robert, seventh High Stewart, became King of Scots in 1372. There was treacherous and sanguinary infighting within the Royal House in the early fifteenth century, especially in the reign of James I, who was, as it happens, an important partron of Anglo-Scottish arts, having married into the Chaucerian House of Lancaster.

Families of the House of Stewart fall into one of two categories: The pre-royal Stewarts, who branched off the main stem before the Stewarts inherited the throne of the Scots; and the royal but illegitimate (at least officially) descendants of the Stewart kings. Branches of the Stewarts, royal and pre-royal, settled over wide areas of Scotland, especially in Galloway and Renfrewshire in the Lowlands, but in various parts of the Highlands as well. The Highland Stewarts adopted Gaelic ways, and lived with the traditional mix of lowland feudalism and highland clanship, with important bonds of association being drawn up from time to time between the various branches throughout the land. The Stewarts of Appin formed a clan, and inherited the Lordship of Lorn from the MacDougals. There were other important branches in Atholl, Moray, Aberdeenshire, Banffshire and Balquhidder. Steuart and Stuart are simply French-influenced forms, owing to the absence of "w" in that language: These forms do not, broadly speaking, indicate a special line of descent.

The *Tobins* (*Toibin*—Norman-French "*St. Aubyn*") take their name from the town of St. Aubyn in Brittany. They came to Ireland in the wake of the twelfth-century Anglo-Norman invasion, and by 1200 were settled in counties Tipperary and Kilkenny, spreading later into the neighboring counties of

Cork, Limerick and Waterford. They became very influential in County Tipperary, the head of the family being known as Baron of Coursey. They formed a warlike sept, after the Gaelic fashion, in the fourteenth century, and were dreaded by later English settlers. Ballytobin, near Callan in County Kilkenny, is named after them.

The Flemings (Pleamonn) descend from Richard le Fleming, a Flemish knight who obtained from Hugh de Lacy a grant of the Barony of Slane and other estates in County Meath, which remained in his family down to the Cromwellian and Williamite confiscations of the seventeenth century. The head of the family was created Lord Slane in 1537, and Viscount Longford in 1713. His armorial motto is written in Gaelic, and translates as "May the King live forever" (Bhear na Righ gan).

The Inneses (Innis) descend from Berowald Flandrensis, a Flemish knight, who was granted the Barony of Innes, in Moray, by Malcolm IV in 1160 after marrying the daughter of its native thane (thus the "three Moray stars," differenced blue on silver, of the Innes arms). This barony included all the coastal territory between the Spey and the Lossie. Berowald's grandson, Walter de Ineys, had a charter from the King in 1226. The ninth Baron, Sir Alexander Innes of that Ilk married the daughter of the last Thane of Aberchirder in the early fifteenth century, thus acquiring additional lands not far to the east in Buchan. Their son Walter, tenth of Innes, built the great tower of Kincairdy Castle. A branch of the family appears in Caithness in 1507, and other branches acquired Innermarkie and Balveny not far to the south of Innes. The Inneses were regarded as a clan by the Privy Council in 1579.

The Leslies take their name from the Barony of Leslie in the Garioch in central Aberdeenshire. They descend from Bartholf, a Flemish knight, who obtained the Barony of Leslie in the second half of the twelfth century. He probably married into a native line, for his son was given the distinctively Celtic name Malcolm. This Malcolm was constable of the Royal castle of Inverurie, and was formally granted the Barony of Leslie by a charter by Earl David, brother of William of the Lion. By subsequent marriages his line acquired the Rothes, a considerable territory not far away in the lowlands of Moray, and thus the Leslies became an important territorial family in the North. They also acquired lands in central Fife and on the south side of the Firth of Tay, the latter by an Abernethy heiress. A branch settled early in France, where they became the De Lisle Viscounts de Fussy. Sir Andrew Leslie, who married the Abernethy heiress, was one of the Scottish barons that in 1320 signed the famous letter to the Pope asserting Scottish independence. His younger son Walter married the daughter of the Earl of Ross and was given the earldom by the King, who seized it from the male-line of the House of Ross. The earldom soon passed deviously from the family by another heiress, into the hands of the Stewarts. Sir Andrew's great-grandson was in 1437 created Earl of Rothes.

The Prendergasts (de Priondargas) take their name from a parish in Pembrokeshire. Maurice de Prendergast was one of the Flemish knights who accompanied Strongbow to Ireland in the original Anglo-Norman invasion of the twelfth century. He and his descendants obtained large grants of land in different parts of the south and west of Ireland. The principal branches of this powerful family held wide lands in what are now the counties of Wexford, Kilkenny, Tipperary, Limerick, Mayo and Galway. Some of the Mayo branch adopted the Gaelic patronymic *MacMorris (Mac Muiris)* or *Fitzmaurice*, while a branch of those in County Kerry adopted the form *MacShearhoon (Mac Searthuin)*.

The Roches (de Roiste), a Flemish family from Wales, came to Ireland with the Anglo-Norman invasion, and settled in Wexford in the late twelfth century. The Roches became numerous as landholders in the area, and branches of the family settled in counties Cork and Limerick. Roche of Rochesland was one of the principal gentlemen of Wexford in 1598. In Cork they acquired by marriage the district around Fermoy, which came to be known as Crioch Roisteach, or Roche's Country. The head of this branch was known as Baron Fermoy. The Roches of Limerick were an important merchant family in that city, and several were prominent in its defense against the English in 1651. There are a number of places called Rochestown in Ireland, six in Wexford alone, and two more in Kilkenny.

The Sutherlands (Sutherlarach) and *Murrays (Moireach* – Latin: *de Moravia)* descend from Freskin, son of Ollec, a Flemish knight with lands in what is now Pembroke in Wales. He was granted by David I, King of Scots, the lands of Strabrock in West Lothian and also Duffas in conquered Moray. Freskin or his son William intermarried with the Picto-Scottish Royal House of Moray, in whose defeat he was taking part, following the Norman custom of consolidation by intermarriage. At about this time the southern part of Caithness was being wrested from the Norse who had long controlled that northern extremity, and the resultant territory (known as "Sudrland" or "the South-Land" by those northwardly-oriented Northmen) was given before the year 1211 to Hugh of Moray, son of William, by William the Lion, King of Scots. William, younger brother of Hugh of Moray, Lord of Sutherland, was ancestor of the great family of *Murray*, while Hugh's own son William of Sutherland was made Earl of Sutherland about the year 1235. His line became chiefs of the Pictish tribe that originally inhabited Caithness before the coming of the Vikings, and to them the earls were always known as the lords of the Catti (cat is the root meaning), the tribal designation from which Caithness ("peninsula of the Catti") takes its name. Hence the "wild-cat" crest of the Sutherland chiefs, similar to that of the nearby Clan Chattan (see Chapter VII), the Picto-Scottish Erainnian clan with whom they probably shared a Pictish connection. The earls fought for the Royal House of Bruce, and but for the death of the fifth earl's son by Margaret Bruce, heiress of the House of Bruce, it would have

been the Sutherlands and not the Stewarts who became kings of Scots. Nevertheless the earls of Sutherland rose to great power in the North, and exercised
something approaching royal authority in their earldom.

As for the *Murrays*, the main line acquired the Lordship of Bothwell by
marriage to an Oliphant heiress (the Oliphants descend from an Anglo-
Norman knight and friend of David I). These Bothwell Murrays were very important in the wars of the thirteenth and fourteenth centuries as patriots, but
the lordship of Bothwell passed away from the family in 1360 in the female line
(through an heiress) to the Douglases (the Douglases were essentially a
Lowland family of Flemish origin, although the power of the Red Douglases,
the chief branch of the family after 1455, was partly derived from the Stewart
earldom of Angus, which they inherited in the late fourteenth century: Afterwards Douglases appear holding lands and titles in the lowlands of Fife and
on lower Don-side and Dee-side in the northeast). By two "Bands of Association" in the late sixteenth century, however, the various Murray lairds from
all over Scotland (Sutherland and Moray, Perthshire, Stirlingshire, and the
Lowlands) recognized the Tullibardine branch (see Chapter IV) as chief and
pledged allegiance to Sir John Murray, first Earl of Tullibardine (the Tullibardine branch had been vested in the chiefly arms of Murray by the Lord Lyon
King of Arms in 1542). Among those signing one or the other of these Bands
were the Morays of Abercairney in Strathearn, Perthshire, and the Murrays
of Polmaise in Stirlingshire, both of whom nonetheless claim senior male-line
descent. Also in the Bands were the Murrays of Cockpool in Dumfriesshire,
the Murrays of Cobairdy in Buchan, and the Murrays of Falahill and
Blackbarony on the Borders.

The House of Tullibardine had originally been discouraged for aiding
Balliol in the early fourteenth century, but was raised to favor again as a result
of the Gowrie Conspiracy at the expense of the Ruthvens. The Murray earls
of Tullibardine soon inherited the Stewart earldom of Atholl in Perthshire,
and thus the Murray earls of Atholl, later dukes of the same, became leaders
of the various clans and baronial families of Atholl, who were now their feudal
tenants. This resulted in a unique mix of clanship and feudalism, placing clan
and family groups within a greater feudal context. After the fourteenth century fall of the House of Strathearn from their position as the native leaders
of the Perthshire region, the Stewart earls of Atholl in northern Perthshire had
gladly attempted to fill the void left by their demise. With the coming of the
South-Perthshire Tullibardine line to Atholl in the early seventeenth century
(and given their female-line connection to the House of Strathearn) there came
a jelling of a natural regional unity behind the Murray dukes of Atholl, who
led the Athollmen and the South-Perthshire gentry to a kind of regional na-
tionhood: Itself set between the regional spheres of the Gordons of Huntly in
the northeast, and the hostile Campbells of Argyle to the west.

The Barretts (Baroid—Cork, *Baireid*—Mayo) came to Ireland with the

Anglo-Norman invasion and settled as two families of the same Welsh stock, one of which, seated at Castle Barrett, became influential in central County Cork, where they were large landowners down to the year 1691. In that year the then head of the Cork family, Colonel John Barrett, was deprived of 12,000 acres for raising a regiment of infantry for King James' Irish army. The Cork Barretts had already suffered loss of land under earlier English encroachments, and originally had been proprietors of the whole of what is now the Barony of Barrett, formerly known as Barrett's Country.

The Mayo Barretts had settled in the northwest of that county, in the Barony of Tirawley, where they became numerous and powerful. They came to form a clan in the Gaelic fashion, the head of which was known as Mac Bhaitin Baireid (Mac Watten Barrett). There were two sub-clans of the Barretts, the *Clan Aindriu,* or *MacAndrews* settled between Lough Conn and the River Moy and the *Clan Toimin,* or *MacTimins.*

The *Blakes (de Blaca:* Norman-French *"le Blac")* are a Cambro-Norman family, that is, an Anglo-Norman family of Welsh origin. They came in the fourteenth century to form one of the Tribes of Galway, the wealthy mostly Norman merchant families of that city, their ancestor being Richard Caddell, alias le Blake, who was sheriff of Connacht in 1303. It was not until the seventeenth century that the surname Blake finally supplanted the original name, which was Caddell, and throughout their history in Galway the family is referred to as "Caddell, alias le Blake," or vice-versa. The Blakes were long prominent in Galway's government and ecclesiastical activity. The Blakes became extensive landowners in County Galway, and two of them were outstanding figures in the seventeenth century: Sir Richard Blake was chairman of the Assembly of Confederate Catholics at Kilkenny in 1647, and Francis Blake was on the Supreme Council. A branch of the Blakes settled in County Kildare, where their presence is reflected by the existence of three townlands called Blakestown.

The *Joyces (Seoigh)* are of Welsh origin, and came to Ireland in the wake of the Anglo-Norman invasion. The first of the family recorded in Ireland was Thomas de Joyce, who married the daughter of the O'Brien Prince of Thomond in 1283 and then took her by sea to Galway, where he settled in a wild mountainous tract on the Mayo border of the generally desolate region known as "Iar Connacht," which means west of Connacht. This territory became known as Joyce's Country (Duthaigh Seoghach), now the Barony of Ross in County Galway. Here they came to form a clan-group on the Gaelic model, and while initially under the overlordship of the O'Flahertys, they became a power in their own right, and were known as a race of very large men. Some of them became known as *Cunnagher.* A branch of the Joyces became established as one of the Tribes of Galway City (see above).

The *Clann Uighilin* or *MacQuillans (Mac Uighilin)* descend from a family of Welsh origin which came to Ireland soon after the Anglo-Norman invasion and settled in Antrim in the late twelfth century. Branches of this family, known then as the de Mandevilles, settled in Waterford and Tipperary where the name became *Mansfield* (another family of Anglo-Norman origin, the de Mandywells, became Mandevilles in Tipperary). The main line, having settled in the north of County Antrim, in the area known as the Route, became known as the MacQuillans, and very early became a completely Gaelicized sept on the native model, their chief being known as Lord of the Route. Their chief seat was at the castle of Dunluce. In 1315 their then chief joined Edward Bruce, and during that century they ranked as hereditary high constables of Ulster. Their predominant position in northeastern Ulster was further consolidated by their participation in the warlike actions of the Northern Ui Neill during the fifteenth century, and their chiefs were sometimes referred to as princes of Dal Riada. In 1541 Rory Og MacQuillan, the then chief declared that no "captain of his race" ever died in his bed.

The MacQuillans met with major defeats at the hands of the MacDonnells, after which their power was greatly reduced, and many of them were dispersed. The last Lord of the Route, a later Rory Og MacQuillan, partly recovered from the initial English confiscations in Ulster, and died in 1634. A Captain Rory MacQuillan was an officer in O'Neill's infantry in King James II's Irish Army in the late seventeenth century.

The Rices (Ris) are a Welsh family (called Rhys in Wales) that settled in the south of Ireland in the fourteenth century, and became influential merchants and landowners near Limerick City and near Dingle in County Kerry. They were prominent in the civic government of Limerick, Cork and Waterford, but suffered heavily under the Cromwellian confiscations of the mid-seventeenth century, especially in Kerry. Afterwards, several leading members of the family became famous as Wild Geese, that is, as Irish soldiers in Europe, and some of the Kerry branch settled in France and became successful bankers.

The Taaffes (Tath) were an important Cambro-Norman family, that is, they were one of the families of Welsh origin who joined in the Anglo-Norman invasion of the late twelfth century. Their ancestors settled in Louth in the late thirteenth century. They were prominent in the Pale, and later in the wars against the O'Neills, for which service they were granted wide tracts of confiscated land in Sligo. They later lost everything for their loyalty to the Stewarts. Other important Anglo-Norman families in Louth included the *Darditzes* (Dairdis) or *Dardeses* of Darditz-rath in Louth, and also the Catholic and pro–Irish *Teelings (Taoiling)* of counties Louth and Meath.

The Walshes (Breathnach) of southeastern Ireland mostly descend from Haylen Walsh, alias Brenach (both names mean "a welshman," Brenach is from the Gaelic), or from his uncle David: the former being the son of a Cambro-Norman invader of 1172 known as Philip the Welshman, the latter being Philip's brother. They settled in southwest Kilkenny, where the family gave its name to the Walsh Mountains. They spread also into Leix, Waterford and

Dublin. Castle Hayl or Hoel (Haylen's Castle) in Kilkenny was a stronghold. Many espoused the Irish cause beginning in the late sixteenth century, and as a result many lost their wide lands during the wars of the seventeenth century.

The Savages (Sabhaois) are an Anglo-Norman family originally planted in the Ards of County Down by Sir John de Courcy in 1177. They became completely Gaelicized from the fifteenth century onwards, and were prominent on the Irish side in the wars against Elizabeth. The Four Masters record the name as Mac an tSabhaisigh – "the son of The Savage." The Savages retained considerable property down to the revolution of 1689.

Finally, there were a number of families of Anglo-Norman genesis that formed important baronial houses in the border regions surrounding the Perthshire Highlands from the later middle ages onwards. The *Haldanes (or Haddens)* of Gleneagles in Perthshire descend from a cadet of the Anglo-Norman house of *Howden* or *Hauden* of that Ilk (the barony of Hadden or Halden) in Roxburghshire. This younger son married the heiress of the family of de Gleneagles in Perthshire, and thus became possessed of the estate of Gleneagles. They became representatives of this extinct family, and adopted their arms as their own. Aylmer de Haldane de Gleneagles rendered homage in 1296. The Haldanes of Gleneagles were barons of some consequence from that time onwards, into the seventeenth century, though the name is now rare in Perthshire. The quartering of Lennox and Menteith in their arms reflects the early fifteenth century marriage of John Haldane of Gleneagles to the eldest granddaughter of Margaret (wife of Robert Menteith of Rusky), one of the heiresses of the earldom of the Lennox in the late fourteenth century. David Hadden, tutor (laird) of Gleneagles is mentioned in 1614. The Haldanes of Lanrick, Stirlingshire, were cadets of Gleneagles.

The *Butters* or *Buttars* of Gormack (just east of Dunkeld) in Perthshire and later Pitlochry and Kinnaird (and later also Faskally) in Atholl appear as landowners in the area as early as 1331, when Adam Butir is on record, and in 1360 William Butyr and Patrick Butirr are mentioned as collectors of contributions in Gowrie (Perthshire). Their name apparently refers to the practice of archery, which is performed at the *butts*, that is, at the target range (the crest of the Butter arms is comprised of two hands holding a drawn bow and arrow). Between 1432 and 1444, Finlay and Patrick Butter served on inquests with other local lairds (landowners) such as Sir David Murray of Tullibardine and Malcolm Drummond of Stobhall, Patrick Rattray of that Ilk, Finlay Ramsay of Bamff and Malcolm Moncreiffe of that Ilk. The Butters were followers of the House of Atholl (see Murray).

The *Ramsays* are, according to tradition, originally from Huntingdonshire, where *Ramsey* (Latin: *de Rameseia*) is a name derived from a local place. The first of the name recorded in Scotland is Simund de Ramesie who witnessed a charter to the Abbey of Holyrood (Edinburgh) before 1175, and probably in the time period of about 1153 to 1165. Symone de Ramsay witnessed a charter by Gilbert, Earl of Strathearn before 1198, and William de Rameshej witnessed a charter by William the Lion before 1200. William de Ramessay appears as de Dalwussy (Dalhousie near Edinburgh) in about 1235, and Sir Alexander Ramsay of Dalhousie appears in 1342, (the family were later earls of Dalhousie). Michael de Ramesay was Sheriff of Fife in 1395. By the middle of the thirteenth century the Ramsays appear as landowners in Angus, dividing into several branches during the fourteenth century.

The Reids (Ruadh) of Colliston in Buchan and the Reid Barons of Strathloch are early fifteenth-century branches of the Ramsays, and probably descend from Patrick Reid (Red Patrick) Ramsay, who apparently married the heiress of Strathloch in Atholl, a granddaughter of the chief of the Robertson. The Strathloch family adhered to the Robertsons.

The Fothringhams of Powrie in Angus held large estates in that county, and had a cadet family, the Fotheringhams of Ballindean, seated in Perthshire. They descend from Henry de Fodringhay or Foddrynghame, deputy of the sheriff of Perth in 1358, who received the lands of Balewny, near Dundee, from Robert II before 1377. They take their name, originally Fotheringhay (Fotheringham is a corruption caused by the resemblance of the final "ay" to "m" in old records) from the manor and castle of Fotheringhay in Northamptonshire in England, owned in the twelfth century by the Royal House of Scotland. Prince David, before he became King David I in 1124 was closely associated with these estates, and that is why so many Anglo-Norman families in Scotland came from Northamptonshire. Hugh de Foderingeye of the County of Perth rendered homage in 1296. Walter de Fodringgeye was one of the executors of the will, in 1291, of Dervorgilla, wife of John Balliol, the competitor for the Scottish Crown, and was later associated with the son, Edward Balliol, with whom he came north in the latter Balliol's invasion of Scotland in 1332.

The Stirlings of Keir appear about 1160, and branches of the family came to hold wide lands north of the town of Stirling and around Cadder in Stirlingshire. They take their name from the town of Stirling. Gilbertus de Striuelin and Walter de Striveling were witnesses for King David in 1136, while Peter de Striuelin appears as a witness to a gift to the Abbey of Hollyrood in Edinburgh in 1158. Sir John Stirling of Moray swore fealty in 1291, and was probably the ancestor of the Stirlings of Edzell, whose large highland district of Glenesk in North Angus passed through an heiress to the Lindsays. King James III was probably killed by Stirling of Keir after the battle of Sauchieburn, after he had burned Stirling of Keir's tower (castle-house) a few days before. A branch of the family settled early in Nairnshire.

Appendix I

The Coats of Arms

Regarding the armorial shields listed in this appendix,, these are arms that had ancient and tribal significance, as opposed to arms that were later assumed by an individual as a part, for instance, of a nonhereditary British knighthood. The symbols used are often highly significant within the tribal-dynastic sphere, in a uniquely Gaelic way. Some common abbreviations are: ar. = argent, az. = azure, betw. = between, gu. = gules, quart. = quarterly, sa. = sable, 1 & 4 = first and fourth, and 2 & 3 = second and third. Sources are listed in the bibliography.

Abernethy Or, a lion rampant gu. surmounted of a ribbon sa.
Arthur Gu. a chevron between three rests (or Clarions) or.
Barrett Barry of ten per pale ar. and gu. counterchanged.
Barry Ar. three bars gemels gules.
Bisset Az. a bend ar.
Blake Ar. a fret gu.
Brodie Ar. a chevron gu. between three mullets az.
Browne Or an eagle displayed with two heads sa.
Buchan Ar. three lions' heads erased sa.
Buchanan Or, a lion rampant sa., armed and langued gu. within a double tressure flory-counter-flory of the second.
Burke Or a cross gu., in the dexter canton a lion rampant sa.
Butler Quart.: 1 & 4, Or a chief indented az., 2 & 3, Gu. 3 covered cups or.
Butter Ar. a cross sa. between four human hearts proper (Gormack).
Callendar Sa. a bend between six billets or.
Cameron Gu., three bars or.
Campbell Quart., 1 & 4, Gyrony of eight, or and sa., 2, Ar. a lymphad, sails furled sa., 3, or, a fess chequy azure and ar. (Glenorchy branch).
Campbell Gyrony of eight, ermine and gu. (Loudoun branch).
Campbell Quart., 1, or, a hart's head cabossed sa., attired gu., 2, Gyrony of eight, or & sa., 3, ar. a galley, 4, per fess az. & gu. a cross or. (Cawdor).
Campbell Quart., 1 & 4, Gyrony of eight, or & sa.; 2 & 3, Ar., a galley, sails furled sa., flag & pennons gu. (Lochow).
Chisholm Gu., a boar's head, couped or.
Colquhoun Ar., a saltire engrailed sa.

Condon Ar. a lion rampant gu. langued and armed az.

Creagh Ar. a chevron gu. between three laurel branches vert, on a chief az. as many bezants.

Cumming Az. three garbs or.

Cusack Per pale or and az., a fess counterchanged.

Dalton Az. a lion rampant guardant ar. charged on the shoulder with a crescent sa. between five fleurs-de-lis or.

Darcy Az. semee of crosses crosslet and three cinquefoils ar.

Dardes, Darditz Ermine a fess sa.

Davidson Quart., 1 & 4, Ar., on a fess az., between a dexter hand couped accompanied by two pheons in chief and a pheon in base, gu., a buck lodged or, 2 & 3, Az., a wolf's head erased or, armed and langued gu.

de Courcy Ar. three eagles displayed gu. ducally crowned or.

Dillon Ar., a lion passant between three crescents gu.

Drummond Or, three bars wavy gu.

Dunbar Gu. a lion rampant ar. within a bordure of the second charged with eight roses of the first.

Dundas Ar. a lion rampant gu.

Durie Az. a chevron between three crescents ar.

Erskine Azure a bend between six cross crosslets fitchee (mar).

Fagan Per chevron gu. and ermine, in chief three covered cups or.

Farquharson Quart., 1 & 4, Or, a lion rampant gu., armed and langued az., 2 & 3, Ar., a fir tree growing out of Mount in base fructed proper, on a chief gu., the Royal standard of Scotland is displayed bendwise on a canton of the field, a hand issuing from the sinister side holding a dagger also proper, point downwards.

Ferguson Az., a round buckle ar. traversed by a baton of the second tipped sa., between three boars' heads erased or, langued gu.

Fitzgerald Ar. a saltire gu.

Fitzgibbon Ermine a saltire gu., on a chief ar., three annulets of the second.

Fitzpatrick Sa., a saltire ar., on a chief az. three fleur-de-lis or.

Fleming Vair a chief chequy or and gu.

Forbes Az., three bears' heads couped ar., muzzled gu.

Fothringham Ermine, three bars gu.

Fox Ar. a lion rampant and in chief two dexter hands couped at the wrist gu.

Fraser Quart., 1 & 4, Az., three fraises ar., 2 & 3, Ar., three antique crowns gu.

French Ermine a chevron sa.

Galbraith Gu. three bears' heads erased ar. muzzled az.

Gordon Quart., 1, Az., three boars' heads couped or, 2, Or, three lions' heads erased gu., 3, Or, three crescents within a double tressure flory-counter-flory gu., 4, Az., three fraises ar.

Graham Quart., 1 & 4, Or, on a chief sa. three escallops of the first. 2 & 3, Or, fess chequy azure and argent, in a chief a chevron gu. (Menteith).

Graham Quart., 1 & 4, Or, on a chief sa. three escallops of the first. 2 & 3, Ar., three roses gu. (Montrose branch).

Grant Gu., three Eastern or antique crowns or.

Gunn Ar. a galley of three masts, her sails furled and oars in action sable flags gu. within a bordure az. on a chief of the third a bear's head of the first, muzzled of the second between two mullets of the field.

Hackett Az. three hake fishes haurient in fess ar., on a chief of the second three shamrocks proper.

Haldane Quart., 1 & 4, ar. a saltire engrailed sa., 2, LENNOX; 3, MENTEITH.

Hamilton Quart., 1 & 4, gu. three cinquefoils pierced ermine, 2 & 3, Ar., a ship with sails furled and oars sa.

Hay Ar., three escutcheons, gu.

Innes Ar., three stars az.

Jordan Ar. a fess sa., in base a lion passant of the last.

Joyce Ar. an eagle with two heads displayed gu., over all a fess ermine.

Kavanagh Ar. a lion passant gu., in base two crescents of the last.

Keating Ar. a saltire gu. between four nettle leaves vert.

Keith Ar. on a chief gu. three palets or.

Kinnaird Gu. a saltire between four crescents or.

Kinsella Ar. a fess gu. between in chief two garbs of the last and in base a lion passant sa.

Lacy Or a lion rampant purpure.

Lamont Az., a lion rampant ar.

Lennox Ar. a saltire gu. between four roses of the last, barbed vert.

Leslie Quart., 1 & 4, Ar. on a bend az. three buckles or, 2 & 3, Or, a lion rampant gu. debruised with a ribbon sa.

Lindsay Quart., 1 & 4, Gu., a fess chequy ar. and az., 2 & 3, Or, a lion rampant gu. debruised with a ribbon sa.

Livingston ar. three cinquefoils (or gullyflowers) gu. within a double tresure flory counterflory vert (Linlithgow).

Livingston Ar. on a bend between three gullyfllowers gu. an anchor of the first, a double tresure flory counterflory vert (Kinnaird).

Logie Ar. two chevronells sa. between three roses gu.

Lynch Az. a chevron between three trefoils slipt or.

Lyon Ar. a lion rampant az. armed and langued, within a double tresure flory counterflory gu.

MacAlister Or, an eagle displayed gu., armed sa.; on its breast a galley, sails furled, oars in action of the last, all within a bordure of the third charged with three crosscrosslets fitchy ar.

MacArthur Az., a cross moline ar. between three antique or Eastern crowns Or.

MacAulay Gu., two arrows in saltire ar. surmounted by a fess chequy of the first and second, between three buckles or, within a bordure indented or.

MacAuliffe Ar. three mermaids with combs and mirrors in fess az. between as many mullets of the last.

MacAwley Ar. a lion rampant gu. armed and langued az. in chief two dexter hands couped at the wrist of the second.

MacBain Quart., 1, Or, a lion rampant gu., 2, Ar., a dexture hand couped in pale gu., 3, Ar., a sword in pale proper, 4, A lymphad az. sails furled proper, oars in saltire gu. and flagged of the last.

MacBrady Sa., in the sinister base a dexter hand couped at the wrist proper pointing with index finger to the sun in splendour in dexter chief or.

MacCabe Vert a fess wavy between three salmon naiant argent.

MacCann Az. fretty or, on a fess argent a boar passant gu.

MacCaron Ar. a lion rampant and in chief two dexter hands couped at the wrist gu.

MacCartan Vert a lion rampant or, on a chief ar. a crescent between two dexter hands couped at the wrist gu.

MacCarthy Ar. A stag trippant gu. attired and unguled or.

MacClancy Ar. two lions passant guardant in pale gu.

MacCoghlan Ar. three lions passant guardant gu. crowned or.

MacColgan Az. a lion rampant or between three pheons points down ar.

MacConsidine Per pale sa. and gu., three lions passant guardant in pale per pale or and ar., armed azure.

MacCorquodale Ar. a demi-stag gu. naissant out of a fesse tortile of the second and first.

MacCostello Or three fusils az.

MacCotter Az. three evetts in pale proper.

MacCurtin Vert in front of a lance in pale or a stag trippant ar. attired or between three crosses crosslet or, two and one, and as many trefoils slipt ar. one and two.

MacDermot Ar. on a chevron gu. between three boars' heads erased az. tusked and bristled or as many cross crosslets of the last.

MacDonald Quart., 1, Ar., a lion rampant gu., armed or, 2, Or, a dexter hand couped fesswise, holding a cross crosslet fitchy gu., 3, Or, a lymphad or galley, oars in saltire sa., and in base a salmon naiant proper, in sea vert., 4, Ar., an oak tree surmounted by an eagle displayed or (Clanranald).

MacDonald Or, an eagle displayed gu. surmounted of a galley sails furled and oars in action sa. (Macdonald of Macdonald).

MacDonald Quart., 1, Ar., a lion rampant gu., 2, Or, a hand in armour holding a cross crosslet fitchy gu., 3, Ar., a row galley (or lymphad), the sails furled sa., 4, Vert, a salmon naiant in fess proper (Sleate).

MacDonell Or, an eagle displayed gu., surmounted by a galley (biorlin) sa., sails furled, in dexter chief a hand couped of the second; sinister a cross crosslet fitchy of the third (Glengarry branch).

MacDonell Or, a lion rampant gu., a canton, ar., charged with a dexter hand couped fessways proper holding a cross crosslet fitchy of the second (Keppoch branch).

MacDonlevy Ar. on a mount in base proper a lion gu. and a buck of the second rampant combatant supporting a dexter hand couped at the wrist of the third.

MacDonnell Az. an ancient galley sails set and flags flying ar. between in chief a cross calvary in three grieces or, between in the dexter an increscent of the second and in the sinister a dexter hand couped at the wrist appaumee proper and in base a salmon naiant of the second (Clare).

MacDonnell Quart., 1, Or a lion rampant gu., 2, Or, a dexter arm issuant from the sinister fess point out of a cloud proper, in the hand a cross crosslet fitchee erect az., 3, Ar. a lymphad sails furled sa., 4, Per fess az. and vert a dolphin naiant proper (of the Glens).

MacDonogh Per chevron invected or and vert, in chief two lions passant guardant gu. in base a boar passant ar. armed and bristled of the first langued of the third.

MacDougal Quart., 1 and 4, Az., a lion rampant ar., 2 & 3, Or, a lymphad (or galley) sa., with a beacon on the topmast proper.

MacDuff Or, a lion rampant gu.

MacEachern A shield gyronny of eight or and sa. suspended from the mast of a lymphad sa.

MacEnery Ar. an eagle displayed vert.

MacEvoy Per fess az. and per pale or and ermine a fess gu. issuant therefrom a demi-lion ar., in the dexter base a dexter hand couped at the wrist of the fourth.

MacFarlane Ar., a saltire waved and cantoned with four roses gu.

MacFie Per fess nebuly az., and or, in chief a two-handed sword ar. hilted and pommelled of the second, & in base a lymphad sa., under sail of the third.

MacGarry, Garrighy Ar. a lion rampant between four trefoils slipt vert, in chief a lizard passant vert.

MacGenis Vert a lion rampant or, on a chief ar. a dexter hand erect couped at the wrist gu.

MacGeoghegan Ar. a lion rampant between three dexter hands couped at the wrist gu.

MacGeraghty Ar. on a mount vert an oak tree proper, in chief two falcons volant gu.

MacGilfoyle Az. two bars ar.

MacGillivray Quart., 1, Or, a cat-a-mountain sejant guardant proper, his dexter fore-paw on the ground his sinister fore-paw in a guardant posture & his tail reflexed under his sinister paw, 2, Ar. a dexter hand couped at the wrist apaumy gu., 3, Az., a salmon naiant Ar., 4, Or, a galley sailing sinister-wise Az., its oars in saltire & flagged gu.

MacGillycuddy Gu. a wyvern or.

MacGorman Az. a lion passant between three swords erect ar.

MacGovern Az. a lion passant or, in chief three crescents of the last.

MacGrath Quart., 1, Ar. three lions passant gu., 2, Or, a dexter hand lying fessways couped at the wrist proper holding a cross formee fitchee az., 3, Gu. a dexter hand lying fessways couped at the wrist proper holding a battle-axe or, 4, Ar. an antelope trippant sa. attired ar.

MacGregor Ar., an oak tree eradicated in bent sinister proper, surmounted by a sword az., hilted and pommelled or, in bend supporting on its point, in the dexter canton, an antique crown gu.

MacHugh Ar. a saltire vert between a dexter hand couped at the wrist in chief gu., two trefoils slipt of the second in fess and a boat with oars proper in base (Galway).

MacHugh Vert a lion rampant or, in chief a fleur-de-lis between two annulets ar. (Munster).

MacIan Or, a galley, sails furled, oars in action sa., between, in fess, dexter, an eagle displayed gu., and sinister, a buckle of the last (Ardmamurchan).

MacInerney Ar. three lions passant in pale gu. armed and langued az (Clare).

MacInnes Quart., 1, Az. a castle of two towers or windows and port gu.; 2 & 3, Or on a sea in base undy az. ar. a lymphad vert flag and five visible oars gu., 4, gyronny of eight sa. and or; over all a cross vert charged with a mill-rhind between four pheons ar. accompanied by two cross crosslets in the flanks and as many cross crosslets fitche, all of the last, in chief and base of the said cross.

MacIntyre Quart., 1 and 4, Or, an eagle displayed gu. armed and langued sa., 2, ar. a galley, her sails furled sa. flags gu.; 3, ar. a sinister hand couped fess-ways, gu. holding a cross crosslet fitche sa.

MacIvor Quart., 1st, gyronny of eight or and sa.; 2nd, ar. a dexter hand couped fesseways, grasping a dagger in pale gu.; 3rd, ar. a galley, her sails furled and oars in action sa.; 4th, quart. or and gu. a bend sa.

MacKay Az., on a chevron between three bears' heads couped ar. and muzzled gu., a roebuck's head erased, between two hands holding daggers, all proper.

MacKenna, Kenny Vert a fess ar. between three lions' heads affrontee or.

MacKenzie Az., a stag's head cabossed or.

MacKeogh Ar. a lion rampant gu., in the dexter chief a dexter hand couped at the wrist and in the sinister a crescent both of the second (Connacht).

MacKeown Ar. two lions rampant combatant sa. supporting a dexter hand couped at the wrist gu., in chief four mullets of eight points gu., in base waves of the sea therein a salmon naiant all proper.

MacKinnon 1, Vert, a boar's head erased ar., holding in its mouth the shankbone of a deer proper, 2, Az., a castle triple-towered and embattled ar., masoned sa., windows and portcullis gu., 3, Or. a lymphad, sails furled, the oars saltirewise sa., flags flying gu., 4, Ar., a dexter hand couped fess-wise, holding a cross crosslet fitchy sa.

MacKintosh Quart., 1, Or, a lion rampant gu., 2, Argent, a dexter hand couped fesswise, grasping a man's heart proper, 3, Az., a boar's head couped or, 4, Or, a lymphad az., oars erect in saltire gu.

MacLachlan Quart., 1, Or, a lion rampant gu., 2, Ar., a dexter hand couped in fess, holding a crosslet patte in pale gu., 3, Or, a galley, oars in saltire sa. in a sea proper, 4, Ar., in base in the sea undy, vert a salmon naiant proper.

MacLaine Quart., 1, Ar., a lion rampant gu., 2, Az., a tower ar., 3, Or, a dexter hand couped in fess gu., holding a cross crosslet fitchy az., 4, Or, a lymphad proper, in base vert a salmon naiant proper.

MacLaren, Laurin Or two chevronnells gu., a lymphad sails furled sa. in base.

MacLean Quart., 1, Ar., a rock gu., 2, Ar., a dexter hand couped fesswise gu., holding a crosslet fitchy in pale az., 3, Or, a lymphad, oars in saltire, sails furled sa., flagged gu., 4, Ar., a salmon naiant proper, and in chief two eagles' heads erased respectant gu.

MacLeish Or two chevrons gu. a canton sa.

MacLeod Quart., 1 & 4, Az., a castle triple-towered and embattled ar., masoned sa., windows and porch gu., 2 & 3, gu., three legs armed, conjoined, and flexed at the knees ar. (Harris branch).

MacLeod Or, a burning mountain proper, in the dexter and sinister chief points two crosses patte fitchy gu. (Lewis branch).

MacLoughlin Per fess az. and gu., in chief a lion rampant or between two swords erect ar. pommels and hilts or, in base three crescents ar. (Tirconnell).

MacLoughlin Per fess, the chief two coats, 1, Ar. three dexter hands couped at the wrist gu., 2, Ar. a lion rampant gu. armed and langued az., the base wavy az. and ar. a salmon naiant proper (Meath).

MacLysaght Ar. three spears erect in fess gu., on a chief az. a lion passant guardant or.

MacMahon Ar. an ostrich sa. holding in the beak a horse shoe or (Oriel).

MacMahon Ar. three lions passant reguardant in pale gu. armed and langued az. (Thomond).

MacManus Vert a griffin sergreant or, in chief three crescents ar.

MacMillan Or, a lion rampant sa., in chief three mullets azure.

MacNab Sa., on a chevron ar., three crescents vert, in base an open boat with oars ar., sailing in a sea proper.

MacNally Gu. an arm in armour proper garnished or and embowed couped at the shoulder holding in the hand a battle-axe of the second between six martlets ar. three and three palewise, in the centre chief point an ancient Irish crown or.

MacNamara Gu. a lion rampant ar., in chief two spearheads or.

MacNaughton Quart., 1 & 4, Ar., a hand fesswise proper, holding a cross crosslet fitchy az., 2 & 3, Ar., a castle embattled gu.

MacNeil Quart., 1, Vert, a lion rampant or, 2, Ar., in base the sea, with a castle issuant therefrom proper, 3, Or, a lymphad, sails furled sa., 4, Or, a dexter hand palewise couped gu., within an orle of nine fetterlocks (Barra).

MacNeil Quart., 1 & 4, Az., a lion rampant, armed and langued gules, 2, Ar., a sinister hand couped fessways in chief gu., in base wavy, az., a salmon naiant ar., 3, Or, a galley, oars in saltire gu., on a chief gu., three mullets or (Gigha).

MacPherson Party per fess or and az., a lymphad of the first flagged gu. sails furled, oars in action proper, in the dexter chief point a dexter hand couped fesswise grasping a dagger erect palewise gu., and in the sinister a cross crosslet fitche gu.

MacQuarrie Quart., 1 & 4, vert three towers embattled in chief ar., 2 & 3, ar. 3 ar. three cross crosslet fitchee.

MacQueen Ar. three wolves' heads couped sa.

MacQuillan Gu. a wolf rampant ar., a chief or.

MacRae Ar., a fess az., between three mullets in chief and a lion rampant in base gu.

MacRannall Vert a lion rampant between three escallops or.

MacShanly Az., a lion passant or, in chief three estoiles of the last.

MacSheehy Quart., 1, Az. a lion passant guardant ar., 2, Ar. three lizards vert, 3, Az. three pole-axes in fess or, 4, Ar., a ship with three masts sa.

MacSweeney Or on a fess vert between three boars passant sa. a lizard argent.

MacTernan, Tiernan Ermine two lions passant gu.

Maguire Vert a white horse fully caparisoned thereon a knight in complete armour on his helmet a plume of ostrich feathers his right hand brandishing a sword all proper.

Malcolm Ar. on a saltire az. between four stags' heads erased gu., five mullets or.

Martin Az. a cross calvary on three grieces ar., the dexter arm terminating in a sun in splendour or, the sinister in a decrescent ar.

Matheson Gyronny of eight sable and gules, a lion rampant or, armed & langued az.

Mentieth Or, a bend chequy az. and sa. (Stewart branch).

Menzies Ar., a chief gu.

Moncreiffe Ar. a lion rampant gu. a chief ermine.

Moray Quart., 1 & 4, az. three stars ar. within a double tressure fllory counter-flory or; 2 & 3, or, two chevronells gu., for STRATHEARN.

Morris Or a fess dancettee, in base a lion rampant sa.

Morrison Per bend sinister Gules and Ar., a demi-lion rampant issuant Or, armed and langued Az., holding in his paws a battle-axe, the shaft curved, of the Third, axe-head of the Fourth in chief, in base, issuing from the sea undy, Vert and Or, a tower sa., windows and port Or, over all a bend sinister embattled Az., charged with an open crown Or, jewelled gu., between two fleurs-de-lys Argent.

Munro Or, an eagle's head erased gules.

Murray Az., three mullets ar., within a double tressure flory.

Nagle Ermine on a fess az. three lozenges or.

Napier Ar. a saltire engrailed between four roses gu. barbed vert.

Nugent Ermine two bars gu.

O'Aherne Vert, three herons ar.

O'Beirne Ar. an orange tree eradicated and fructed proper, in base a lizard vert, in the dexter base point a saltire couped gu. on a chief az. the sun in his splendour or and a crescent of the first.

O'Boylan Ar. an eagle displayed sa. armed or.

O'Boyle Or an oaktree eradicated vert.

O'Branagan Per pale gu. and ar. a sinister hand erased at the wrist between three crosses moline counterchanged.

O'Brennan Ar. a lion rampant az., in chief two dexter hands couped at the wrist apaumee gu. (Connacht).

O'Brennan Gu. two lions rampant combatant supporting a garb all or, in chief three swords two in saltire points upwards and one in fess point to the dexter, pommels and hilts of the second (Ossory).

O'Brien Gu., three lions passant guardant in pale per pale or and ar.

O'Byrne Gu. a chevron between three dexter hand couped at the wrist ar.

O'Cahan Az. on a fess per pale gu. and ar. between in chief out of the horns of a crescent, a dexter hand couped at the wrist and apaumee, surmounted by an estoile between on the dexter a horse counter-saliant, and on the sinister a lion rampant each also surmounted by an estoile, and in base a salmon naiant all ar. on the dexter side three lizards passant bend sinisterways gu. and on the dexter an oak tree eradicated vert, over all an escutcheon ar. charged with a cross calvary on three grieces proper.

O'Cahill Ar. a whale spouting in the sea proper.

O'Callaghan Ar. in base a mount vert on the dexter side a hurst of oak trees issuant therefrom a wolf passant towards the sinister all proper.

O'Carroll Sa. two lions rampant combatant or armed and langued gu. supporting a sword point upwards proper pommel and hilt or.

O'Carry Az. a lion passant guardant or.

O'Casey Ar. a chevron between three eagles heads erased gu.

O'Cassidy Per chevron ar. and gu., in chief two lions rampant and in base a boar passant both counterchanged.

O'Cleary Or three nettle leaves vert.

O'Coffey Vert a fess ermine between three Irish cups or.

O'Concannon Ar. on a mount in base proper an oak tree vert, perched on the top thereof a falcon proper, two cross crosslets fitchy in fess az.

O'Connell Per fess ar. and vert a stag trippant proper between three trefoils slipped counterchanged.

O'Connor Vert a lion rampant double queued and crowned or (Kerry).

O'Connor Ar. on a mount in base an oak tree all proper (Keenaght).

O'Connor Vert a stag trippant ar (Corcomroe).

O'Connor Per pale vert and ar., in the dexter a lion rampant to the sinister or, in the sinister on a mount in base vert an oak tree proper (Sligo).

O'Connor Ar. on a mount in base vert an oak tree acorned proper (Faly).

O'Connor Erm. an oak tree eradicated and acorned proper (Roe).

O'Connor Ar. an oak tree vert (Don).

O'Conrahy Quart., 1, Vert three goats passant ar., 2, Ar. a lion rampant gu., 3, Gu. three escallops ar., 4, Vert a cock statant proper.

O'Cornyn Per fess ar. and ermine a fess gu. in chief a demi lion rampant sa.

O'Corrigan or a chevron between two trefoils slipt in chief and in base a lizard passant vert.

O'Crean, Creghan Ar. a wolf ramant sa. between three human hearts gu.

O'Crowley Ar. a boar passant az. between three crosses crosslet gu.

O'Cullane Ar. two lions rampant combatant proper.

O'Cullen Gu. on a chevron between three dexter hands erect couped at the wrist ar. a garb of the first between two trefoils slipt vert.

O'Cullinan Ar. a stag springing gu. attired and unguled vert, in base a dexter hand appaumee couped at the wrist proper.

O'Daly Per fess ar. and or a lion rampant per fess sa. and gu., in chief two dexter hands couped at the wrist of the last.

O'Davoren Ar. a sword erect in pale distilling drops of blood proper pommel and hilt or.

O'Dea Ar. a dexter hand lying fessways couped at the wrist cuffed indented az. holding a sword in pale all proper, in chief two snakes embowed vert.

O'Dempsey Gu. a lion rampant ar., armed and langued az. between two swords points upwards of the second pommels and hilts or one in bend dexter the other in bend sinister.

O'Dinneen, Denning Az. two swords in saltire points upwards ar. pommels and hilts or between four roses or.

O'Doherty Ar. a stag springing gu. on a chief vert three mullets of the first.

O'Donegan Ar. three ermine spots in pale sa. between four lions rampant, those in dexter chief and sinister base gu., and those in sinister chief and dexter base of the second.

O'Donnell Or issuing from the sinister side of the shield an arm fessways vested az. cuffed ar. holding in the hand proper a passion cross gu.

O'Donnellan Ar. an oak tree eradicated proper, on the sinister side a slave sa. chained to the stem gu.

O'Donnelly Ar. two lions rampant combatant supporting a dexter hand couped at the wrist apaumee gu., in base the sea therein a salmon naiant proper.

O'Donoghue Vert two foxes rampant combatant ar., on a chief of the last an eagle volant sa.

O'Donovan Ar. issuing from the sinister side of the shield a cubit dexter arm vested gu. cuffed of the first the hand grasping a scian in pale the blade entwined with a serpent all proper.

O'Doran per pale sa. and ar. a boar passant counterchanged, on a chief az. three mullets of the second.

O'Dowd Vert a saltire or, in chief two swords in saltire points upwards the dexter surmounted of the sinister ar. pommels and hilt or.

O'Dowling Ar. a holly tree eradicated proper, on a chief az., a lion passant between two trefoils slipt or.

O'Doyle Ar. three bucks' heads erased gu. attired or, within a border compony or and az.

O'Driscoll Ar. an ancient galley sails furled sa.

O'Duany, Devany Ermine a fox passant sa., in chief two crescents of the last.

O'Dugenan Ar. on a mount in base vert an oak tree, the stem entwined with two serpents interwoven and erect respecting each other all proper.

O'Dunne Az. an eagle displayed or.

O'Dwyer Ar. a lion rampant gu. between three ermine spots.

O'Fahy Az. a hand couped at the wrist fessways in chief proper holding a sword paleways argent pommel and hilt or point downwards pierced through a boar's head erased of the last.

O'Fallon Gu. a greyhound rampant ar. holding between the forepaws a tilting spear point to the dexter or.

O'Farrell Vert a lion rampant or.

O'Finnegan Gu. two lions rampant combatant ar. supporting a sword in pale blade wavy point upwards proper.

O'Flaherty Ar. two lions rampant combatant supporting a dexter hand couped at the wrist all gu., in base a boat with eight oars sa.

O'Flanagan Ar. out of a mount in base vert an oak tree proper, a border of the second (Roscommon).

O'Flynn Az. a wolf passant ar., in chief three bezants.

O'Fogarty Az. two lions rampant combatant supporting a garb all or, in dexter base a crescent ar., in sinister base a harp of the second stringed of the third.

O'Friel Gu. in dexter fess a garb or, in sinister fess a dexter hand couped at the wrist fessways proper grasping a cross calvary on three grieces ar., in chief three mullets of the second.

O'Gallagher Ar. a lion rampant sa. treading on a serpent in fess proper between eight trefoils vert.

O'Galvin, Gallivan Gu. three salmon haurient ar.

O'Gara Ar. three lions rampant az., on a chief gu. a demi-lion rampant or.

O'Gormley Or, three martlets gu., two and one.

O'Grady Per pale gu. and sa. three lions passant per pale ar. and or.

O'Griffey Sa. a griffin segreant or, langued and armed gu.

O'Hagan Quart., ar. and az., in 1, a shoe proper, on a canton per chevron gu. and ermine three covered cups or, in 2, a flag of the first charged with a dexter hand of fourth, 3, a lion rampant of the sixth, and 4, a fish naiant proper.

O'Halloran Gu. a horse passant ar. saddled and bridled proper, on a chief of the second three martlets az.

O'Hanlon Vert. on a mount in base proper a boar passant ermine.

O'Hanly Vert a boar passant ar. armed hoofed and bristled or, between two arrows barways of the second headed of the third, that in chief pointing to the dexter and that in base to the sinister.

O'Hanraghty Az. a griffin passant wings elevated or.

O'Hanrahan Gu. a lizard passant in fess or, in chief a trefoil slipped between two holly leaves ar. in base a garb of the second.

O'Hara Vert on a pale radiant or a lion rampart sa.

O'Hart Gu. a lion passant guardant or, in base a human heart ar.

O'Hartagan Az. a lion rampant or holding in each forepaw a dagger ar. pommels and hilts of the second.

O'Hea Ar. a dexter arm lying fessways couped below the elbow vested gu. turned up of the first grasping in the hand a sword in pale entwined with a serpent descending all proper.

O'Heffernan Per fess vert and gu., on a fess or a lion passant guardant az., in chief three crescents or.

O'Hegarty Ar. an oaktree eradicated proper, on a chief gu. three birds of the first beaked and legged sa.

O'Hennessy Gu. a boar passant proper (Clare-Cork).

O'Hennessy Vert a stag trippant ar. between six arrows, two, two, and two saltireways or (Offaly).

O'Heyne Per pale indented or and gu. two lions rampant combatant counterchanged.

O'Hickey Az. a lion passant guardant or, on a chief ermine a bend sa.

O'Higgin, Higgins Ar. guttee de poix on a fess sa. three towers of the first.

O'Horan Vert three lions rampant two and one or.

O'Houlihan Az. a tower or supported by two lions rampant argent, in base two crescents of the last, on a chief of the third three annulets gules.

O'Kearney Ar. three lions rampant gu., on a chief az. between two pheons of the first a gauntletted hand fessways or holding a dagger erect proper pommel and hilt or.

O'Keeffe Vert a lion rampant or, in chief two dexter hands couped at the wrist erect and apaumee of the last.

O'Keevan Vert a saltire or, between in chief and in base a lizard passant of the last, and in fess two daggers erect ar. pommels and hilts gold.

O'Kelly Az. a tower triple-towered supported by two lions rampant ar., as many chains descending from the battlements between the lion's legs or.

O'Kennedy Sa. three helmets in profile proper.

O'Kiernan Vert on a chevron ar. three leopards' faces gu.

O'Kinneally Gu. a stag statant ar.

O'Laylor Or a lion rampant guardant gu.

O'Lanigan Az. on a palet ar. between two lions rampant regarding each other or, each between three fleurs-de-lis, two and one, of the second, three trefoils in pale vert.

O'Leary Ar. a lion passant in base gu., in chief a ship of three masts sa. sails set proper from the stern the flag of St. George flotant

O'Lee Ar. an oak tree eradicated proper on a fess wavy az. a fox's head erased of the first between two fish naiant or.

O'Lonergan Ar. on a chevron az. three estoiles or, in chief two arrows in saltire points downwards gu.

O'Loughlin Gu. a man in complete armour facing the sinister shooting an arrow from a bow all proper.

O'Lynch Ar. a cross sa. between four lions rampant gu. armed and langued az.

O'Lynn Quart., ar. and gu. four dexter hands couped at the wrist counterchanged (branch of O'Lynn).

O'Lynn Per fess ar. and gu. a sword in pale between two dexter hands couped at the wrist, one in chief the other in base counterchanged (branch).

O'Madden Sa. a falcon volant seizing a mallard ar.

O'Maher Az. two lions rampant combatant or, supporting a sword ar. pommel and hilt of the second, in base two crescents of the third.

O'Mahony Quart., 1 & 4, Or a lion rampant az., 2, per pale ar. and gu. a lion rampant counterchanged, 3, Ar. a chevron gu. between three snakes tongued proper.

O'Malley Or a boar passant gu.

O'Malone Vert a lion rampant or between three mullets ar.

O'Mannin Gu. three crescents ar. a border ermaine (or ar.).

O'Meara Gu. three lions passant guardant in pale per pale or and ar., a border az. charged with eight escallops ar.

O'Meehan Gu. on a chevron ar. three bucks' heads erased of the field attired or, in base a demi-lion rampant ar.

O'Moledy Vert a lion rampant double queued and crowned or, between three close helmets in profile ar.

O'Molloy Ar. a lion rampant sa. between three trefoils slipt gu.

O'Molony Az., on the dexter side a quiver of three arrows, on the sinister a bow erect all or.

O'Monahan Az. a chevron between three mullets or.

O'Mooney Ar. a holly tree eradicated vert thereon a lizard passant or, a border compony counter compony of the first and second.

O'Morchoe Ar. an apple tree eradicated fructed proper, on a chief vert a lion passant or.

O'More Vert a lion rampant or, in chief three mullets of the last.

O'Moriarty Ar. an eagle displayed sa.

O'Moroney Az. a chevron or between three boars' heads couped ar. langued gu.

O'Mulconry Az. a ancient book open indexed edged or, a chief embattled of the last.

O'Mullally, Lally Ar. three eagles displayed gu. two and one each holding in the beak a sprig of laurel proper between as many crescents, one and two, az.

O'Mullen Ar. a dexter hand couped at the wrist in fess gu. holding a dagger in pale proper between three crescents gu.

O'Mulroony Ar. a dexter hand couped at the wrist and erect gu. a border az. charged in the dexter chief with an open book proper.

O'Mulryan Gu. three griffins' heads erased ar.

O'Mulvihil Per fess ar. and gu., in chief two lions rampant combatant az. supporting a dexter hand couped at the wrist gu. and in base a salmon naiant proper, in base an Irish harp or stringed ar. between two battle-axes proper.

O'Murphy Quart., ar. and gu., on a fess sa. between four lions rampant counterchanged three garbs or.

O'Naghten Quart., 1 & 4, Gu. three falcons close proper, 2 & 3, Vert three swords ar. pommels and hilts or, one in pale point downwards the others in saltire points upwards.

O'Neill Ar. two lions rampant combatant gu. supporting a dexter hand couped at the wrist of the last, in chief three estoiles of the second, in base waves of the sea therein naiant a salmon all proper.

O'Neill Per fess wavy the chief ar. the base representing waves of the sea, in chief a dexter hand couped at the wrist gu. in base a salmon naiant proper (Claneboy).

O'Nolan, Knowlan Ar. on a cross gu. a lion passant between four martlets of the first, in each quarter a sword erect of the second.

O'Phelan Ar. four lozenges in bend conjoined az. between two cotises of the last, on a chief gu. three fleur-de-lis of the first.

O'Quigley Gu. an orle ar., over all a bend erminois.

O'Quin Vert a pegasus passant wings elevated ar., a chief or (branch of O'Farrell).

O'Quin Gu. a hand couped below the wrist grasping a sword all proper between in chief two crescents ar. and in base as many serpents erect and respecting each other tails nowed or (Clare).

O'Quinlan Per pale ermine and or two lions rampant combatant between in chief a mullet surmounted of a crescent and in base a dexter hand couped at the wrist and erect all gu.

O'Regan Or a chevron ermine between three dolphins az.

O'Reilly Vert two lions rampant combatant or supporting a dexter hand couped at the wrist erect and apaumee bloody proper.

O'Riordan Quart., 1 & 4, Gu. out of clouds in the sinister side a dexter arm fessways proper holding a dagger in pale ar. pommel and hilt or, 2 & 3, Ar., a lion rampant gu. against a tree in the dexter couped proper.

O'Rourke Or two lions passant in pale sa.

O'Scanlan Per fess indented ar. and az. three lions rampant counterchanged.

O'Shaughnessy Vert a tower triple towered ar. supported by two lions rampant combatant or.

O'Shea Per bend indented az. and or two fleur-de-lis counterchanged.

O'Sheehan Az. on a mount in base vert a dove ar. holding in the beak an olive branch proper.

O'Shiel Ar. a lion rampant between two dexter hands couped at the wrist erect apaumee in chief and a mullet in base all gu.

O'Sheridan Or a lion rampant between three trefoils vert.

O'Sullivan Per fess, the base per pale, in chief or a dexter hand couped at the wrist gu. grasping a sword erect blade entwined with a serpent proper between two lions rampant respecting each other of the second, on the dexter base vert a stag trippant or, on the sinister base per pale ar. and sa. a boar passant counterchanged (main branch).

O'Sullivan Per pale ar. and sa., a fess between in chief a boar passant and in base another counter passant all counterchanged armed hoofed and bristled or (Beare branch).

O'Toole Gu. a lion passant ar.

Ogilvy Ar., a lion passant guardant gu., crowned with an imperial crown, and collared with an open crown or.

Power Ar. a chief indented sa.

Prendergast Vair on a chief or, three oak leaves vert.

Purcell Or a saltire between four boars' heads couped sa.

Ramsay Ar. an eagle displayed sa. beaked and membered gu.

Rattray Az. three cross crosslets fitchee or.

Reid Ar. an eagle displayed sa. beaked and membered or, charged on the breast with an escutcheon of the last (Colliston, Fife).

Reid Quart.,1 & 4, ar. an eagle displayed gu. beaked and armed az., 2 & 3, gu. a dagger erect in pale proper between three wolves' heads erased ar. (Strathloch).

Rice Quart., 1 & 4, per pale indented ar. and gu., 2 and 3, az. a lion rampant or.

Robertson Gu., three wolves' heads erased arr., armed and langued az.

Roche Gu. three roaches naiant in pale ar.

Ross Gu., three lions rampant, two and one ar.

Rothe Or, on a mount in base proper a stag trippant ar. attired gu. in front of an oak tree vert.

Ruthven Ar. three pallets gu.

Sarsfield Per pale ar. and gu. a fleur-de-lis counterchanged.

Savage Ar. six lions rampant sa. langued gu.

Scrymgeour Gu. a lion rampant or, armed and langued az. holding in the dexter paw a scymitar ar.

Sinclair Quart., 1, Az., a ship at anchor within a double tressure flory-counter-flory, her oars erect in saltire or, 2 & 3, Or, a lion rampant gu., 4, Az., a ship under sail or, over all a cross engrailed, quartered, dividing the four quarters ar. and sa.

Skene Gu., three sgians (or daggers) palewise in fess ar., hilted and pommelled or, surmounted of as many wolves' heads or.

Spalding Ar. a two-handed sword in pale az.

Spens Or, a lion rampant gu. surmounted of a bend sa. charged with three lozenges ar.

Strathearn Gu. two chevronells or.

Steuart Or, a lion rampant gu. between three mullets az. over all a fess chequy ar. and of the third (Dalguise, Atholl—Royal).

Steuart Quart., 1 & 4, Or, a lion rampant within a double tressure flory-counter-flory gu., 2 & 3, Or, a fess chequy az and ar. all within a bordure engrailed of the first (Ballechin, Atholl—Royal).

Stewart Quart., 1 & 4, Or, a fess chequy az. and ar., 2 &3, Ar., a galley, sails trussed up, flags, gu., and oars in action (Appin).

Stewart Quart. 1 & 4, Or, a fess chequy az. and ar., 2 & 3, Ar., a lymphad, oars in action sa. (Grandtully, Atholl).

Stewart Quart., 1 & 4, Or, a lion rampant gu., armed and langued az., within a double tressure flory-counter-flory gu., 2, Or, a fess chequy az. and ar., in chief a mullet gu., 3, Ar. a saltire gu. cantoned with four roses of the last, all within a bordure engrailed compony az. and ar. (Ardvorlich, Balquhidder—Royal).

Stewart Quart., 1 & 4, or, a fess chequy az. and ar. surmounted by a lion rampant gu., 2 & 3, az. three garbs or (Garth, Atholl—Royal).

Stirling Ar. on a bend sa. three buckles or (Keir).

Stuart Or, a fess chequy az. and ar. within a double tressure flory-counter-flory gu. (Marquis of Bute—Royal).

Sutherland Gu., three mullets or, within a tressure flory-counter-flory of the first.

Taaffe Gu. a cross ar. fretty az.

Teeling Quart. per fesse indented or and gu.

Tobin Az. three oak leaves ar.

Tyrie Sa. on a chevron ar. a lion rampant az. between two torteaux.

Urquhart Or, three boar's heads erased gu., armed proper and langued azure.

Wall, Faltagh Az. a lion rampant between three crosses crosslet or.

Walsh Ar. a chevron gu. between three broad arrow heads points upwards sa.

Appendix II

A List of Surnames

There are over a thousand families listed here. The names are in their Anglicized form, that is, the most generally representative forms in English. Several categories of names appear, including names of the families covered in Part II, by ethnic group; important variant forms of names found in Part II; and names of families which are direct branches of one of the families dealt with in Part II, as opposed to more distantly related *tribal* branches. Included in this latter category are blood-related septs of the Scottish clans. (Scottish clan septs can be of two kinds; firstly there are the male-line branches, the identifiable of which are covered here, but then secondly there were those not related in the male line, yet who nonetheless followed the chief of the clan, adhering to him for protection. This reflects Scottish clanship's slightly different development in this regard, as discussed in Part I.)

Finally, it should be noted that in some cases more than one distinct sept bore the same name in English or Gaelic or both, and when one or more of such families are dealt with while others of the same name are not, confusion may arise. To avoid confusion, those not dealt with are listed here but marked "IVL" (indeterminate, various localities), which generally indicates that these families simply did not fall within the main Gaelic tribal sphere, either because they resided outside the Gaelic area, or else because they did not form a cohesive group with the level of real political significance common to the tribal and clan families listed in Part II, hence their exclusion from further consideration. They are included to show, for instance, that all O'Neills are not necessarily of the great Ulster clan, or O'Neill might be the name of a minor family or of some other clan, or even of a family with no historical or tribal significance. In this way I have cross-referenced family names throughout the Gaelic area, so that accuracy might be maintained.

For the genealogist, connection with a particular family bearing such an often-used name must be made on a territorial basis (e.g., if your MacInerney great-grandmother was from County Clare, then that shows her to be Dalcassian, and not of the famous Roscommon family of hereditary abbots or

171

erenaghs). If a family is only known to originate in a metropolitan area such as Dublin, or Cork City, then a family tradition must be extant to determine the origin of the family (unless a family connection to the city is very old). The same is true if the families in question lived in areas adjacent to each other, though this is relatively rare for families of the same name. For the most part the genealogist's track is straightforward when logic and some sense of history are employed. For Scottish families, holding a sept-name is often a better indication of actual descent than holding the clan chief's name itself, unless a knowledge of one's exact connection to the chiefly line is known (see remarks in Part I, Chapter I). This again reflects the particular differences of Scottish clanship. In addition, many Scottish families also appear in Ulster after the sixteenth century, as a result of large-scale immigration. The genealogist will find this cross-referenced appendix invaluable, and a further look to the bibliography is also advised, especially where doubt may exist. Also, when using this, name-forms should be searched with and without the prefixes "O" and "Mac."

Families	Ethnic Group	Branch of
Abbot		MacNab
Abbot	IVL – Ireland	
Abernethy		MacDuff
Alexander		MacAlister
Alexander	IVL – South Scotland	
Anderson		Ross
Anderson	IVL – South Scotland	
Ardencaple	Gaels	MacAulay
Arthur (Limerick)	Vikings	
Arthur	IVL – South Scotland	
Bain		MacKay
Balquhidder	Cruithne	
Barrett	Normans	
Barron		Fitzgerald
Barron	IVL – Mayo, Angus	
Barry	Normans	
Bartholomew		MacFarlane
Bartholomew	IVL – South Scotland	
Baxter		MacMillan
Baxter	IVL – South Scotland	
Bell		MacMillan
Bell	IVL – South Scotland	
Bisset	Normans	
Black		Lamont
Black		MacGregor
Black	IVL	
Blake	IVL – Mayo, Fermanagh	
Blake	Normans	Tribes of Galway
Bohannon	IVL – Clare	

Bohannon		Buchanan
Bolan, Boland	IVL – Mayo, Sligo, Clare	
Bolan, Boland	Gaels	O'Beolain (Drumcliffe)
Bolan, Boland	Gaels	O'Brolan
Bowie		MacDonald (Clan Donald)
Boyle	IVL-South Scotland	
Brady		O'Grady
Brady	IVL-Leinster	
Brallaghan		O'Brollaghan
Brandon	Normans	Fitzmaurice (Kerry)
Brandon	IVL	
Brien	IVL	
Brieve		Morrison
Brodie	Cruithne	
Brodie (Argyle)		O'Brollaghan
Brolochan (Argyle)		O'Brollaghan
Brown		Lamont
Brown	IVL-South Scotland	
Browne	IVL-Ireland	
Browne	Normans	Tribes of Galway
Bruce	Normans	
Buchan	Cruithne	
Buchanan	Gaels	
Burke, Bourke	Normans	
Burness, Burnes, Burns		Campbell
Burness, Burnes, Burns	IVL – South Scotland	
Burns		O'Beirne
Burns		O'Byrne
Burns	IVL-Ireland (not Ulster)	
Butler	Normans	
Butter, Buttar	Normans	
Byrne	IVL	
Caddell		Campbell
Caddell		Blake
Cairney	Gaels	O'Beolain
Calder		Campbell
Callaghan	IVL-Oriel	
Callendar, Callander	Normans	
Cameron	Erainn	
Campbell	Erainn	
Carney	(Rare)	Fox
Carney	(Rare)	O'Neill (Ulster)
Carney		O'Kearney (Mayo, Tipperary)
Carron	IVL-Ulster	
Carry	IVL-Ulster, Galway	
Carthy		MacCarthy
Carthy		O'Carry
Carthy	IVL – Connacht	
Cattanach		MacPherson

Cavan		O'Keevan
Cawley		MacAwley (Fermanagh)
Chalmers		Cameron
Cheyne, Chesney	IVL – Ulster	
Cheyne	IVL – Northeast Scotland	
Chisholm	Normans	
Clarke		O'Cleary
Clarke		O'Hara
Clarke	IVL	
Cleary		O'Hara
Coffey	IVL – Connacht, Kerry, Tipperary	
Cogley		O'Quigley
Collier, Colyear		Robertson
Collier, Colyer	IVL – Ireland	
Collins		O'Cullane
Collins	IVL – Ireland	
Colquhoun	Normans	
Colson		MacDonald (Clan Donald)
Comrie		MacGregor
Condon	IVL	
Condon	Normans	
Conlon, Connellan		O'Quinlan
Conlon, Connellan	IVL – North Connacht	
Conn		MacDonald (Clan Donald)
Conn	IVL – South Scotland	
Conry		O'Mulconry
Conry	IVL – Galway	
Cowan		Colquhoun
Cowan		MacKeown
Cowan	IVL – Ireland, S. Scotland	
Cowhey	IVL – Connacht	
Cowhey, Cowhig		O'Coffey
Creagh	Erainn	
Creagh	IVL – Munster	
Crean, Crehan, Creghan	IVL – Leinster, Galway, South Ireland	
Creghan, Crehan		O'Crean
Crehan	IVL-Ulster	
Crerar		MacKintosh
Cullen		MacQuillan
Cullen		O'Cullane
Cullen	Gaels	O'Cullinan
Cullen	IVL – Ireland, South Scotland	
Cumming	IVL – Ireland	
Cumming, Comyn, Cummin	Normans	
Cunnagher		Joyce

Currie		MacPherson
Currie		O'Daly
Currie	IVL—Scotland	
Cusack	IVL	
Cusack	Normans	
Dallas, Doles		MacPherson
Dalton	Normans	
Darcy	IVL—Connacht	
Darcy	Normans	
Darditz, Dardes	Normans	
Davidson	Erainn	
Davis		O'Morchoe
Davis	IVL—Ireland	
Daw		O'Dea
Deane		Tribes of Galway
Deane	IVL—Donegal, Tipperary	
de Courcy	Normans	
Deignan, Dignam		O'Duigenan
Dewar		MacNab
Dewar		Menzies
Dillon	IVL	
Dillon	Normans	
Dinnes		Innes
Dochart		MacGregor
Donachie		Robertson
Donaldson, Donald		MacDonald (Clan Donald)
Donleavy		Buchanan
Donnelson, Donillson		MacDonald (Clan Donald)
Doody		O'Dowd
Dougherty		O'Doherty
Douglas	Normans	
Dove, Dow		Buchanan
Downing		O'Dinneen
Downing	IVL—Cork, Kerry, Limerick	
Doyle (Roscommon)		MacDougal
Doyne		O'Dunne
Drummond	Cruithne	
Drummond	IVL-Ireland	
Duff	IVL—Ireland, Scotland	
Dunbar	Gaels	
Duncan	IVL—Ireland	
Duncan, Duncanson		Robertson
Dundas	Gaels	
Dunning		O'Dinneen
Dunning	IVL—Britain	
Durie	Cruithne	
Dyce		Skene
Elder		MacPherson

Elder	IVL – S. Scotland, Ireland	
Enrick, Eanrig		Gunn
Erskine	Cruithne	
Fagan		O'Hagan
Fagan	IVL – Ireland	
Fagan	Normans	
Faltagh, Wall	Normans	
Fant		Tribes of Galway
Farquharson	Erainn	
Fergus	IVL – Ireland	
Fergusson, Fergus	Erainn	
Fergusson, Fergus	IVL – Northeast & South Scotland, Ireland	
Fernon		O'Heffernan
Ferries		Fergusson (Ulster)
Ferris		Fergusson (Buchan)
Ferris		O'Moriarty
Ferris	IVL – Scotland, Kerry	
Finlay, Finlayson		Farquharson
Fitzgerald	Normans	
Fitzgibbon	Normans	
Fitzmaurice		Fitzgerald
Fitzmaurice		Prendergast
Fitzpatrick	Erainn	
Fleming	IVL	
Fleming	Normans	
Fletcher		MacGregor
Fletcher	IVL – Ireland	
Forbes	Cruithne	
Fotheringham		Fothringham
Fothringham	Normans	
Fox	Gaels	
Fox	IVL – Cork, Sligo, Limerick	
Fraser	IVL – Ireland	
Fraser	Normans	
French	Normans	Tribes of Galway
Frissell, Frizell		Fraser
Frissell, Frizell	IVL – Munster	
Gaffney (SW Ulster)		MacCaron
Gaffney	IVL	
Galbraith	Laigin	
Gallie		Gunn
Gallie	IVL – South Scotland	
Gallivan		O'Galvin
Ganley, Gantley		MacShanly
Garrahy		MacGarry
Garrahy		MacGeraghty
Gaunson		Gunn
Gawley (Connacht)		MacAwley (Fermanagh)
Geary		O'Gara

Georgeson		Gunn
Gilbert	IVL – Leinster	
Gilbert, Gilbertson		Buchanan
Gilbride		MacDonald (Clan Donald)
Gilbride	IVL – West Ulster	
Gilchrist		MacLachlan
Gilchrist		Ogilvy
Gilchrist	IVL – North Connacht, Longford	
Gilfillan		MacNab
Gilfillan	IVL – Ireland	
Gillan, Gillon		MacLean
Gillanders		Ross
Gillanders	IVL – North Ireland	
Gillespie, Gillies		MacPherson
Gillespie, Gillies	IVL – S. Scotland, Ireland	
Gilmore		Morrison
Gilmore	IVL – Ulster	
Gilzean		MacLean
Ginnaw, Ginnane		MacKenna
Glaughlin		MacLoughlin (Ulster)
Glencairnie	Cruithne	
Gloughlin		MacLoughlin (Dublin)
Gordon	IVL – Ireland	
Gordon	Normans	
Gorman		O'Gormley
Graham	Normans	
Graham		O'Gormley
Graham	IVL – East Connacht	
Grannell (Wexford)		MacRannall
Grant	Normans	
Gray		O'Rourke
Gray		Stewart
Gregor		MacGregor
Gregory		MacGregor
Grierson		MacGregor
Griffin		O'Griffey
Griffin	IVL – Connacht, Offaly	
Grimes		O'Gormely
Grimes	IVL – Connacht, South Ireland	
Growney		MacCaron
Guckian	IVL – Ulster	
Guckian		Hackett
Guinness		MacGenis
Gunn	IVL – Ulster	
Gunn	Vikings	
Hackett	IVL – Ulster	
Hackett	Normans	
Haldane, Halden	IVL – South Scotland	

Haldane, Hadden	Normans	
Hamilton	Normans	
Handrahan		O'Hanrahan
Hanratty		O'Hanraghty
Hare		MacGarry
Hare	IVL – Ireland	
Haren, Harhan		O'Hanrahan
Haren, Harhan	IVL – Clare, Connacht, Oriel	
Hart	IVL – Ulster, South Scotland	
Hay		O'Hea
Hay	IVL – Ireland	
Hay	Normans	
Hearne		O'Aherne
Heas		O'Hea
Henchy		O'Hennessy
Henderson		Gunn
Henderson		MacKeown
Henderson	IVL – West Scotland	
Henry		MacNaughton
Henry	IVL – South Scotland	
Hewison		MacDonald (Clan Donald)
Hiffernan, Hernon		O'Heffernan
Holland		O'Houlihan
Horan, Haughran		O'Hanrahan
Hylan		O'Phelan
Hynes		O'Heyne
Inches		Robertson
Innes		MacInnes
Innes	IVL – Ireland	
Innes	Normans	
Innie		Innes
Isles		MacDonald (Clan Donald)
Jameson		Gunn
Jameson	IVL – West Scotland	
Jennings	Normans	Burke
Johnson		Gunn
Johnson		MacIan (Glencoe)
Johnson		MacIan (Ardnamurchan)
Johnson	Gaels	O'Neill (Ulster)
Jordan	IVL – Ireland	
Jordan	Normans	
Joy		Joyce
Joy	IVL – Ireland	
Joyce	Normans	Tribes of Galway
Kane		O'Cahan
Kavanagh	Laigin	
Kay		Davidson
Kealaghan	IVL – Oriel	

Keane		O'Cahan
Keane	IVL – Galway, South Ireland	
Kearns		O'Kieran
Keating	IVL – Limerick, Ulster	
Keating	Normans	
Keavan	IVL – Cork	
Kee	IVL – West Ulster	
Keevane		O'Keevan
Keevane	IVL – Cork	
Kegley		O'Quigley
Kehoe		MacKeogh (Leinster)
Keith	Normans	
Kelly	IVL – Scotland	
Kennagh		MacKenna
Kennealy		O'Kinneally
Kennedy	IVL – South Scotland	
Kennelly		O'Kinneally
Kennelly	IVL – West Cork	
Kennethson, Kenneth		MacKenzie
Kenny		MacKenna
Kenny	IVL – Ireland	
Kerin		O'Kieran
Kermode	IVL-Munster	
Kermode	Gaels	MacDermot
Kevane		O'Keevan
Kevane	IVL – Cork	
Kevans		O'Keevan
Kilpatrick		Fitzpatrick
Kilpatrick	IVL – South Scotland	
Kindellan		O'Quinlan
King		MacGregor
King	IVL – Ireland	
King	IVL – Ireland, Aberdeen	
Kiniry		MacEnery
Kinnaird	Normans	
Kinsella	Laigin	
Kirkpatrick		Fitzpatrick
Kirkpatrick	IVL – South Scotland	
Kirwan		Tribes of Galway
Knowlan		O'Nolan
Lachlan, Lauchlan		MacLachlan
Lacy	IVL – Wexford	
Lacy	Normans	
Lally		O'Mullally
Lambie		Lamont
Lambie	IVL – Angus	
Lamondson		Lamont
Lamont, Lammon	Gaels	
Lanigan, Lenigan		O'Flanagan (Offaly)

Landers		Lamont
Larnach		MacLaren
Leash		Lacy
Leckie	Gaels	
Lee	IVL--Ireland	
Lennox	Gaels	
Lenny, Lennie		Buchanan
Leslie	IVL--Ireland	
Leslie	Normans	
Lindsay	IVL--Ireland	
Lindsay	Normans	
Linklater		Sinclair
Livingston	Normans	
Livingstone	Gaels	
Logie	Cruithne	
Londrigan		O'Lonergan
Lorrigan		O'Lonergan
Love		MacKinnon
Love	IVL--Ireland	
Lucas, Luke		Lamont
Lucas, Luke	IVL--Ireland, South Scotland	
Lynch	Normans	Tribes of Galway
Lyon		Lamont
Lyon	IVL--South Scotland	
MacAdam		MacGregor
MacAdam	IVL	
MacAdam	Normans	Barry
MacAfee		MacFie
MacAlarry		O'Harra
MacAldonich		Buchanan
MacAlduie		Lamont
MacAleevy		MacDonlevy
MacAlister	Laigin	MacDonald (Clan Donald)
MacAllan		MacDonald (Clanranald)
MacAllan		MacFarlane
MacAllan		MacKay
MacAllan	IVL--South Scotland	
MacAlpin		MacGregor
MacAndeoir		MacNab
MacAndrew		Ross
MacAndrew	Normans	Barrett
MacAngus		MacInnes
MacAnully, Knally		MacNally
MacArthur	Laigin	
MacAskill		MacLeod
MacAulay		MacLeod (Lewis)
MacAulay, MacAwlay	Gaels	

MacAuliffe		MacCarthy
MacAuse		MacFarlane
MacAuslan		Buchanan
MacAwley, MacAuley		Maguire
MacAwley, MacAuley	Gaels	
MacAy		Davidson
MacBain	Erainn	
MacBarron	Gaels	O'Neill (Ulster)
MacBarron		Fraser
MacBaxter		MacMillan
MacBean		MacBain
MacBeath		MacBain
MacBeath	IVL—Islay & Mull, Scotland	
MacBeolain		Ross
MacBrady	Laigin	
MacBrannan		O'Brannan
MacBride	,	MacDonald (Clan Donald)
MacBride	IVL—West Ulster	
MacBrieve		Morrison
MacBrolachan		O'Brollaghan
MacBurie		O'Daly
MacCabe		MacLeod
MacCahan	IVL—Clare	
MacCainsh, MacCansh		MacInnes
MacCall, MacColl		MacDonald (Clan Donald)
MacCallum		MacLeod
MacCalman, Colman		Buchanan
MacCalum		MacLeod
MacCann	IVL—Ireland (Rare)	
MacCann	Laigin	
MacCara		MacGregor
MacCarney	Gaels	O'Neill (Ulster)
MacCaron	Gaels	
MacCarra		MacGregor
MacCarron	IVL—Donegal	
MacCartan	Cruithne	
MacCarthy	Gaels	
MacCarthy	IVL—Donegal	
MacCheyne, Mac-Chesney		MacShane
MacClancy	IVL—Clare	
MacClancy		O'Rourke
MacCleary		O'Cleary
MacCleary		O'Hara
MacCleish	IVL—South Scotland	
MacClery	IVL—Scotland	
MacClymont		Lamont

MacCoghlan	Laigin	
MacColgan	IVL – Derry	
MacColgan	Laigin	
MacColl		MacDonald (Clan Donald)
MacCombie		MacKintosh
MacConachie		MacGregor
MacConachie		Robertson
MacConachie	IVL – Ireland	
MacConn	IVL – Ulster	
MacConnach		MacKenzie
MacConnall, MacConnell		MacDonald (Clan Donald)
MacConnochy		Campbell
MacConsidine		O'Brien
MacCorquodale		MacLeod (Lewis)
MacCorquodale	Vikings	
MacCostello	Normans	
MarCotter	Vikings	
MacCoul		MacDougall
MacCowan		Colquhoun
MacCoy (Ulster, Tipperary)		MacKay
Mac Cracken		MacNaughton
MacCraith		MacRae
MacCrays		MacGrath
MacCreath, MacCrie		MacRae
MacCreath, MacCrie	IVL – South Scotland	
MacCulreavy		O'Rourke
MacCunn		MacQueen
MacCurtin	Erainn	
MacDaid		O'Doherty
MacDaniell		MacDonald
MacDavid		Davidson
MacDavid		MacDermot
MacDavie	Normans	Burke
MacDermid		Campbell
MacDermid		MacDermott
MacDermid	IVL – Ireland	
MacDermot	Gaels	
MacDermott		Campbell
MacDermott	IVL – Ireland	
MacDiarmid		Campbell
MacDonachie		Robertson
MacDonald	Laigin	
MacDonell		MacDonald
MacDonlevy	Erainn	
MacDonnell		MacDonald
MacDonnell		O'Brien
MacDonnell	IVL – Fermanagh	

MacDonagh, MacDonough		MacDermot
MacDonagh, MacDonough	Gaels	O'Flaherty
MacDonagh, MacDonough	Gaels	MacCarthy
MacDougal	Laigin	
MacDowell		MacDougal
MacDowell	IVL – South Scotland	
MacDuff	Gaels	
MacDuffie		MacFie
MacEachan		MacDonald (Clanranald)
MacEachern		MacDonald (Clan Donald)
MacEarachar		Farquharson
MacEchern	IVL – Cavan	
MacEnery	Erainn	
MacEvoy	IVL – Ireland	
MacEvoy	Laigin	
MacEwen		MacLachlan
MacEwen	IVL – South Scotland	
MacFarlane	Gaels	
MacFarlane	IVL – Ireland	
MacFarquhar		Farquharson
MacFergus		Fergusson
MacFie	Erainn	
MacGarry, Garrihy		O'Flaherty
MacGeachie		MacDonald (Clanranald)
MacGeever (Donegal)		MacIvor
MacGenis, MacGuinness	Cruithne	
MacGeoghegan	Gaels	
MacGeraghty, Gerty	Gaels	
MacGhie, MacGhee		MacKay
MacGibbon	Normans	Burke
MacGibbon	Normans	FitzGibbon
MacGilchrist		MacLachlan
MacGilchrist		Ogilvy
MacGilfoyle	Erainn	
MacGilligowie		Lamont
MacGillivour		MacGillivray
MacGillivray	Erainn	
MacGillonie	Erainn	Cameron
MacGillycuddy		O'Sullivan Mor
MacGilpatrick		Fitzpatrick
MacGilvernock		Graham
MacGiver		Maguire
MacGivern		O'Neill (Ulster)
MacGlashan		Stewart
MacGlashan	IVL – West Ulster	

MacGlasrich		Campbell
MacGloughlin		MacLoughlin
MacGloughlin	IVL – Meath	
MacGorman	Erainn	
MacGorry		MacDonald (Clan Donald)
MacGovern, Magauran	Gaels	
MacGowan, Gowan, Gow	IVL – Ireland	
MacGowan, Gow	MacPherson	
MacGowan, Goun	MacDonald	
MacGowran		MacGovern
MacGrath		MacRae (East Ulster)
MacGrath	Erainn	
MacGrath	IVL – Donegal	
MacGreal		MacNeill
MacGregor	Erainn	
MacGreusich		Buchanan
McGrory		MacLaren
MacGuffie		MacFie
MacGuire		Maguire
MacGuire, MacGauran		MacQuarrie
MacGuirk, MacGurk		O'Neill (Ulster)
MacHackett		Hackett
MacHaffie, MacHaffy		MacFie
MacHardy		Erskine
MacHay		Davidson
MacHendry		MacNaughton
MacHenry		MacEnery
MacHenry	IVL – Ireland	
MacHugh		O'Flaherty
MacHugh		O'Quin
MacHutcheon, MacHugh		MacDonald (Clan Donald)
MacIan		Gunn
MacIan		MacDonald (Ardnamurchan)
MacIan		MacDonald (Glencoe)
MacIldowie		Cameron
MacIlduy		MacGregor
MacIlduy	IVL – Hebrides	
MacIlvernoch		Graham
MacIlvride		MacDonald (Clan Donald)
MacIlwhom		Lamont
MacIlwraith		MacDonald (Clan Donald)
MacIlwraith	IVL – Ireland	
MacIndeoir		Buchanan
MacIndeor		Menzies

MacInerney	Erainn	
MacInerney, Nerney		O'Brannan (Roscommon)
MacInnes		Innes
MacInnes		MacGenis
MacInnes	Erainn	
MacIntaylor		Cameron
MacIntosh		MacKintosh
MacIntyre	Laigin	
MacIver		Campbell
MacIver		Robertson
MacIvor		Campbell
MacKay	Gaels	
MacKeamish		Gunn
MacKean, MacKain		MacIan (Ardnamurchan)
MacKearney	Gaels	O'Neill (Ulster)
MacKechnie		MacDonald (Clanranald)
MacKee (Ulster)		MacKay
MacKendrick		MacNaughton
MacKenna	Gaels	
MacKenzie	Cruithne	
MacKeogh	IVL – Tipperary	
MacKeogh	Laigin	
MacKeogh	Laigin	O'Kelly
MacKeown	IVL – South Scotland	
MacKeown	IVL – Sligo, Leitrim	
MacKeon	Normans	
MacKerras, MacKersey		Fergusson
MacKichan		MacDougall
MacKie	IVL – South Scotland	
MacKiernan	Gaels	O'Connor
MacKiernan		O'Rourke
MacKernan		Maguire
MacKimmie, Kimm		Fraser
MacKinlay		Buchanan
MacKinlay		Farquharson
MacKinnell		MacDonald (Clan Donald)
MacKinney		MacKenzie
MacKinney		MacKinnon
MacKinning, MacKinven		MacKinnon
MacKinnon	Erainn	
MacKinny		MacKenna
MacKinny		MacKinnon
MacKintosh	Erainn	
MacKnight		MacNaughton
MacKnight	IVL – Ireland	
MacLandrish		Ross
MacLachlan	Gaels	
MacLaghlan		MacLachlan
MacLaine		MacLean
MacLamond		Lamont

MacLaren, MacLaurin	Cruithne	
MacLaughlan (Ulster)	Gaels	
MacLean	Erainn	
MacLeay	Gaels	
MacLeay	IVL – Sutherland	
MacLee		O'Lee
MacLee	IVL – Ireland	
MacLeish	Cruithne	
MacLeister		MacGregor
MacLeod	Vikings	
MacLise	IVL – Ireland, South Scotland	
MacLoughlin (Ulster)	Gaels	
MacLoughlin	Gaels	
MacLucas		Lamont
MacLucas, MacLugash		MacDougall
MacLure		MacLeod
MacLure	IVL – Galloway	
MacLysaght		O'Brien
MacMahon		O'Brien
MacMahon	Laigin	
MacMakan		Matheson
MacManus	Gaels	O'Connor
MacManus	Laigin	Maguire
MacMartin, Martin	Erainn	Cameron
MacMartin	IVL – South Scotland	
MacMaster		MacKiernan (O'Rourke)
MacMaurice		Buchanan
MacMillan	Cruithne	
MacMoriarty	IVL – Roscommon	
MacMorran		MacKinnon
MacMorris		Fitzgerald
MacMorris		Prendergast
MacMorris	IVL	
MacMurchie, Murchison		MacDonald (Clan Donald)
MacMurchie, Murchison	IVL – Scotland	
MacMurdoch		MacDonald (Clan Donald)
MacMurdoch		MacPherson
MacMurphy		MacDonald (Clan Donald)
MacMurphy	IVL – Ulster	
MacMurray	IVL-Donegal	
MacMurray, Moray		Murray
MacMurrich	IVL – Scotland	
MacMurrich		MacPherson
MacNab	Erainn	
MacNair		MacFarlane
MacNair		MacNaughton

MacNally	Erainn	
MacNally, Nally	IVL – Connacht	
MacNamara	Erainn	
MacNaughton	Erainn	
MacNee		MacGregor
MacNee	IVL – Ireland	
MacNeil, MacNeill	Gaels	
MacNichol		Campbell
MacNichol	IVL – Tyrone	
MacNiven		MacNaughton
MacNully		O'Lynn
MacNulty		MacDunlevy
MacNuyer		Buchanan
MacOmie		MacKintosh
MacOran		Campbell
MacPatrick		MacLaren
MacPatrick, Patrick		Lamont
MacPeter		MacGregor
MacPetrie		MacGregor
MacPhail		MacKay
MacPhail		MacPherson
MacPhee		MacFie
MacPherson	Erainn	
MacPhilbin		Burke
MacQuarrie	Erainn	
MacQueen	Gaels	
MacQuillan	Normans	
MacQuire		MacQuarrie
MacQuistan		MacDonald (Clan Donald)
MacQuoid	IVL – Ireland	
MacQuoid, MacQuey		MacKay
MacRae	Cruithne	
MacRaith, Mac-Reach		MacDonald
MacRannall	Erainn	
MacRedmond		Burke
MacRitchie		MacKintosh
MacRob		Gunn
MacRobert, MacRobbie		Robertson
MacRory		MacLaren
MacRory	IVL – Ulster	
MacRory, MacRorie		MacDonald (Clan Donald)
MacRury, MacRuer		MacDonald (Clan Donald)
MacShane	Gaels	O'Neill (Ulster)

MacShanly	Gaels	
MacSheehy		MacDonald
MacShemis		Fraser
MacSorley	Laigin	MacDonald (Islay)
MacSorley	Erainn	Cameron
MacSorley	Gaels	Lamont
MacSweeney		MacQueen
MacSwyde, Mac-Swen		MacQueen
MacTaggart		Ross
MacTary		Innes
MacTavish		Campbell
MacTear, MacTier		MacIntyre
MacTernan, Tiernan		O'Rourke
MacThomas		MacKintosh
MacTimin	Normans	Barrett
MacTire, Mac-Tier		MacIntyre
MacTire, Mac-Tyre		Ross
MacTournor		Lamont
MacVurrich		MacPherson
MacVurrich	IVL – Scotland	
MacVurrich		O'Daly
MacWalter		Burke
MacWalter		MacFarlane
MacWattie		Buchanan
MacWhannell		MacDonald (Clan Donald)
MacWilliam		MacQuillan
MacWilliam	IVL – Scotland	
MacWilliam		MacLeod (Harris)
Madigan		O'Madden
Magauran		MacGovern
Maguire	Laigin	
Mahaffy		MacFie
Mahon	IVL – Ireland	
Malcolm		MacLeod
Malcolm	IVL – Ireland	
Malcolmson		MacLeod
Malloch		MacGregor
Mallon, Mallin		O'Mellan
Manning	IVL – Cork, Dublin	
Manning		O'Mannin
Mannion		O'Mannin
Mansfield		MacQuillan
Manson		Gunn
Mara		O'Meara
Marnoch		Innes

Martin	IVL – Ireland, Hebrides	
Martin	Normans	Tribes of Galway
Martin		O'Neill (Ulster)
Masterson, MacMaster		Buchanan
Masterson	IVL – Ireland, South Scotland	
Matheson	Cruithne	
Mathison	IVL – South Scotland	
Mavor		Innes
Mawhannon		Buchanan
Meikleham		Lamont
Melville	IVL – Ulster	
Melville, Mulville		O'Mulvihil
Mentieth		Graham
Mentieth		Stewart
Menzies	Normans	
Middleton		Innes
Middleton	IVL – Ireland, South Scotland	
Molloy	IVL – Ireland	
Moncreiffe	Gaels	
Monk		O'Monahan
Monk	IVL – Hebrides	
More	IVL – Munster, Connacht	
Moroney		O'Mulroony
Morris	IVL – Ireland	
Morris, Morrissey	Normans	Tribes of Galway
Morris		Fitzmaurice (Mayo)
Morris		Fitzmaurice (Kerry)
Morrison		MacLeod
Morrison	IVL – Ireland, Harris, South Scotland	
Mullen	IVL	
Munro, Monroe		O'Cahan
Munroe, Monroe		O'Mellan
Munroe, Monroe	IVL – Mayo	
Murchison, MacMurchie		Buchanan
Murchison, MacMurchie		MacDonald (Clan Donald)
Murphy		Kinsella
Murphy		O'Morchoe
Murphy	IVL – Ireland	
Murray	Normans	
Murray	IVL – Ireland	
Nagle, Nangle		MacCostello
Neilson		MacKay
Neilson	IVL – South Scotland	
Nerney		MacInerney (Roscommon)
Nicholson	Cruithne	
Nicholson	IVL – South Scotland	

Nolan		O'Houlihan
Nolan	IVL – Fermanagh, Kerry	
Norman		MacLeod
Norman	IVL – Meath	
Nugent	IVL – Meath, Cavan	
Nugent	Normans	
O'Aherne	Erainn	
O'Beirne	Gaels	
O'Beirne	IVL – Mayo	
O'Beolain, O'Bolan	Gaels	
O'Bolan	IVL – Clare	
O'Boylan	Laigin	
O'Boyle	Gaels	
O'Branigan, Brangan	Gaels	
O'Brannan, Brennan	Laigin	
O'Brennan	Erainn	
O'Brennan	Gaels	
O'Brennan	IVL – Galway, Kerry	
O'Brennigan		O'Branagan
O'Brien	Erainn	
O'Brien	IVL – Connacht, Leinster	
O'Brolachain (Argyle)		O'Brollaghan
O'Brolan	Gaels	
O'Brollaghan	Gaels	
O'Byrne		O'Beirne
O'Bryne	Laigin	
O'Cahan	Gaels	
O'Caherney		Fox
O'Cahill	Erainn	
O'Cahill	IVL – Galway, Kerry	
O'Callaghan	Gaels	
O'Callaghan	IVL – Mayo	
O'Cannon, O'Canannain	Gaels	O'Donnell
O'Cannon	IVL – Galway	
O'Carroll	IVL – Ireland	
O'Carroll	Laigin	
O'Carroll		MacBrady
O'Carry	Gaels	
O'Casey	IVL – Limerick, Cork	
O'Casey	Laigin	
O'Cassidy	Laigin	
O'Cleary	Gaels	
O'Coffey	Erainn	
O'Coghlan	IVL – Cork	
O'Colgan		MacColgan
O'Colgan	IVL – Derry	
O'Concannon	Laigin	
O'Connell	Erainn	
O'Connell	IVL – Gallway, Derry	
O'Connor	Erainn	
O'Connor	Gaels	

O'Connor	IVL – Oirghialla	
O'Connor	Laigin	
O'Connor	Laigin	
O'Conrahy		MacCoghlan
O'Cornyn	Erainn	
O'Corrigan	Laigin	
O'Crean	Gaels	
O'Crowley		MacDermot
O'Cullane	Erainn	
O'Cullen	Laigin	
O'Cullinan, Cullen	Gaels	
O'Cullinan	IVL – Cork	
O'Cullinane	IVL – Cork	
O'Daly	Gaels	
O'Davoren	Erainn	
O'Dea	Erainn	
O'Dempsey	Laigin	
O'Devany	IVL – West Ulster	
O'Dinneen, Denning	Erainn	
O'Doherty	Gaels	
O'Donegan	IVL – Tipperary	
O'Donnell	Gaels	
O'Donnell	IVL – West Munster, Galway	
O'Donnellan	IVL – Tyrone, Offaly	
O'Donnellan	Laigin	
O'Donnelly	Gaels	
O'Donnelly	IVL – Galway, Cork	
O'Donoghue	Gaels	
O'Donohoe	IVL – Galway, Cavan	
O'Donovan	Erainn	
O'Donovan	IVL – Cork, Tipperary	
O'Doran	Cruithne	
O'Dowd	Gaels	
O'Dowd	IVL – Derry	
O'Dowling	Cruithne	
O'Dowling	IVL – Cork, Leinster	
O'Doyle	Vikings	
O'Driscoll	Erainn	
O'Duany, Devany		O'Gara
O'Duggan	IVL – Cork	
O'Duigenan, Deignan	Gaels	
O'Dunne	Laigin	
O'Durack	Erainn	
O'Dwyer	Erainn	
O'Fahy	Laigin	
O'Fallon	IVL – Offaly	
O'Fallon	Laigin	
O'Farrell	Erainn	
O'Finnegan	Gaels	

O'Finnegan	IVL–Cavan	
O'Flaherty	Gaels	
O'Flanagan	Gaels	
O'Flanagan	Laigin	O'Boylan
O'Flanagan	Laigin	O'Carroll
O'Flynn	Erainn	
O'Flynn	IVL–Galway, Cork	
O'Fogarty	Erainn	
O'Friel	Gaels	
O'Gallagher	Gaels	
O'Galvin	Erainn	
O'Gara	Laigin	
O'Garriga		MacGarry
O'Gormley	Gaels	
O'Gormley	IVL–Connacht	
O'Grady	Erainn	
O'Grady	IVL–Connacht	
O'Griffey	Erainn	
O'Hagan	Gaels	
O'Hagan	IVL–South Ulster	
O'Halloran	IVL–Clare	
O'Halloran	Vikings	
O'Hanlon	Laigin	
O'Hanley	Laigin	
O'Hanraghty	Laigin	
O'Hanrahan	Erainn	
O'Hara	Laigin	
O'Hart	Gaels	
O'Hartagan	Erainn	
O'Hea	Erainn	
O'Heffernan	Erainn	
O'Hegarty	Gaels	
O'Hegarty	IVL–Tipperary	
O'Hennessy	Erainn	
O'Hennessy	Laigin	
O'Heyne	Gaels	
O'Hickey	Erainn	
O'Higgin, Higgins	Gaels	
O'Hoey	IVL–Meath	
O'Hoey		MacDonlevy
O'Holohan	Laigin	O'Hennessy
O'Horan	Laigin	
O'Houlihan	Gaels	
O'Kearney		Fox
O'Kearney	Gaels	
O'Keeffe	Gaels	
O'Keevan	Gaels	
O'Kelly	IVL–Ireland	
O'Kelly	Laigin	
O'Kennedy	Erainn	
O'Kennedy	IVL–Galway	

O'Kiernan	Laigin	
O'Kinneally	Erainn	
O'Lalor, Lawlor	Cruithne	
O'Leary	Erainn	
O'Lee	Gaels	
O'Lonergan	Erainn	
O'Loughlin		MacLoughlin (Ulster)
O'Loughlin	Erainn	
O'Lynch	Cruithne	
O'Lynch	IV—Donegal, Connacht, Munster	
O'Lynn	Laigin	
O'Madden	Laigin	
O'Maher		O'Carroll
O'Mahony	Gaels	
O'Malley	Erainn	
O'Malone	Gaels	O'Connor
O'Mannin	Cruithne	
O'Meara	Erainn	
O'Meehan	IVL—Louth, Clare, Galway	
O'Meehan		MacCarthy
O'Mellan		O'Neill (Ulster)
O'Moledy		O'Farrell
O'Molloy	Gaels	
O'Molloy	Gaels	O'Connor
O'Molony	Erainn	
O'Monahan	Laigin	
O'Mooney	Laigin	O'Connor
O'Morchoe	Laigin	
O'More	Cruithne	
O'Moriarty		O'Donoghue
O'Moroney	Erainn	
O'Mulconry	Gaels	O'Connor
O'Mulderry		O'Donnell
Muldrew, Muldragh		O'Mulderry
O'Mullally	Laigin	
O'Mullen		O'Concannon
O'Mullen	IVL—Ulster	
O'Mulroony	Laigin	
O'Mulryan	Laigin	
O'Mulvihil	Gaels	O'Connor
O'Murphy		Kinsella
O'Naghten, Naughton	Laigin	
O'Naghten, Naughton	IVL—Clare	
O'Neill	Gaels	
O'Neill	IVL—South Ireland	
O'Nihill	Erainn	
O'Nolan		O'More
O'Phelan	Erainn	
O'Quigley	Gaels	
O'Quin		O'Farrell

O'Quin	Erainn	
O'Quin	IVL – Ulster	
O'Quinlan	Gaels	
O'Rahilly	Gaels	O'Neill (Ulster)
O'Regan	Gaels	
O'Regan	IVL – Limerick, Cork	
O'Reilly	Gaels	
O'Riordan		O'Carroll
O'Rourke	Gaels	
O'Scanlan	Gaels	
O'Scanlan	IVL – Sligo	
O'Shanahan	Erainn	
O'Shaughnessy	Gaels	
O'Shea	Erainn	
O'Sheehan	Laigin	
O'Sheridan	Gaels	
O'Shiel, O'Sheill	Gaels	
O'Sullivan	Gaels	
O'Sweeney		MacSweeney
O'Toole	IVL – Ulster	
O'Toole	Laigin	
O'Tracy		MacGorman
O'Tracy	IVL – Galway	
Ogilvy	Cruithne	
Oliphant	Normans	
Oynie		Innes
Parlane		MacFarlane
Patrick	IVL – Ulster, South Scotland	
Paul		MacKay
Paul		MacPherson
Polson		Ross
Power	Normans	
Prendergast, Pendergast	Normans	
Purcell	Normans	
Quillen		O'Cullane
Quillen		O'Cullen
Quillen	IVL – Ireland	
Quinlivan		O'Quinlan
Ramsay	Normans	
Rattray	Cruithne	
Reardon		O'Carroll
Redmond		Burke
Redmond	IVL – Ireland	
Reid	IVL – South Scotland, Ireland	
Reid		Ramsay
Reidford, Redford		Innes
Revie		MacDonald
Reynolds		MacRannall
Reynolds	IVL	

Rice	IVL—Louth	
Rice	Normans	
Risk		Buchanan
Ritchie		MacKintosh
Ritchie		MacPherson
Ritchie	IVL—South Scotland	
Robertson	Gaels	
Robison, Robson		Gunn
Roche	IVL—Ireland	
Roche	Normans	
Ronaldson, Ronald		MacDonald
Rorison		MacDonald
Rose		O'Cahan
Rose	IVL—Limerick	
Ross	Gaels	
Ross	IVL—South Scotland	
Rothe, Ruth	Normans	
Ruskin		Buchanan
Ruthven	Vikings	
Ryan		O'Mulryan
Ryan	IVL—Leinster, Roscommon	
Sage		Savage
Sanderson		MacDonald (Glengarry)
Sarsfield	Normans	
Savage	Normans	
Savage	IVL—South Scotland	
Savage	IVL—Cork, Kerry	
Scrymgeour		MacDuff
Shane		O'Farrell
Shaw		MacKintosh
Shearhoon		Prendergast
Shields, Sheilds		O'Shiel
Shinnock, Shinnach	Gaels	Fox
Shinnock, Shinnach	IVL—Sligo, Cork	
Shoye		Joyce
Simpson		Fraser
Sinclair	Normans	
Sinclair	IVL—Argyle, Perthshire	
Skene		
Skerret		Tribes of Galway
Spalding	Normans	
Spens, Spence		MacDuff
Spittal		Buchanan
Steuart, Stuart		Stewart
Stewart	Normans	
Stirling	Normans	
Strathearn	Cruithne	
Sutherland	Normans	
Swanson		Gunn
Taaffe	Normans	
Taggart	IVL—Ulster	

Taggart		MacTaggart
Taylor		Cameron
Taylor	IVL – Ireland, South Scotland	
Taylor, MacIntaylor		Cameron
Teeling	Normans	
Thomason		MacFarlane
Thompson, Tawesson		Campbell
Tiernan	IVL – Mayo, Roscommon, Westmeath	
Tobin	Normans	
Tonnochy		Robertson
Tosh, Tossack		MacKintosh
Toward, Towart		Lamont
Turner		Lamont
Turner	IVL – South Scotland	
Tyre		MacIntyre
Tyrie	Cuithne	
Ultagh		MacDonlevy
Urquhart		Forbes
Waldron		MacCostello
Waldron	IVL – Meath	
Wall, Faltagh	Normans	
Walsh	IVL – Ireland	
Walsh	Normans	
Weir		MacFarlane
Weir		MacNaughton
Weir	IVL – Ireland	
Wemyss, Weems		MacDuff
Whelan		O'Phelan
Whelan	IVL – Ulster	
White		Lamont
White		MacGregor
White	IVL	
Wier		Buchanan
Wier	IVL – North Ireland	
Williamson		MacKay
Williamson	IVL – South Scotland, Angus	
Wilson		Innes
Wilson	IVL – South Scotland	
Wilson, Williamson		Gunn
Wright		MacIntryre
Wright	IVL – Ireland, South Scotland	
Yule, Yuill		Buchanan
Yule, Yuill	IVL – Angus, Aberdeen	
Yunie		Innes

Bibliography

Adam, Frank. *The Clans, Septs and Regiments of the Scottish Highlands.* 8th ed. Baltimore: Genealogical Publishing Company, 1970.

Alcock, Leslie. *Economy, Society and Warfare Among the Britons and Saxons.* Cardiff: U of Wales P, 1987.

Alexander, James W. "The English Palatinates and Edward I," *Journal of British Studies.* 22 (Spring 1983): 1-22.

Almquist, Bo, et al., eds. *The Heroic Process: Form, Function and Fantasy in Folk Epic.* Dun Laoghaire: Glendale, 1987.

Anderson, Alan and Marjorie O. Anderson, eds. *Adomnan's Life of Columba.* London: Thomas Nelson and Sons Ltd., 1961.

Anderson, Marjorie O. *Kings and Kingship in Early Scotland.* Rev. ed. Edinburgh: Scottish Academic Press, 1980.

Anderson, Rasmus B., ed. *The Norse Discovery of America.* New York: Norroena Society, 1911.

Anderson, William. *The Scottish Nation.* 3 vols. Edinburgh: Fullerton, 1869.

Ashe, Geoffrey. *Camelot and the Vision of Albion.* New York: St. Martin's, 1971.

Bain, Robert. *The Clans and Tartans of Scotland.* Ed. Margaret O. MacDougall. 6th ed. Glasgow: Collins, 1977.

Bannerman, John. *Studies in the History of Dalriada.* Edinburgh: Scottish Academic Press, 1974.

Barber, Richard. *The Figure of Arthur.* Totowa: Rowman and Littlefield, 1973.

Barrows, G.W.S. *The Anglo-Norman Era in Scottish History.* Oxford: Clarendon, 1980.

_____. *The Kingdom of the Scots.* New York: St. Martin's, 1973.

_____. *Kingship and Unity.* Toronto: U of Toronto P, 1981.

Black, George Fraser. *Surnames of Scotland.* New York: New York Public Library, 1946.

Blair, Peter Hunter. *Anglo-Saxon Northumbria.* Ed. M. Lapidge and P. Hunter Blair. London: Variorum Reprints, 1984.

Bloom, Harold, ed. *Dr. Samuel Johnson and James Boswell.* New York: Chelsea, 1986.

Bord, Colin, and Janet Bord. *Earth Rites.* London: Granada (Paladin), 1982.

Bosner, Wilfred. *An Anglo-Saxon and Celtic Bibliography, 450-1087.* 2 vols. Berkeley: UCP, 1957.

Brown, Jennifer M., ed. *Scottish Society in the Fifteenth Century.* New York: St. Martin's 1977.

Burke, John B. *A Genealogical and Heraldic List of the Landed Gentry of Ireland.* London: 1912.

Burke, Sir John Bernard. *A Genealogical History of the Dormant, Abeyant, Forfeited, and Extinct Peerages of the British Empire.* London: William Clowes, 1962.

_____. *Burke's Genealogical and Heraldic History of the Peerage, Baronetage and Knightage.* London: Burke's Peerage, Ltd., 1967.

Burke, Sir Bernard. *Burke's Genealogical and Heraldic History of the Landed Gentry.* 18th ed. London: Burke's Peerage, 1969.

_____. *The General Armory.* Baltimore: Genealogical Publishing Company, 1969.

Burleigh, J.H.S. *A Church History of Scotland.* London: Oxford UP, 1960.

Burns, G.N. *A Welcome to Gaelic.* Dunkeld: Norman Burns, 1983.

Butler, Alban. *Butler's Lives of the Saints.* Ed. Herbert Therston and Donald Attwater. London: Burns & Oates, 1981.

Byrne, Francis John. *Irish Kings and High-Kings.* New York: St. Martin's, 1973.

Campbell, John Lorne, ed. *Highland Songs of the Forty-Five.* Edinburgh: Scottish Gaelic Texts Society, 1984.

Carney, James. *Studies in Irish Literature and History.* Dublin: Institute for Advanced Studies, 1955.

Carney, James, trans. *Medieval Irish Lyrics.* Los Angeles: U of California P, 1967.

Chadwick, H.M. *Early Scotland.* New York: Octagon, 1974.

_____, Nora K. Chadwick, and Kenneth Jackson. *Studies in Early British History.* Cambridge: Cambridge UP, 1959.

Chadwick, Nora K. *The British Heroic Age.* Cardiff: U of Wales P, 1976.

_____. *Celtic Britain.* London: Thames and Hudson, 1963.

_____. *The Celts.* New York: Penguin, 1982.

_____. *The Druids.* Cardiff: U of Wales P, 1966.

Chapman, Malcolm. *The Gaelic Vision in Scottish Culture.* Montreal: McGill-Queen's UP, 1978.

Christie, J. "The MacNayres, the Cardneys, and the Stewarts, Lairds of Foss." *Scottish Notes and Queries.* 12 (1899): 129–31.

Clarke, Maude Violet. *Fourteenth Century Studies.* Freeport: Books for Libraries Press., 1967.

Coghlan, Ronan. *Pocket Dictionary of Irish Myth and Legend.* Belfast: Appletree, 1985.

Cowan, Samuel. *Three Celtic Earldoms; Atholl, Strathearn, Menteith.* Edinburgh: Norman MacLeod, 1909.

Craig, David. *Scottish Literature and the Scottish People, 1680–1830.* London: Chatto & Windus, 1961.

Crawford, Barbara E. *Scandinavian Scotland.* Atlantic Highlands: Humanities Press, 1987.

Cross, Tom Peete, and Clark Harris Slover, eds. *Ancient Irish Tales.* New York: Henry Holt, 1936.

Cumont, Franz. *The Mysteries of Mithra.* Trans. Thomas J. McCormack. New York: Dover, 1956.

Cunningham, A.D. *A History of Rannoch.* Elgin: A.D. Cunningham, 1984.

Curle, C.L. *Pictish and Norse Finds from the Brough of Birsay.* Edinburgh: Society of Antiquaries of Scotland, 1982.

Curriculum Development Unit. *The Celtic Way of Life.* Dublin: O'Brien, 1976.

Davis, R.H.C. *A History of Medieval Europe.* Rev. ed. London: Longman, 1980

De Blacam, Aodh. *Gaelic Literature Surveyed.* New York: Barnes and Noble, 1974.

De Breffny, Brian, ed. *Ireland, a Cultural Encyclopedia.* New York: Facts on File, 1983.

_____. *The Irish World.* New York: Abrams, 1977.

Delaney, John T. *Dictionary of Saints.* Garden City: Doubleday, 1980.

DePaor, Liam and Marie DePaor. *Early Christian Ireland.* London: Thames and Hudson, 1958.

Dickinson, W. Croft. *Scotland from the Earliest Times to 1603.* 3rd ed. Oxford: Clarendon, 1977.

Dillon, Myles. *Celts and Aryans: Survivals of Indo-European Speech and Society.* Simla: Indian Institute of Advanced Study, 1975.

_____. *The Cycles of the Kings.* London: Oxford UP, 1946.

_____. *Early Irish Literature.* Chicago: U of Chicago P, 1948.

_____, and Nora K. Chadwick. *The Celtic Realms.* 2nd ed. London: Weidenfeld and Nicholson, 1972.

Dinneen, Patrick S., ed. *Irish-English Dictionary.* Dublin: Irish Text Society, 1927.

Donaldson, Gordon. *Scotland: Church and Nation Through Sixteen Centuries.* New York: Barnes and Noble, 1973.

_____. *Scottish Kings.* New York: John Wiley, 1967.

_____. *Scottish Historical Documents.* New York: Barnes & Noble, 1970.

Donaldson, Gordon and Robert S. Morpeth. *A Dictionary of Scottish History.* Edinburgh: John Donald, 1977.

_____. *Who's Who in Scottish History.* New York: Barnes and Noble, 1973.

Dowden, Rev. D.D. *The Bishops of Scotland, Being Notes on the Lives of All the Bishops, Under Each of the Sees, Prior to the Reformation.* Glasgow: James Maclehose, 1912.

Dwyer, John, Roger A. Mason and Alexander Murdoch, eds. *New Perspectives on the Politics and Culture of Early Modern Scotland.* Edinburgh: John Donald, 1980.

Edwards, Robert Dudley. *Church and State in Tudor Ireland, A History of the Penal Laws Against Irish Catholics, 1534-1603.* New York: Russel and Russel, 1972.

Edwards, Ruth Dudley. *An Atlas of Irish History.* 2nd ed. New York: Methuen, 1981.

Eyre-Todd, George. *Medieval Scottish Poetry.* London: Sands and Co., 1892.

_____. *The Highland Clans of Scotland.* Charleston: Garner, 1969.

Farmer, David Hugh. *The Oxford Dictionary of Saints.* Oxford: Oxford UP, 1982.

Fell, Barry. *Bronze Age America.* Boston: Little, Brown, 1982.

Fenton, Alexander and Hermann Palsson. *The Northern and Western Isles in the Viking World.* Edinburgh: John Donald, 1984. 265-79.

Finlay, Ian. *Columba.* London: Victor Gollancz, 1979.

Flower, Robin. *The Irish Tradition.* Oxford: Clarendon, 1966.

Foley, John Miles, ed. *Oral Traditional Literature.* Columbia: U of Missouri P, 1986.

Ford, Patrick K., trans. *The Mabinogi and Other Medieval Welsh Tales.* Berkeley: U of California P, 1977

Fowler, J.T., ed. *Vita S. Columbae.* By Adamnan. Oxford: Clarendon Press, 1894.

Friell, J.G.P. and W.G. Watson, eds. "Pictish Studies." *B.A.R.* 125 (1984).

Gibbs, Vicary, ed. *The Complete Peerage of England, Scotland, Ireland, Great Britain and the United Kingdom.* By G[eorge] E[dward] C[okayne]. 13 vols. London: The St. Catherine Press, 1912.

Glassie, Henry. *Irish Folk History, Texts from the North.* Philadelphia: U of Penn. P, 1982.

Gordon, J.F.S. *The Book of the Chronicles of Keith, Grange, Ruthven, Cairney, and Botriphnie.* Glasgow: Robert Forrester, 1880.

Green, Alice Stopford. *History of the Irish State to 1014.* London: Macmillan, 1925.

_____. *The Irish Nationality.* New York: Henry Holt, 1911.

Harbison, Peter. *Guide to National Monuments in the Republic of Ireland.* Dublin: Gill and MacMillan, 1982.

Harrison, Richard J. *The Beaker Folk: Copper Age Archeology in Western Europe.* New York: Thames and Hudson, 1980.

Hieatt, Constance B., Trans. *Beowulf and Other Old English Poems.* New York: Bantam, 1983.

Higham, Nick. *The Northern Counties to AD 1000.* New York: Longman, 1986.

Hill, George Birkbeck, ed. *Boswell's Life of Johnson*. By James Boswell. 6 vols. Oxford: OUP, 1934.

Historical Manuscripts Commission. *The Manuscripts of the Duke of Athole, K.T., and the Earl of Home*. London: Stationery Office, 1891.

Hoagland, Kathleen, ed. *1000 Years of Irish Poetry*. Old Greenwich: Devin-Adair, 1975.

Holweck, Frederick George. *A Bibliographical Dictionary of the Saints*. Detroit: Gale Research, 1969.

Hughes, Kathleen. *The Church in Early Irish Society*. Ithaca: Cornell UP, 1966.

Hyde, Douglas. *A Literary History of Ireland*. New York: Barnes and Noble, 1967.

Innes, Sir Thomas. *Scots Heraldry*. 2nd ed. Edinburgh: Oliver and Boyd, 1956.

Jackson, Kenneth H. *The Gaelic Notes in the Book of Deer*. Cambridge: Cambridge UP, 1972.

————. *The Gododdin: The Oldest Scottish Poem*. Edinburgh: Edinburgh UP, 1969.

Jenkins, David and Mark Visocchi. *Mehdelssohn in Scotland*. New York: Chappell, 1978.

Johnson, Samuel. *A Journey to the Western Islands of Scotland*. Ed. Peter Levi. New York: Penguin, 1984.

Johnston, W. Ltd. *The Scottish Clans and Their Tartans*. Toronto: Musson, 1936.

Joyce, P.W. *A Short History of Gaelic Ireland*. London: Longmans, Green, 1924.

————. *A Social History of Ancient Ireland*. 2 vols. New York: B. Blom, 1968.

Knott, Eleanor, and Gerald Murphy. *Early Irish Literature*. New York: Barnes and Noble, 1966.

Knox, H.T. *History of the County of Mayo to the Close of the Sixteenth Century*. Dublin: 1908.

Kratzmann, Gregory. *Anglo-Scottish Literary Relations, 1430–1550*. Cambridge: Cambridge UP, 1980.

Kurten, B. "Dance of the Tiger: A Paleomystery." *Science Digest*. 90 (1982): 76–77.

Laing, Lloyd, ed. "Studies in Celtic Survival." *B.A.R.* 37 (1977).

————, and Jennifer Laing, ed. *The Origins of Britain*. New York: Scribner's 1980.

Leneman, Leah. *Living in Atholl: A Social History of the Estates, 1685–1785*. Edinburgh: Edinburgh UP, 1986.

Lethbridge, T.C. *Herdsmen & Hermits*. Cambridge: Bowes and Bowes, 1950.

Lewis, Samuel. *A Topographical Dictionary of Ireland*. 2 vols. Port Washington: Kennikat Press, 1970.

Lindsay, Hon. John. *The Lives of the Lindsays*. London: J. Murray, 1858.

Lindsay, Maurice. *History of Scottish Literature*. London: Robert Hale, 1977.

Llwelyn, Morgan. *Lion of Ireland*. New York: Playboy, 1979.

Logan, Patrick. *Irish Country Cures*. Belfast: Appletree, 1985.

Lonigan, Paul R. "Shamanism in the Old Irish Tradition." *Eire-Ireland*. 20.3 (1985): 109–129.

Lord, Albert B. *The Singer of Tales*. Cambridge: Harvard UP, 1960.

MacCana, Proinsias. *Celtic Mythology*. New York: Hamlyn, 1970.

————. "Irish Literary Tradition." *A View of the Irish Language*. Dublin: Stationery Office, 1969.

Mac Firbisigh, Dubhaltach. *Chronicon Scotorum . . . to A.D. 1135*. Ed. W.M. Hennessy. London, 1866.

————. *Annals of Ireland, Three Fragments*. Dublin, 1860.

McIan, R.R. *The Clans of the Scottish Highlands*. New York: Knopf, 1980.

MacKenzie, W. MacKay. *The Mediaeval Castle in Scotland*. New York: Benjamin Blom, 1972.

McKitterick, Rosamond. *The Frankish Kingdoms Under the Carolingians.* New York: Longman, 1983.

McLaren, Moray. *Bonnie Prince Charles.* New York: Saturday Review, 1972.

McLynn, Frank. *The Jacobites.* London: Routledge & Kegan Paul, 1985.

MacLysaght, Edward. *Irish Families, Their Names, Arms and Origins.* 3rd ed. New York: Crown Publishers, 1972.

_____. *The Surnames of Ireland.* 5th ed. Dublin: Irish Academic Press, 1980.

MacLeod, C.I.N. *Highland Scottish Folklore and Beliefs.* Antigonish: Formac, 1975.

McNeill, John T. *The Celtic Churches.* Chicago: Chicago UP, 1974.

MacVeigh, James. *The Scottish Nation; or, the Historical and Genealogical Account of all Scottish Families and Surnames.* 3 vols. Dumfries: James MacVeigh, 1889.

Manning, Susan. "Ossian, Scott, and Nineteenth-Century Scottish Literary Nationalism." *Studies in Scottish Literature* 17 (1982) 39–54.

Metropolitan Museum of Art. *Treasures of Early Irish Art, 1500 B.C. to 1500 A.D.* Ed. Polly Cone. New York: Metropolitan Museum of Art, 1977.

Meyer, Kuno. *Death Tales of the Ulster Heroes.* Dublin: Hodges, Figgis, 1906.

Miket, Roger and Colin Burgess, eds. *Between and Beyond the Walls.* Edinburgh: John Donald, 1984.

Mitchison, Rosalind. *A History of Scotland.* 2nd ed. New York: Methuen, 1982.

_____. *Lordship to Patronage, Scotland 1603–1745.* London: Edward Arnold, 1983.

Moncreiffe, Sir Iain. *The Highland Clans.* Rev. ed. New York: Clarkson, 1982.

Moody, T.W., and F.X. Martin, eds. *The Course of Irish History.* Cork: Mercier, 1961.

Morris, John. *The Age of Arthur.* New York: Scribner's, 1973.

Morrison, Alex. *Early Man in Britain and Ireland.* New York: St. Martin's, 1980.

Murray, Margaret Alice. "Organizations of Witches in Great Britain," *Folklore* 28 (September 1917): 228–58.

_____. *The Witch-Cult in Western Europe.* Oxford: Oxford UP, 1921.

_____. "Witches and the Number Thirteen," *Folklore* 31 (September 1920): 204–209.

Mylne, Alexander. *Rentale Dunkeldense.* Trans. Robert Kerr Hannay. Edinburgh: Scottish Historical Society, 1915.

_____. *Vitae Dunkeldensis Ecclesiae Episcoporum.* Edinburgh: Bannatyne Club, 1831.

Nagy, Joseph Falaky. "Orality in Medieval Irish Narrative: An Overview." *Oral Tradition* 1 (1986): 272–301.

_____. *The Wisdom of the Outlaw.* Berkeley: U of California P: 1985.

"Neanderthal Flower Medicine." *Science Digest.* 79 (1976): 10.

Noble, Rev. Mark. *An Historical Genealogy of the Royal House of Stuarts.* London: Faulder, 1795.

Nicholson, Ranald. *Scotland, The Later Middle Ages.* New York: Barnes & Noble, 1974.

Nicholson, Edward W.B. *Goldspie, Contributions to Its Folklore.* Norwood: Norwood Editions, 1975.

Nelson, Harry. *Introduction to Physical Anthropology.* New York: West Publishing, 1979.

Nicolaisen, Wilhelm F. *Scottish Place Names.* London: Batsford, 1976.

Norton-Taylor, Duncan. *The Celts.* New York: Time-Life Books, 1974.

O Dalaigh, Aengus. *The Tribes of Ireland Together with an Historical Account of the Family of O'Daly.* Ed. John O'Donovan. Dublin, 1852.

O'Donovan, John, ed. *Annala Rioghachta Eireann: Annals of the Kingdom of Ireland . . . to 1616.* By the Four Masters. Dublin: 1851.

_____. *The Tribes & Customs of Hy Many & Hy Fiachrach.* Dublin: 1843–44.

O'Driscoll, Robert, ed. *The Celtic Consciousness.* New York: Braziller, 1982.

O Faolain, Sean. *The Silver Branch*. New York: Books for Libraries Press, 1968.

O'Flaherty, Roderick. *A Chorographical Description of West or H-iar Connacht*. Ed. James Hardiman. Dublin, 1846.

O Muirithe, Diarmaid. *The English Language in Ireland*. Cork: Mercier, 1978.

Ong, Walter J. *Orality and Literacy*. New York: Methuen, 1985.

O'Rahilly, T.F. *Early Irish History and Mythology*. Dublin: Dublin Institute for Advanced Studies, 1957.

O'Suilleabhain, Sean. *A Handbook of Irish Folklore*. Detroit: Singing Tree, 1970.

Palsson, Hermann and Paul Edwards, trans. *Orkneyinga Saga*. New York: Penguin Books, 1984.

Paul, Sir James Balfour. *An Ordinary of Arms Contained in the Public Register of All Arms and Bearings in Scotland*. Edinburgh: W. Green, 1893.

_____. *Heraldry in Relation to Scottish History and Art*. Edinburgh: Douglas, 1900.

_____. *The Scots Peerage*. 9 vols. Edinburgh: D. Douglas, 1904-14.

"Pedigree of the Family of Stewart of Stenton, Co. Perth." *The Scottish Antiquary*. Vol. 7, pp. 103-108.

Pepper, John. *Illustrated Encyclopedia of Ulster Knowledge*. Belfast: Appletree, 1985.

_____. *Ulster-English Dictionary*. Belfast: Appletree, 1985.

_____. *Ulster Phrase Book*. Belfast: Appletree, 1985.

Polome, Edgar C., ed. *Old Norse Literature and Mythology*. Austin: U of Texas P, 1969.

Prebble, John. *Mutiny: Highland Regiments in Revolt, 1743-1804*. New York: Penguin, 1985.

Quiggin, Edmund Crosby. *Poems from the Book of the Dean of Lismore*. Cambridge: Cambridge UP, 1937.

Ralston, Ian and Jim Inglis, eds. *Foul Hordes*. Aberdeen: Anthropological Museum, 1984.

Readers' Digest Assn. *The Readers' Digest Complete Atlas of the British Isles*. London: Readers' Digest Assn., 1965.

Reed, James. *Sir Walter Scott: Landscape and Locality*. London: Athlone, 1980.

Rhett, Beatriz Mariscal de. "The Structure and Changing Functions of Oral Traditions." *Oral Tradition* 2 (1987): 645-66.

Rhys, John, and David Brynmore-Jones. *The Welsh People*. New York: Greenwood, 1969.

Roche, Richard. *The Norman Invasion of Ireland*. Dublin: Anvil, 1970.

Root, Margaret E. *Dunkeld Cathedral*. Edinburgh: Her Majesty's Stationery Office, 1950.

Ross, Anne. *The Folklore of the Scottish Highlands*. Totowa: Rowman and Littlefield, 1976.

Ross, John R. *The Great Clan Ross*. Lindsay: John Deyell, 1968.

Royle, Trevor. *The Macmillan Companion to Scottish Literature*. London: Macmillan, 1984.

Saul, George Brandon. *Traditional Irish Literature and Its Backgrounds*. Lewisburg: Bucknell UP, 1970.

Scotland of Old. Map. Edinburgh: John Bartholomew, 1975.

Severy, Merle. "The Celts, Europe's Founders." *National Geographic*. 151.5 (1977): 582-633.

Sjoestedt, Marie-Louise. *Gods and Heroes of the Celts*. Trans. Myles Dillon. Berkeley: Turtle Island Foundation, 1982.

Smyth, Alfred P. *Warlords and Holy Men*. London: Edward Arnold, 1984.

_____. *Scandinavian York and Dublin*. 2 vols. Dublin: Templekieran, 1975-79.

_____. *Scandinavian Kings in the British Isles 850–880*. Oxford: Oxford UP, 1977.

Stewart, Donald C. *The Setts of the Scottish Tartans, with Descriptions and Historical Notes*. Edinburgh: Oliver and Boyd, 1950.

Stewart, Elizabeth. *Dunkeld, An Ancient City*. Dunkeld: Norman Burns, 1979.

Stewart, John. *The Stewarts*. Edinburgh: Johnston and Bacon, 1973.

Stuart, Margaret and James Balfour Paul. *Scottish Family History*. Baltimore: Genealogical Publishing Company, 1983.

Thomas, Charles. *Celtic Britain*. London: Thames and Hudson, 1986.

Thomson, Derick S., ed. *Companion to Gaelic Scotland*. Oxford: Blackwell Reference, 1983.

_____. "Gaelic Literary Interactions with Scots and English Work: A Survey." *Scottish Language* 5 (1986): 1–14.

Waddell, Helen. *The Wandering Scholars*. 7th ed. (Rev.) New York: Henry Holt, 1934.

Wahlgren, Erik. *The Vikings and America*. New York: Thames and Hudson, 1986.

Walsh, Paul. *Irish Chiefs and Leaders*. Dublin: Sign of the Three Candles, 1960.

Walton, Evangeline. *The Children of Llyr, the Second Branch of the Mabinogion*. New York: Ballantine, 1977.

Watson, Roderick. *The Literature of Scotland*. New York: Schocken Books, 1985.

Watson, William J. *The History of the Celtic Place-Names of Scotland*. Edinburgh: Blackwell, 1926.

Watt, Donald Elmslie Robertson. *A Biographical Dictionary of Scottish Graduates to A.D. 1410*. Oxford: Clarendon, 1977.

Weaver, Kenneth S. "The Search for Our Ancestors." *National Geographic*. 168.5 (1985): 560–623.

Whitlock, Dorothy, ed. *The Anglo-Saxon Chronicle*. London: Eyre and Spottiswoode, 1961.

Whitlock, Dorothy and Rosamond McKitterick, eds. *Ireland in Early Medieval Europe*. Cambridge: Cambridge UP, 1982.

Whittington, G. and I.D. Whyte, eds. *An Historical Geography of Scotland*. New York: Academic Press, 1983.

Wilson, Daniel. *The Archeology and Prehistoric Annals of Scotland*. Edinburgh: Sutherland and Knox. 1851.

Woodward, John and George Burnett. *A Treatise on Heraldry, British and Foreign*. Rutland: Charles E. Tuttle, 1969.

Wormald, Patrick, ed. *Ideal and Reality in Frankish and Anglo-Saxon Society*. Oxford: Oxford UP, 1983.

Woulfe, Rev. Patrick. *Irish Names and Surnames*. Baltimore: Genealogical Publishing Company, 1969.

Index

Made in the USA
Coppell, TX
25 September 2021

62995057R00125